D1505253

A
YEAR OF THE
HUNTER

OTHER WORKS IN ENGLISH
BY CZESLAW MILOSZ

Beginning with My Streets
Bells in Winter
The Captive Mind
Collected Poems
Conversations with Czeslaw Milosz
(by Ewa Czarnecka and Aleksander Fiut)
Emperor of the Earth
Happy as a Dog's Tail: Poems by Anna Swir
The History of Polish Literature
The Issa Valley
The Land of Ulro
Native Realm
Nobel Lecture
Post-War Polish Poetry (anthology)
Provinces
The Seizure of Power
The Separate Notebooks
Unattainable Earth
Visions from San Francisco Bay
With the Skin: Poems of Aleksander Wat
The Witness of Poetry

A
YEAR OF THE
HUNTER

by

CZESLAW MILOSZ

TRANSLATED BY MADELINE G. LEVINE

FARRAR, STRAUS AND GIROUX

NEW YORK

LIBRARY OF CONGRESS CATALOGING-IN-PUBLICATION DATA
Miłosz, Czesław.
[Rok myśliwego. English]
A year of the hunter / Czeslaw Milosz ; translated by Madeline G.
Levine.
p.   cm.
1. Miłosz, Czesław—Biography.   2. Poets, Polish—20th century—
Biography.   I. Title.
PG7158.M5532A3713   1994   891.8'58709—dc20 [B]   93-49598 CIP

$\mathcal{P}$REFACE

Why this eccentric title? First and foremost, to honor the memory of a book
I loved when I was a schoolboy, a book that had the identical title. Its author
was Włodzimierz Korsak, who has never been considered a writer, but who
was well known among nature lovers, especially lovers of that nature whose
primeval beauty adorned the lands of the former Grand Duchy of Lithuania.
There were innumerable Korsaks among the gentry, especially in Belorussia
("Every shrub holds a Korsak"). He came from the Vitebsk region. After the
First World War, he found himself in Poland and selected forestry as his
profession, but he also wrote. *On the Trail of Nature*, a novel for young
readers set in Korsak's native region, is the story of two boys' summer vacation.
His novel *In the Wilderness*, which has a romantic theme, shows the same
regression in time and the same landscapes. Both these works are about
hunting and observing the local fauna. Korsak would often illustrate his
descriptions with pen-and-ink drawings which were very lovely but which
nevertheless prove that he was interested not so much in art as in accuracy
and faithfulness to details. I owe him so much of my knowledge about birds
and four-footed animals that I consider it appropriate to pay him homage
by borrowing his title.

Korsak's *The Year of the Hunter* is a calendar of things that need to be
done by months; it is, quite simply, a hunting handbook, although, to be
sure, it is geared mainly to the forested expanses of Northern Europe. My
book has nothing at all in common with this topic, I assure you, but it has
a great deal in common with the calendar form. It is the diary of one year
in my life: from August 1987 to August 1988. But since I repeatedly returned

in these entries—which I recorded daily or every few days—to distant events and people whom I once knew, the past and the present are interwoven in these pages.

I spent that year in Berkeley, but not only in Berkeley, for I made frequent trips to Europe and to various locations in the States to read my poetry. That is why many of the entries were written aboard airplanes or in airports. There were fewer of these trips than earlier in the decade, but still, I traveled assiduously.

There is also another explanation for the title. My youthful dreams of excursions "on the trail of nature" were never fulfilled, and yet I did become a hunter, although of a different sort: my game was the entire visible world and I have devoted my life to trying to capture it in words, to making a direct hit with words. Alas, the present year of the hunter brings, in the main, reflections on the incommensurability of aspirations and accomplishments, despite the existence of an entire shelf of books written by me. I repeat to myself a poem by Robinson Jeffers that I translated into Polish a long time ago, and I see more clearly than ever before that I could well have adopted it as the motto for all my creative work:

LOVE THE WILD SWAN

"I hate my verses, every line, every word.
Oh pale and brittle pencils ever to try
One grass-blade's curve, or the throat of one bird
That clings to twig, ruffled against white sky.
Oh cracked and twilight mirrors ever to catch
One color, one glinting flash, of the splendor of things.
Unlucky hunger, Oh bullets of wax,
The lion beauty, the wild-swan wings, the storm of the wings."
—This wild swan of a world is no hunter's game.
Better bullets than yours would miss the white breast,
Better mirrors than yours would crack in the flame.
Does it matter whether you hate your . . . self? At least
Love your eyes that can see, your mind that can
Hear the music, the thunder of the wings. Love the wild swan.

A
YEAR OF THE
HUNTER

*A*UGUST 1, 1987, *B*ERKELEY

Unending amazement, every day. I am beginning the seventy-seventh year of my life. I repeat this over and over again and cannot persuade myself that it is really so. And that what is happening now inside me and around me is not happening somewhere else, but right here, in Berkeley, California (so far from Wilno).

A beautiful summer, very few foggy days as yet, and even when there is fog, it burns off around midday. The flowers on the patio are growing like crazy: heliotrope, lobelia, petunias, New Guinea impatiens. The princess tree has been in bloom for a month and will keep on flowering until late autumn. The Italian buckthorn that we planted last year is still scraggly; it's been chewed up by the deer, who have also eaten all the flowers on the neighbors' shrubs.

Last night we took the mountain road up Grizzly Peak again. Cars were parked on the shoulders, the people admiring the expansive view down toward the bay, the bridges, San Francisco, Oakland, the celebrated colors of the local sunsets, this time delicate, like an Oriental painting, dusted with gray. Then a sauna and a swim in the pool under the dark sky, turning on our backs and looking up at the stars, although it's always an open question: Is it a star, a plane, or a spaceship?

*A*ugust 2, 1987

"I did not know that the Berkeley Hills would be my last," says my poem. Maybe they won't be, since nothing is certain as long as one is alive, but it seems likely that that's how it will be. Wilno is Atlantis. I cannot imagine living in Poland either, even though I visited there in the period of relative freedom under Solidarity. Paris became depopulated when my three friends died one after the other: Zygmunt Hertz, Father Józef Sadzik, Kot Jeleński. Anyhow, wherever I live, it will always be in a state of disengagement, just as here, where I hardly have any reason to descend into the city.

Books and dictionaries. There would be enough material in my life for a novel, but I am glad that I don't write novels. Perhaps it's a Nobel Laureate's conceit to think that my fame is narrow, limited to readers of poetry. Certainly, I would prefer it if print runs of my books were larger, but I value the providential equanimity inscribed in my destiny: never too much fame, just the right amount.

The virtue of a novel lies in the possibility of describing our relations with other people without pointing a finger at them; in other words, affording them adequate protection. In writing a diary or a journal, you don't have that privilege; it's as if you cast aside all scruples, as many people do today.

Without my permission and for reasons known only to them, the Warsaw newspaper *Polityka* has dug up and reprinted "Elegy," an article of mine from the late forties. Even the Warsaw correspondent for *The New York Times*, Michael Kaufman, has written about this article, because it describes, among other things, the chairoplane next to the walls of the Warsaw Ghetto. So, it's being treated as a continuation of the discussion unleashed by Jan Błoński's article in *Tygodnik Powszechny* [The Universal Weekly], about Polish indifference. Kaufman translates the word "karuzela" literally, as carousel, which implies horses with children riding in circles, while this was actually a chairoplane, with couples soaring into the sky. But the chairoplane is not well known.

I had completely forgotten about the existence of my article and read it as if it were written by someone else. One more proof that we are not conscious of either our good or our bad deeds, which means that we know very little about ourselves and, if it is correct to assume that there will be no Judgment Day, neither we ourselves nor anyone else will ever know. In this article, which I don't particularly like, my compassion is authentic.

It is only natural that I should play at being the judge of my own deeds, always pondering the degree of my self-awareness. For how is one to distinguish obsessions, illusions, symbolic acts from truthful evaluation? I know only too well that guilt feelings and constant self-accusation are the mark of an egomaniac and that a fundamental principle should be to arm oneself against egomania by the best possible knowledge of its enticements.

𝒜ugust 3, 1987

I shall copy out something I wrote in my notebook two years ago, because it is connected with what I observed yesterday:

Marek Zaleski's book, *The Adventure of the Second Avant-garde*. It's exactly as if I were discovering myself in another, distant incarnation. Denial: This can't be me. And yet it is me. Curiosity, because I come across quotes from articles, from letters, that I had completely forgotten I ever wrote. I also discover the logic of my alienation. Just because my slender volumes of poetry, and my colleagues', appeared in editions of one hundred or three hundred copies, that doesn't mean they had that many buyers. In those days I was convinced that we write for perhaps twenty or thirty individuals, for our fellow poets; that belief is returning. Right beside us, thousands are waiting, attentively pricking up their ears whenever a poem mentions politics, poised to adopt us under the condition that we serve the cause. A leftist cause, obviously. On the bottom is the great mass of those who read nothing because they are illiterate or barely literate, the mass for whom television was invented. Somewhat higher, a clear-cut division: On one side, progressivism, leftist inclinations, an openness to innovation, snobbery, a dubious intellectualism, the shifting borderline between Polish and Yiddish (in Wilno, between Yiddish and Russian)—because that entire milieu was eighty percent Jewish. On the other side, right-wing tendencies, ritual Catholicism, an absence of intellectual interests. My fate was determined by a traumatic distaste for the latter camp. Warm, getting warm, in a moment

I'll find the key, because I said "traumatic." An intellectual confronting primitives? A Jew confronting goyim? A wise man versus fools? A mystic versus believers in the religion of the folk, in which the Mother of God plays an ancillary role? Unquestionably, alluding to my Lithuanian ancestry was one more way of cutting myself off from my real or imagined arch-Polish persecutors. I am probably being unjust, but I am not interested in a sociological or political analysis of that era. That is how I felt at the time. But where, in fact, is the key to my trauma?

That whole avant-garde was laughable; a few lost young people, absolutely marginal in the daily life of a couple of university towns, even more so in the life of the entire country. That daily life has vanished: the jobs, the amusements, the loves, the marriages, the births, the undiscoverable stories of millions of individuals. Then a literary critic comes along, and confers reality on what must take the place of that distant real life, solely because it survives in language. Even though it's no longer possible to verify what deformations reality was subjected to in the thoughts and writings of the avant-garde poets, who were probably rife with assorted traumas, just as I was. My imagination conjures up particular individuals who, contemporaneously with me, experienced the world in a totally different dimension than I did, through different ideas and different sensual perceptions.

Isaac Bashevis Singer writes about Poland in the nineteen-thirties in his autobiographical *Love and Exile*. I was never in the Jewish writers' club in Warsaw, but even so I had formed an opinion. It was a time when young Jews were leaving the faith and customs of their fathers, not for freethinking and liberalism, but directly for Communism and the fanatical hatreds between Stalinists and Trotskyists that arose out of that new faith. There is no lack of similarities between my alienation and Singer's. The son of a rabbi, he had had a religious upbringing, was already secularized, but was sufficiently complex to perceive the cult of Moloch within the Communism of his fellow writers; he did not get along very well with the Zionists and developed an art of distance in a void: a writer in Yiddish, but for whom? When Hitler came to power in Germany, Singer's milieu was certain that Germany would soon occupy Poland. Singer left for America in 1934 and for many years, as he himself says, he suffered from an inability to write—the logical outcome, it would seem, of a loss that turned out to be providential, because in searching for the ground under his feet he discovered the traditional Jewish world of his childhood. And, most of all, the great metaphysical questions that had preoccupied him since childhood. I, too, during my émigré crisis, searched for the forever-lost country of my child-hood. Throughout his life, Singer, whose narrative gift I truly envy, circled around one question: How can God permit so much evil? The Jewish tragedy, Job's crying out on behalf of the millions of victims, is transposed in his work, concealed, although his revulsion at sinful humanity, complicitous in the crimes of Hitler and Stalin, openly erupts in his short late novel, *The Penitent*. The indictment of God, the palpable awareness of the Devil's presence, belief in Providence—just as in my writing. When I read *The Penitent*, I said to myself that Singer has the same attitude toward Hassidic orthodoxy that I have toward orthodox Catholicism. That is the source of my true kinship with Singer, which is stronger than with any other living prose writer, Polish or American. Nobel Prizes for two alienated men.

Yes, it's hard to believe that the following quotes from Singer's novel *Shosha* did not issue from my pen; that we wrote about the same thing at the same time, but without agreeing to do so:

> I elaborated to Shosha the theory that world history was a book man could read only forward. He could never turn the pages of this world book backward. But everything that had ever been still existed. Yppe lived somewhere. The hens, geese, and ducks the butchers in Yanash's Court slaughtered each day still lived, clucked, quacked, and crowed on the other pages of the world book—the right-hand pages, since the world book was written in Yiddish, which reads from right to left.

> Where did all the years go to? Who will remember them after we're gone? The writers will write, but they'll get everything topsy-turvy. There must be a place somewhere where everything is preserved, inscribed down to the smallest detail. Let us say that a fly has fallen into a spiderweb and the spider has sucked her dry. This is a fact of the universe and such a fact cannot be forgotten. If such a fact should be forgotten, it would create a blemish in the universe.

*A*UGUST 4, 1987

About May in Europe. Arrival by plane in Paris on the afternoon of the third; destination, rue de l'Université. A television crew from a cultural program shows up the next morning. During the taping, a phone call, with news of Kot Jeleński's death, which was inevitable, expected at any moment for the last few weeks. Nothing intelligent comes to mind other than picturing the many situations in which his absence will be painful. He was so needed. By many people, by me. My consciousness of this is deflected by writing an obituary for *Le Monde* at Leonor's request and by a trip to Lille to attend a conference on "Les Confins orientaux de l'ancienne Pologne." Throughout the three days of active participation, in the back of my mind are thoughts about everything that is connected with the year 1944–45, with the final end of the Kresy,* and astonishment that such a conference is possible here, after more than forty years, with so many fine papers, including papers written by professors from Poland. An awareness of the fabric of time itself, of change taking place by degrees.

Rainy, chilly, like most of May; in Lugano, too, where the PEN convention began on the tenth. Jeanne's presence is the sole attraction; both of us are delivering opening addresses. My complete indifference throughout the convention, neither hot nor cold, even when they take us by bus to La Scala in Milan for a (bad) piano recital and a reception hosted by the great fashion house of Crizia.

A short stay at Jeanne's home in Geneva; rain. By car with Jeanne to Lausanne to visit "Grandma," as I have always called Mrs. Irena Vincenz. What a delight. That people like her should also walk this earth. But this spring the earth lost a man who was, for me, a model of integrity as well as a friend: Tadeusz Byrski, the man I worked with at Radio Wilno, has died in Warsaw.

Association based on the same awe for the just, as opposed to *rashaim*, the godless. Byrski was a couple of years older than I. But here Jeanne and I assume the role of "the youngsters," out of habit, just as we used to some thirty years ago.

---

* A term applied to the eastern, ethnically mixed territories of the Polish–Lithuanian Commonwealth; Eastern Marches, or, in French, *confins*.

𝒜ugust 5, 1987

From Geneva to Menton for two days, to the Hôtel l'Aiglon, which I know. Rain here, too. Once again, like a counterpoint, conversations with Nela and Janek. Back to Paris; cloudy and rainy.

Like other people, I was enchanted with Jeleński. I also envied him. What did I envy? His full life, because I believed that he was made of nobler metal than I, despite the part of him that I found murky: his passion for *ragazzi*, which, Leonor told me, existed already in 1950, when they first became acquainted in Rome.

For the past several years I have enjoyed France, but in retaliation for the humiliations I once suffered there. Perhaps I would not have felt so humiliated in the 1950s had I not craved recognition as a poet. A couple of people—Jean Cassou, Supervielle—had some understanding of who I was, but I could sense through my pores the general aura surrounding my person: he's some kind of crank, maybe a little crazy, working at anti-Communism. Gallimard published me because of my Prix Européen, but since it was so hard to find my books in bookstores, it seems as if they were sabotaged in the distribution system. While Camus was alive, I had one ally at Gallimard. When an Italian publisher wrote a letter of inquiry to Gallimard about *The Captive Mind* (I think it was in the late seventies, just before the Nobel Prize), the press replied that the author was unknown. At Gallimard, I would wait in the anteroom, in part because of my possibly exaggerated sensitivity to barely perceptible signs indicating that my place was in the anteroom. I never felt at home there, and it is very important for an author to be able to walk into his publisher's office and be treated as "one of ours." As I am now at Fayard on rue des Saints-Pères.

Sunsets as in the mountains, because the fog creeps out of the ocean, embraces San Francisco, settles on the islands and promontories, so that from here, from up above, it looks like billowing white shoals with the peaks of skyscrapers protruding here and there, fantastic splashes of light, and it grows denser, intensifies, until the sun sets as if behind a mountain range.

The Musée d'Orsay. It would be hard to call my experiences aesthetic. Anyway, I don't know what aesthetic experiences are. My thoughts take two directions:

1. Everything that has accumulated from the middle of the nineteenth century to the present day, the infinite number of lives of human beings subject to physiological changes, to fashions, to the shifts and leaps of history, of individuals who died, each his own kind of death, that enormity which cannot be encompassed by the imagination *and yet* is condensed into a kind of extract; for example, into Degas's dancer, who is herself and who also trails an entire retinue—her family, conversations, beds, kitchens, Paris of that time, year, day. Degas moves me, because there is compassion behind his painting. For the fragile body, for the aspirations of those girls, for their lovers, husbands, for their future adventures, as yet unknown. *Bourgeoises, poules*, great ballerinas. Time is stopped, here, now, along with its potentiality. In the Musée d'Orsay I am interested in realistic painting, prior to Impressionism. I wander through the galleries with a practical aim in mind, too, looking for a picture to reproduce on the cover of the paperback edition of *Unattainable Earth*.

In other words, to return to my theme: in painting, the human time of passing decades persists, condenses, freezes into form, time that is otherwise elusive, untouchable, although some people may object: But what about photographs? Perhaps. I leave it to someone else to ponder why they are not the same thing. For me, it is important that there is a date below each painting.

2. If we think about it seriously, it is unbelievable that from a considerable distance, when we still don't even know the painter's name, we are able to make distinctions and to say who it is. For example, that it is a landscape by Corot. Which means that there exists (I'm not sure how to define it) a tone, a nuance, a melody, which is peculiar to one man only and to no one else, the mark of an individual, and art supplies only a particular occasion for becoming conscious of this, for the painter has managed to express what is his own, but that does not mean that other people lack their own particular note. This may be the sole proof of the immortality of the soul, with due consideration for additional premises, to be sure: that this strictly individual, unique *something* cannot be destroyed forever, because that would be senseless and unjust.

I am beleaguered by unwritten poems that I will never write, pictures, situations, themes, at night, at daybreak.

$\mathcal{A}$UGUST 6, 1987

The billowing fog down below, over San Francisco, foretold a change in the weather. The sea fog chilled us, too; yesterday the sun appeared only around four in the afternoon and by six there was fog again.

My life adventures. A "bard on a swiveling pedestal," as I have called myself. For thirty years an Orwellian non-person in Poland; then, in 1981, a reception given in my honor in the Summer Palace in Łazienki by the Minister of Culture; then again onto the rubbish heap. But my adventure with Oscar Milosz is even more amazing. It's Sunday, May 24, 1987; I've caught a train for Fontainebleau at the Gare de Lyon. A few minutes later and to the right of the tracks, there are the familiar ramparts and trees: my station, Montgeron, flashes by, and later, when the train passes Brunoy and speeds into the fields, I scan the horizon for the cathedral tower of Brie-Comte-Robert.

I boarded the train to Fontainebleau in the summer of 1931. I was twenty years old. We'd come to Paris as a trio—Robespierre (Stefan Jędrychowski), Elephant (Stefan Zagórski), and I, dressed in shirts and shorts, because our knapsacks had sunk in the rapids of the upper Rhine. Oscar had sent me money and advised me to buy a suit in Samaritaine, so I was dressed not too elegantly, but respectably. A young woman sat opposite me. Provincial that I was, I was fascinated with her, a Parisian woman. It isn't true that I'm not thinking about her now, in this train, because I am counting: she must have been around thirty, let's say; add fifty-six years; she would be eighty-six now, so most likely she's been dead for a long time.

At that time, in Fontainebleau, Oscar received me in his room in the Hôtel l'Aigle-Noir. The birds in the cage (or cages) were African sparrows, which he couldn't very well release into the park, but he would never have kept local birds in captivity. My anxious respect, my snobbishness about my French relation, my true delight in *Miguel Mañara* in Bronisława Ostrowska's translation, and my total ignorance of the intertwining of our fates which would bear fruit after many decades. For it was in America that I discovered his correspondence with Christian Gauss. I considered it my duty to publicize his writings, and so I translated *Ars Magna* and *Les Arcanes* into English. I would not have run into difficulties getting them published if they had been fashionable, cheap occultism, which they are not; also, their prediction of the triumph of the Roman Catholic Church put people off. But finally they became part of *The Noble Traveller*, a large volume of his writings, with a foreword by me, which was published in 1985 through the efforts of Christopher Bamford. When I heard about the Nobel, I thought that this was a dispensation on Oscar's behalf, to keep his name alive. And as a matter of fact, in the bookstores in Berkeley, for example, *The Noble Traveller* sits on the shelf alongside my poems.

So, May 1987. Les Amis de Milosz hold an annual commemorative luncheon in that very Hôtel l'Aigle-Noir and I am going there as the newly elected honorary president of this society, upon the death of Jean Cassou. It is probably the only sunny day in May. We place flowers on his grave, which bears a new inscription in Lithuanian and in French: "The first representative of independent Lithuania in Paris." The small crowd is made up of Frenchmen and Lithuanians. Andrzej, who arrived a few days ago from Warsaw, surprises them by addressing them in pure Lithuanian. Afterward, a tour of Place Milosz and the house where Oscar died, on rue Royale, with a walled garden that the courteous present owner, a retired shoe merchant, allows us to enter. The luncheon takes a long time; there are speeches, then a stroll in the park around the palace where my identity with that young man who was shown around here fifty-six years ago is questionable.

AUGUST 7, 1987

The sun emerged around three in the afternoon and set in golden and red reflections on the swiftly gathering clouds of fog. Shopping for bougainvillea in a nursery on San Pablo. These wanderings of plants and their names: the eighteenth-century French traveler, Bougainville, sailed around the world and gave his name (I don't know if he actually did this himself) to a shrub he discovered in the Antilles.

𝒜UGUST 9, 1987

To Walnut Creek for Ewa's wedding, then the reception in the park in Danville. When I first came to Berkeley in 1960 with Janka and the children, and Alfred Tarski drove us around to show us the area, the countryside began to the east of the Berkeley Hills—chestnut orchards in the valleys; higher up, straw-colored slopes punctuated by black oaks throughout most of the year. Now the city is everywhere: streets and houses covered with green foliage, lawns, tennis courts, swimming pools, parks. Also, the metro, which runs aboveground here, has been extended all the way from San Francisco. I'm not sure that I'm so much in favor of conservation and against development. Those were quite desolate landscapes, with their dry grass and wiry oaks. Because the climate here is different from Berkeley's, the ocean fog doesn't reach this far, the sky is always blue, everything is parched; so, people and greenery go together.

Well then, it has been given to me to see in one lifetime the end of the countryside. What happened here is a pattern for the entire planet, not that it has to look the same everywhere, but a clear pattern is developing, if only with regard to population density. So, housing tracts are scattered over a great distance, preserving relics of the countryside, but already maintained artificially: irrigation, trees, space set aside for sports. Farming is kept separate, but there are no more hamlets.

My rural childhood differed from today's childhoods. Chiefly in the swarms of insects that buzzed, bit, crawled into one's eyes. Bare feet covered with scars and scabs from constant scratching. Crickets hopped in the grass, beetles raced around, red ants (the ones that bite the worst) and black ants of various sizes swarmed, caterpillars of many colors and shapes were found on the leaves, and indoors, on the walls of the kitchen and certain rooms —for example, those near the milking shed—was a black moving coat of flies. The whey in the glass fly traps was thick with layers of drowned flies. Chemical methods have taken care of this entire swarming world that marked my childhood in yet another way, surrounded as it was by a multitude of birds. Today, insectivorous birds have a hard life, although their small number doesn't surprise people who have nothing to compare it to.

AUGUST 10, 1987

There is a particular quality to the light in the North, as I discovered after I folded our tent in a campground in the Canadian Rocky Mountains, in Jasper National Park, from which the first snow (in August) was chasing Janka and me away. It was 1969. From Jasper, the road to Edmonton heads north and then makes a turn. It was there, beside the Athabasca River, that I encountered that quality of northern light which is, after all, so ordinary for many inhabitants of our planet that they fail to notice it. I experienced that sensation for the first time when, shortly before the outbreak of World War II, I traveled from Warsaw to the little town of Głębokie, where my father was working at the time. Głębokie is no farther north than my native district, but it is a lot farther east; perhaps that explains the difference. I have never described this town. Its surroundings were archetypal Belorussia, but in the town itself the Baroque of post-Jesuit churches survived, and in the center, a shtetl like those in Jewish literature and Chagall's paintings; never before or after have I seen such a density of wooden market stalls. It looked like a single wooden sailing vessel divided by partitions into individual stalls.

Accustomed to the California light, I would most likely find it hard to adapt to northern light. That recent gray May in Europe got me down. Yesterday's blue sky (after one o'clock, more or less) assuaged, as it usually does, all those anguishes to which I forbid entry. Although I might, perhaps, have relished a climate like that in the Antilles—violent downpours that last a few minutes, and then the splendor of wet foliage gleaming in the sunlight. In California it almost never rains during the summer months.

AUGUST 11, 1987

My sensitivity to the climate may derive from the fact that my life has passed and now every day is precious. In his old age, Leopold Staff wrote a poem called "The Bridge":

> I didn't believe,
> Standing on the bank of a river
> Which was wide and swift,

That I would cross that bridge
Plaited from thin, fragile reeds
Fastened with bast.
I walked delicately as a butterfly
And heavily as an elephant,
I walked surely as a dancer
And wavered like a blind man.
I didn't believe that I would cross that bridge,
And now that I am standing on the other side,
I don't believe I crossed it.

How did I do it? How did I cross that bridge? An enumeration of my own qualities would sound false, but my judgment of myself is really unfavorable. With a certain tendency to look for genetic disadvantages on the Milosz side. Oscar used to say, "You know, like a Milosz," which meant, "Like a madman." This was in reference to his grandfather, a wounded veteran of the battle of Ostrołęka, who married an Italian singer; to his father, who suffered from clinical paranoia at the end of his life; and to his cousins from the Druja line of the family, who also had quite a few screws loose. True, Oscar's saying this shocked me, because it hit me squarely in my suspicions: Why the resemblance if those Miloszes, from the Czereja as well as the Druja lines, weren't particularly close relations? Could it be a congenital flaw, countered by the powerful blood of the ancient Kunats and the even more powerful blood of the Syruć family?

An artist and an exception to the norm. Since the days of Romanticism, we have been accustomed to this link, even to a link with illness; Thomas Mann placed it at the center of his concerns. Probably under the influence of Romanticism, I hit upon the idea of substitute, compensatory activities, but I really have no sympathy for "sick geniuses." Who knows if my ambition wouldn't have been better nourished by ordinary virtues, even if it meant that I would not create a single work?

Mediocrity as an ideal? Because then there are no guilty feelings about one's own existence. In Berkeley, I derive pleasure from being addressed as "Doctor" or "Professor." The satisfaction of belonging to a respected clan, but without excesses, because, after all, "one pays for everything," as the devil, the assistant manager of the hotel, says in Leszek Kołakowski's play *Hotel Eden.*

Last night, dinner at the Leonard Nathans' and a discussion about how to phrase one's refusal when turning down an invitation to participate in meaningless performances organized in support of international causes. Decency would require us to give the reasons why we think debates about, for example, how to introduce democracy, tolerance, and peace to the planet are a waste of time. But people like to travel to Paris at someone else's expense, and if they refuse, they prefer to do so politely.

$\mathcal{A}$UGUST 12, 1987

Marek prepared the soil and we planted the bougainvillea. It is delicate and doesn't transplant easily. The one that I bought for Nela last year in the old city of Menton was sickly for a long time; it lost its leaves.

So, I am trying to understand my life. I have to confess that my terror of the illness-genius correlation was downright obsessive and it explains many of my decisions. Stubborn, suspicious, stingy, cautious—a real Lithuanian—I was determined to husband my resources within their limits, believing that I would disintegrate if I forgot about my weaknesses. My marriage lasted nearly fifty years, in spite of everything. I chose Janka in order that her eyes, her judgment would govern my behavior, although I caused her much suffering. And perhaps it was from fear of the dark tide of irresponsibility and madness that I imposed so much discipline on myself, was so accurate, precise, punctual that I could almost be taken for a model baker, scientist, or businessman.

In California at the end of the twentieth century, I, with my knowledge of the hells of Europe, am like Mr. Sammler from Saul Bellow's novel. Also with a certain skepticism toward the privilege that American poets appropriate for themselves, the privilege of being certified madmen. Alcoholism, drugs, stays in psychiatric hospitals, suicide—these are supposed to be the signs of exceptionally talented individuals. America has been thrusting them into this since the time of Edgar Allan Poe. This is possible, but it is also possible that the Romantic myth that identifies greatness with deviance received a new stimulus in the shape of the permissive society and now engenders real, not imagined, results. Whenever Robert Lowell landed in a clinic I couldn't help thinking that if someone would only give him fifteen lashes with a belt on his bare behind, he'd recover immediately. I admit, that was envy speaking through me. If I cannot indulge myself, why should he be free to indulge himself?

*A*UGUST 13, 1987

The bay is gray; a bit of sunshine at midday. A sauna and a swim. I live shallowly, barely beneath the surface. Aware that a lot of things are happening in the depths, but preferring not to look. Stupid dreams connected with trivial daytime incidents.

Also, I am distanced from my own body. I am dependent on it (and I think of all those people who depended on their own bodies, just like me). I don't want it to be older than I feel I am inside. Kot Jeleński said I have the face of a forty-year-old man, a lined face, to be sure, the face of someone *qui a beaucoup vécu*. And the magnetism between me and women still functions, and women know, of course, if someone is still in the game or beyond it.

But consciousness observes, from a distance. Dante, dividing human life into periods, said sixty-five is the boundary of old age, after which the age of decay begins. Everyone is living longer today. I can't complain about my body. Nonetheless, with an old car you can expect that the carburetor will fail or the transmission break down at any minute. This union we have with our body—simultaneity and identity and habitation on the outside—is astonishing in and of itself. It is appropriate that the human mind is fascinated by it at the end of the twentieth century. In Milan Kundera's novel *The Unbearable Lightness of Being*, the best part is when Teresa, standing naked in front of the mirror, tries to discover where her soul is located.

In my childhood I often heard the legend of the Miloszes' Serbian roots, which probably arose because our family name is the same as the given name of one of their medieval heroes. In Belgrade, I stayed on Prince Miloš Street. I have been feted in Yugoslavia, they have translated almost all my books, I was elected to the Serbian Academy of Sciences, and now a Yugoslav journalist in Paris tells me that they consider me one of their own. She asked me where I developed such an understanding of Communism, because *The Captive Mind* is "the bible of Yugoslav intellectuals."

Yesterday a book of my poems in Hungarian translation arrived from Budapest, a beautiful edition. It had been blocked for the longest time by the intervention of the Polish Embassy through the Hungarian Ministry of Foreign Affairs. A few days ago, Tomas Venclova sent me a volume of poems and translations by Juozas Kekštas, published in Vilnius, in which I found twenty-six of my own poems. Kekštas died in Warsaw in 1981; he was one of the personalities of my Wilno youth. What a life! Arrested as a Communist by the Polish authorities (he was in the same cell as the Belorussian poet Maksym Tank, whom I knew); arrested again and sent to the concentration camp in Bereza Kartuska; deported to the gulag after the occupation of Vilnius by the Soviet army; then Anders's army, Iran, Iraq, Egypt, Italy. He fought at Monte Cassino, was wounded, decorated; then he emigrated to Argentina, where he worked as a laborer for many years. When he fell ill (paralysis), he moved to Warsaw because he was a Polish citizen, and he lived there for twenty years in a veterans' home.

AUGUST 14, 1987

I would like to free myself from moralizing, but I can't. The Romantic habit of compensation is too strong: Since you would like to be good, but are not, may your books serve the good. But your books are independent of you, ambivalent; sometimes you think they have served the good, at other times you don't. And you envy those who glorified art for art's sake, the artists of the past, and, under a somewhat different label, the artists of today, because they never asked themselves such questions.

AUGUST 15, 1987

I have to seek out the causes of my despair. When someone's life has passed under the sign of public and private misfortunes, it is easy to enumerate them. What does it mean that from childhood I have lived in countries that no longer exist? First, tsarist Russia. Obviously, I wasn't conscious then. But perhaps the fluids of the end do exist, and I was distinctly aware of them in

Rzhev on the Volga that revolutionary autumn of 1917, so that later on I even attempted to capture them in my early poems, but I didn't succeed. Then the 1920 war, images of a battle lost, flight, fate reversed, if only briefly, in the battle on the outskirts of Warsaw. True, my school years are an exception to this because they were normal, but already in my youth there was the growing consciousness that the entire system surrounding me was provisional. I knew that everything was going to disintegrate, but there were two levels of awareness, strangely enough. One was the possibility of an apocalyptic war; the other, which I found more convincing, consciously at least, was an ideological vacuum and within it—but here I again have to refer to currents (fluids)—signs that could be deciphered only by those who were particularly sensitive. I saw Marxism as the sole force that was potentially grounded in reality. It was bringing defeat to Poland, but I could see no countervailing force, and I spoke about this openly with my director at Polish Radio, Halina Sosnowska. She took my words seriously. Later, I saw the end of two countries with my own eyes: independent Poland and independent Lithuania. And soon after that, the end of Europe. Whatever may be the fate of Europe's fabric, limited to the West European peninsula (for comfort, one can refer to the ancient threat of Islam, first from the south through the Saracens, then from the east through the Turks), the impression of Europe's provisional existence in the years after the war reminded me of what I had felt in Poland during the thirties. It was, so to speak, a posthumous existence. In the case of Western Europe, it was the transformation of living countries into a museum and a quiet readiness to accept slavery. (According to the classic Hegelian formula, a slave is a person who wants to live at any cost, even at the cost of his freedom.)

These, then, are the determinant causes of my pessimism. But here, in America, to whom can I bequeathe my "knowledge of the end," of which I myself am somewhat ashamed? First of all, a person who is marked in this way is untrustworthy, even for himself; second, there is such a thing as responsibility for the spoken, and not just the written, word. Since there is no pure diagnosis, every diagnosis also creates reality.

AUGUST 16, 1987

A visit from the gardener, who advises me to transplant the feijoa because there's no way to control their growth under the windows. He also confirms that the pines are healthy and can stand there for another twenty years or so, despite their gigantic height, although there was some talk this winter of their posing a danger to the house because of storms blowing in from the ocean.

Attended an afternoon party at Simon Karlinsky's, where Frank Whitfield was presented with a Festschrift in his honor. I learned that one way to deter deer is to go to the zoo and buy lion or tiger droppings (?).

My "knowledge of the end" has a counterweight in the admiration I feel for people endowed with the virtue of hope. Tadeusz Byrski was one of those. Jerzy Turowicz, too. Pope John Paul II. Endowed with the virtues of faith and hope. But what if someone has very little hope? That's closer to my situation. Is there love in me? It's not for me to judge. The hope of those whom I admire derives from a vision of mankind in Christological movement, so that in the final analysis the defeats inflicted by history (for example, the totalitarian system) do not present an obstacle to the development of human souls and will even produce positive results, although not immediately.

Perhaps Jeanne represents another kind of hope, taken from Jaspers's "philosophical faith." This is faith in the appeal to transcendence inscribed in the very nature of man.

I have received a belated birthday present, Renata's work: a book consisting of a facsimile of my *Three Winters* plus commentaries by various authors on each poem. Holding this book in my hands, I was totally on the side of art, maybe even of art with a capital A. Proud that my poems have their own life. Objects that used not to be and that suddenly emerged through my mediation so that, like Chardin's painting, they will always exist, and whatever may be said about them will exist only in relation to them. And this feeling is intensified by amazement: How could this have emanated from me? For the body and the soul change, undergo various stages, physiological ones, too, and if a past stage should happen to be preserved, it takes you by surprise.

$\mathcal{A}$UGUST 17, 1987

Stefan Kisielewski (Kisiel), in his commentary on my poem "The Gates of the Arsenal":

> For me, Milosz is a poet of fear, fascinating in his lack of faith, his pessimism that arises out of his sense of the fragility, the ephemerality of all worlds, both spiritual and material, and that penetrates to the very marrow of his bones. I believe in the authenticity of his dread; I do not believe in his consolations. Neither in his reasonably leftist, "humanistic," secular consolations nor in his religious supports: mysticisms, Swedenborgs, lands of Ulro. His Old Testament translations? They are a poetic-linguistic costume, a mask for the soul; after all, one has to do something on this earth. "You delude yourself with religion, sir, and tomorrow you will cast it aside."

$\mathcal{A}$UGUST 18–19, 1987

On board a Pan Am plane approaching London, en route to Castel Gandolfo for a papal seminar on Europe. My motivation: courtesy toward the Pope, although I don't have high expectations of what can emerge from the deliberations of old baboons. The seminar papers I read are so-so.

I am very fond of Kisiel (the Old Monkey) and I value him. There is a lot of malicious truth in what he says in that fragment. However, he doesn't take into account a particular, quite fundamental, fact: all my intellectual impulses are religious and in that sense my poetry is religious. Also (and perhaps this is the same thing) it is pro Life and against Nothingness. Although, if we are speaking of Christianity, it is consistently couched in terms of yes and no. His Holiness has noticed this; John Paul II once said to me in a private conversation about *Six Lectures in Verse*, "You always take one step forward and one step back." To which I replied, "Can one write religious poetry in any other way *today*?"

$\mathscr{A}$ugust 25, 1987

After my return from Castel Gandolfo. The feel of Europe in the plane from London to Rome. I run into Leszek Kołakowski as I leave the plane and together we delight in the elation of a group of Italian youths (a school outing?). They are singing, kissing, chanting "Italia," applauding—the very image of freedom and the spontaneous approbation of life. Charming.

We are met at the Rome airport by Krzysztof Pomian and Father Tischner, who, along with Krzysztof Michalski, is one of the organizers of the papal seminar. Jacek Woźniakowski arrives shortly afterward on the plane from Zurich. On the road to Castel Gandolfo, I inhale the odor of smoke; they are burning grass in the fields, the heat is intense after California, it's oppressive, the inside of a furnace. Supper in Casa Nostra, the nuns' pensione, where they are putting us up. A Polish gathering, just what I lack in Berkeley, and I would give a lot to have these Polish conversations over wine more often. Despite all sorts of obstacles, they did take place in Brie-Comte-Robert and Montgeron, although not without Janka's quiet opposition and the worst possible influence on the children. Because, for someone who listens in without knowing exactly what the point is, such conversations sound absurd and their humor has a macabre cast. For me, however, they are and were essential.

The conference is on "Europe and What Europe Has Given Birth To"— combined with my jet lag (there's a nine-hour difference) and also the impossibility of sleeping because of the heat. Every morning a van takes the participants to the papal palace and drives through the gates, saluted by the Swiss Guard in their colorful costumes. The session lasts from ten to one; the Pope, who is present, listens intently. Then it's down to the city for lunch at our nuns' establishment, and my one chance at sleep during the siesta, after which there's an afternoon session, also with the Pope, from four to seven. The palace walls are thick and offer partial protection from the sun, but there is no air-conditioning. The hall opens onto a long terrace from which there is a view of the lake; a breeze stirs the curtain. We sit at a long table, behind microphones; the Pope's table is in a corner, piled with books that he leafs through while listening. The Europeanization of the planet, expounded most interestingly in the not too specialized papers (Europe and India, Europe and Islam). There isn't enough of the broader vision that a German, Professor Robert Spaeman, and Professor George Kline (Russia and the West) demonstrate. The Germanocentrism of the Germans, until finally I have to speak up and talk about the constant German tendency (preceding Nazism and illuminating Hitler's lost war with Russia) to treat whatever is to the east of Germany as "outer darkness." After this session, the Pope praises me ("It was high time someone mentioned that"). Later, I also speak about the film *Shoah* (the indictment of Christianity contained in it) and about the corrosion of the religious imagination as a result of the European revolution, asking how this affects and will affect the particular great religions of mankind.

The Pope's dinners with language groups: English, German, Polish. At the Polish dinner the conversation is uninhibited, almost exclusively about Polish affairs. The Pope talks a lot, there's a great deal of laughter (Father Tischner's highlander jokes).

To close the conference, my bilingual reading at 9 p.m. Saturday, August 22. I am not particularly satisfied with it, I'm sweating, I can't see well because I am standing and there is no podium, just books lying on a table, I lose time looking for the right page, and furthermore I want to read as much as possible in Polish, out of consideration for the Pope.

Duchess Aldobrandini gives a dinner for the conference participants in her villa not far from Castel Gandolfo, but the Polish group arrives only after dinner with the Pope. This Pope, unlike his predecessors, does not cultivate ties with the great Roman families. The fame of the Aldobrandinis dates from the time of Clement VIII. He was a good Pope, the Duchess says, except that he ordered the execution of Beatrice Cenci.

When he bade farewell to the conference participants, the Pope said that while listening to the proceedings he had been thinking constantly of Peter's decision to come to Rome, and that Peter would have been amazed to see what had come of that decision and of Europe.

*A*ugust 26, 1987

The Berkeley climate is a relief. I made notes on Castel Gandolfo as if it were nothing special; that is, as if I weren't convulsed with laughter inside myself at my participation in it and did not have a "Metaphysical Sense of the Strangeness of Existence," which is a single compound feeling that ought to have a separate name so that one would not have to repeat continually and not very precisely: "I am astounded." Consider this: I am, after all, the boy who was so timid that when he was sent to the store he was afraid to utter the words telling what he'd come for. And the same one who, in Krasnogruda, suffered torments because of his lack of social sophistication and knowledge of how to behave at the table. To this day, I still carry within me every minute of my unbounded envy there in Krasnogruda as I watched those tall, handsome, athletic Varsovians—Michał, Zdziś, and Edek—who hung out together. Let us also compare my identity now, in 1987, with myself in, shall we say, 1940. France had just fallen, I had seen the Soviet tanks on Cathedral Square in Wilno, and there I was one summer night waist-deep in a bog, threading my way through the reeds, in total euphoria. Which is incomprehensible to me to this day. I could have gotten eight years in a labor camp for my attempt to escape across the border of the Soviet Union, and everything else would have been different, assuming I survived. Ahead of me was the possibility of Sachsenhausen or Auschwitz. And none of it had any effect on me. Euphoria: an agile body, adventure, danger. From that distant me to myself today; from that Europe to this Europe. What a condensation of history, beyond words. "It could have been worse," says the Pope. What would have been if; what would have been if not. And so on. One of the improbabilities: the resilience of Polish Catholicism, a Polish Pope, a conference such as this one, and on such a topic. And if someone had predicted that I would someday be Professor Emeritus at the University of California, I would have thought: Just to be a professor would be quite an achievement, let alone "emeritus." How much time that title contains!

$\mathscr{A}$UGUST 27, 1987

In the morning, a cold fog dripping from the trees. I awoke to a surprise and disappointment: a deer had eaten all the heliotrope blossoms. They were so abundant, not even professional gardeners have heliotrope like that.

The papacy as a rock on which the pure can take shelter. But sinful people press in upon it from all sides, morally suspect, crazed, grinding their hips to the beat of rock music, open to delirium, crime, and television. From the point of view of the Church, there are entire armies of them, embraced by a universal licentiousness: homosexuals, lesbians, women who have had one or more abortions, men who are responsible for those abortions one way or another; women and men whose means of livelihood are their genitalia; everyone who sleeps with someone outside a Church-licensed matrimonial union; divorced men and divorced women. Isn't that enough? But there are also the uncounted millions of men and women who don't adhere to the ban on contraceptive devices. I compare the papacy, not the Church, to a rock. For where, on which side, are we—we who are baptized in the Roman rite? Don't we recognize ourselves in one of those enumerated categories? And don't we look upon the teachings of the Vatican with respect and humble envy as something that is too elevated for us ordinary mortals?

The Pope in white, a powerful, attractive image of man above the earth, above our monkey-like masses mired in lusts. Were he a dried-out old man, the image would not exert such power; but he is a strapping man, he belongs to the crowd of passersby, while, at the same time, he does not belong. He returns in dreams. Would it be worthwhile, as an American writer has suggested half jokingly, to shoot him, so that a modern Pope would take the place of this conservative, a Pope who would permit contraceptives, would rescind the celibacy of priests, introduce divorce, grant equality to women by giving them the right to become priests? John Paul II as a "sign of refusal." They have already wanted to get rid of him; and we know who.

Certainly, openness is better than phariseeism. But perhaps dams are better than the opening of sluice gates for the wrong reason.

AUGUST 28, 1987

A dream: I am a teacher in an American high school. After the end-of-year exams, the principal (yes, a woman) asks me to address the students. I stand beside her on the podium. I don't know what to say, so I begin to tell them about my own school exams. They start to leave, first one at a time, then practically en masse. I understood that, instead of saying just a few words, I have been nattering away in the most boring talk, and that I am an old fogy.

At Castel Gandolfo, someone told me about the Pope's visit with Agca, the Turkish assassin, in a Roman jail. In the photographs, it looked as if Agca was confessing to the Pope. In reality, he was sharing his worries with him. He had fired from so close that the Pope could have survived only through the intervention of the Mother of God of Fatima; it was her anniversary. Agca, who was superstitious, was now afraid that the Mother of God would take revenge. The Pope had to calm him down, reassuring him that the Mother of God is not in the habit of taking revenge.

I have received a copy of my book *The Witness of Poetry* in an edition put out by the Warsaw publishing house Czytelnik. I compared it with the Polish version published by Kultura in Paris. Quite a few censor's cuts— stupid, but highly informative about what is not permitted.

AUGUST 29, 1987

Fine weather. Fog only down below, over San Francisco. Yesterday, a visit to Dr. Goetsch. It's been two years and three months since he removed a cancerous polyp. I took a chance then and did not agree to major preventive surgery. I received the news quite calmly—not that I didn't think about it, but I was also able to think about something else. Now Dr. Goetsch is proud of his patient; the cancer has not recurred.

"The inevitable extinction of the human person appears to us the ultimate defeat of being; unlike the biological decomposition of the organism, it does not belong to the natural order of the cosmos. Indeed, it violates this order. Order, being empirically inaccessible, may be spoken of only when *contin-* ⟶

gentia rerum is related to a necessary and thus eternal reality" (Leszek Kołakowski, *Religion*).

According to Kołakowski, it is impossible to believe in God without at the
same time believing in immortality, because such a lack of faith denies God.
It is impossible to believe in immortality without at the same time believing
in God, because such a lack of faith denies the very possibility of immortality.
When we feel that our death is real, we are capable of valuing Leibniz's
argument about the world being imperfect, to be sure, but still the best of
all possible worlds, for who would we be, were it not for pain and death?

In my old notebook I find an entry from two years and three months ago:

"My fellow man." One should ponder the meaning of these words
constantly, but our "I" gets in our way, all its boundless ambitions and
fears, so that the other appears to us wrapped up in his selfness, dangerous, mysterious, in his thoughts, desires, actions, and in the recesses
of his body which we stealthily observe. And only in brief moments of
reflection about our own illness or approaching death are we able to
discover our identity, to say to ourselves: but he (she) is I! To make
matters worse, we are divided according to gender and we suspect,
perhaps justifiably so, but perhaps not, that the philosophy of the penis
cannot be the same as the philosophy of the vagina. But, after all, "My
fellow man" means that we are one person inhabiting the planet Earth,
divided according to gender, temperament, strength, appetites, etc.
"What can link me with him?"—a question that includes gratitude to
fate for my not being like that fool, that brute, that criminal. "What
can link me with her?"—for example, that drunken black prostitute on
the street corner, with her gaudy makeup. But when we face the stars,
or our animal neighbors—cats or dogs? Or a butterfly? Only humans
are identical in their desires and gratifications. And, above all, in their
pain. The universality of pain as a guarantee of my (our) nature. And
yet to empathize completely with our fellow man and to know his
misfortunes as if they were our own . . . Only a saint is capable of that.
Even saintliness is insufficient. God must incarnate himself in man. In
one man, and thereby in all.

I have been trying for a long time to comprehend John Paul II. To be
precise, not John Paul II, but his Polishness. An American Jesuit of Polish
descent wrote to me from Perugia after his stay in Poland; he had met so
many real devils and angels there that Dante could have found examples

among them for his book. The Pope represents the pure Poland of sacrificial youth who are like stones thrown by God to erect a rampart—the most noble Poland—but it worries me that this is a Norwidesque Poland. The golden bee. ("I could point her out to you at the ends of the earth!") The poet Cyprian Kamil Norwid is like the Warsaw of his youth: a plain covered with apple orchards and in each orchard a tiny manor house—or so it was described by a foreign traveler, one Johnston, in 1813. The legend of Piast the plowman, angels with blue eyes and flaxen hair, chivalric virtues, bewilderment at the evil of this world. In Norwid there is faith in the unique essence and, I daresay, in the calling of each nation as a tribe (General Bem's funeral in his poem "To the Memory of Bem—a Funeral Rhapsody" is a tribal ritual). Nationalism in the sense of historic formation is expressed more fully in Norwid than in Adam Mickiewicz or Juliusz Słowacki. Norwid is more ethnocentric, and the adherents of nationalism as a political ideology sensed this. Norwid, unlike his romantic contemporaries, was untouched by heresies, he was orthodox in his Catholicism, he spun out meditations on history, fulfilling itself through the sacrifices of individuals so that in the end "martyrdom would become unnecessary on this earth."

AUGUST 30, 1987

The Pope was raised on Mickiewicz and Słowacki and, in my opinion, on Norwid above all. They were still poets of the old Res Publica: Mickiewicz from Lithuania, Słowacki from Ukraine. Despite the Lithuanian origin of his family name, Norwid represents the retreat to ethnic boundaries. Although his sensitivity to history as a system to be deciphered, a procession of suffering but already redeemed humanity, originates in the historical experiences of the Res Publica, more so, to be sure, than from any philosophical readings. His writing is full of historicism, the *storicismo polacco*, as Brzozowski called it, that characterizes Polish literature. In this regard, only Russian literature, perhaps, can rival Polish literature, although it stands at the opposite pole, constantly returning to the idea of Moscow as the Third Rome.

The country's defeat and Norwid's personal defeat—here, suddenly, he is incarnated as the leader of world Christianity setting out to do battle with the forces of darkness. There is something to ponder here and to shudder at; this is a great theme, worthy of a gifted pen. It is doubtful that foreigners can understand anything of this. For every Pole must have a vision of true history, *Civitas Dei*, peering out from behind the deception of secular history. But now someone is seated on Peter's throne who was prepared by Norwid to interpret Russia's centuries-long march to the West as the process of her humanization through the martyrdom meted out by her to Poles above all.

There is a Norwidian messianism which differs from the blasphemous messianism that called Poland the Christ of nations. No collective body can be the Messiah. But particular features of certain countries, revealed in their history, can form a framework for the activity of a larger number of disinterestedly sacrificial spirits than can be found elsewhere.

A dream about an affront to a Russian writer (who resembled Adam Ważyk) and about the duel that would have to take place.

A dream about a long speech that I deliver in Polish; it is not translated, and none of the people in the audience can understand it.

SEPTEMBER 1, 1987

At the nadir of her misery Poland acquired a king, precisely the sort of king she had dreamed of—from the tribe of Piast, a judge beneath an apple tree, not one who was embroiled in the raucous reality of politics. His first capital was in Cracow, with its circle of Catholic intellectuals around *The Universal Weekly* and *The Sign*; his next capital was in Rome. A king who was a bearer of messianic faith, profoundly convinced that a domain of spirits does exist, in which there are clashes, struggles, and triumphs, and that it exists side by side with that other history, the history of living beings, and in close communion with it. Undoubtedly, any other Pope would also have had to believe in the communion of the saints, but he would not necessarily have viewed the collaboration of that world with this one as the very fabric of history. Now, as I write this, I begin to comprehend the degree to which Poland was formed by a daily awareness of the union of the living and the dead. This may go back even further than Christianity, as in the "forefathers" ritual, but it was the Romantic poets who most forcefully extracted this aspect of Christianity. "Everything from the Spirit and for the Spirit." Norwid's "Great Master . . . the Spirit!"

John Paul's journeys to Poland can be understood as an otherworldly battle for her soul. As if every communion among his thousands of listeners in brotherly love, even for a brief moment, moved the heavens, took place both here on earth and up there, in the beyond. Could he have known beforehand that he would be able to lift people out of their collective degradation in a bloodless insurrection? That something akin to Solidarity would arise, appropriate to the peaceful habits of these people? A symbolic response to Stalin's question: "How many divisions does the Pope have?"

Brought up on Mickiewicz, Słowacki, Krasiński, and Norwid, I am grateful for this inheritance that offers the possibility of intuitive insight into the historical dimension. And yet I distrust a Norwidesque Poland. Here I definitely am touching my own raw nerve.

Where is the line between Catholicism and Polishness? Is it possible to draw such a line? To be frank, in virtually every single Pole I can smell the innocence of elevated spiritual rhetoric, which means I share a common language only with demonized Poles, with those who have passed through Marxism, atheism, or some other deviations—ethnic deviations within their family, for example, or sexual ones. How can I place John Paul II, when his philosophical writings, like Norwid's writings, lack the flaw that I find so necessary?

SEPTEMBER 2, 1987

Last Sunday I played the role of indulgent grandpa. Taking the girls (both of them raised without religion) to Mass in Newman Hall, not in order to convert them, but so they might have respect for that sphere. The liberal priest delivered a sermon on the distancing of Christianity from Judaism as a calamity. I asked Marta if the priests in Poland speak out against anti-Semitism in their sermons. Her response: "Once I went to church at summer camp in Szklarska Poręba; he said something about the Jews, but the opposite." After Mass, lunch at Skates overlooking the bay; outside the window, a huge wave and the maneuvering of the sailboats. Marta tells me that on her high-school graduation exam she had to compare any novel with its film version and she chose *The Issa Valley*. "But the film has practically nothing in common with the novel."

The nationalisms of my part of Europe are incredibly pathological. I cannot trust thought that is the product of degradation and of attempts at finding consolation in defeat. If the material world gives you nothing, flee to the realm of the spirit. Norwid's irony masks his self-pity, and that emerges in translations of his poetry into English; for that reason, his position in world poetry is doubtful. If only someone would write a comparative study of three writers who were almost exact contemporaries: Melville, Dostoevsky, Norwid. Despite all the differences between them, including the differences in their backgrounds (the capitalist revolution in Melville's America and the barest beginnings of capitalism in Dostoevsky's Russia), both Melville and Dostoevsky are prophetic because they struggle with the crisis of Christian faith—the former in despair because he cannot believe, and the latter wishing to believe at any price and wrestling with his own devil. Norwid is virtuous, not a speck of demonism, but the question arises: Isn't literature that lacks this admixture too vegetarian a cuisine for us?

If it weren't for the fact that I have experienced Polish nationalism in practice, not just in attractive family trees and traditional dishes, I would look upon it differently. Modern patriotism is usually unaware of what has shaped it; it doesn't call itself nationalism but is eager to speak about the nationalism of its neighbors. In Poland, furthermore, the main ideology was (and probably still is) the so-called national ideology, and the assorted patriots have not comprehended that each of them is *anima naturaliter endeciana*. This term came into being in my Wilno university when Henryk Dembiński, the leader of the Catholic "Renaissance" movement, started drifting to the left. The Church Fathers had called Plato *anima naturaliter christiana* and Dembiński adapted the term, describing the Polish soul as, by nature, *Endek* (after the right-wing nationalist party).

One way or another, Warsaw under the German occupation was the place and time of my encounter with Polish nationalism in its highest intensity, when it acted exclusively as a patriotism that no one had the right to criticize. It carried an entire system of values, and I could not have liberated myself from it; that is, I would have remained in its power, unable to comprehend it from the outside, as it were, were it not for my inner discomfort as a poet, my intuitive perception of a certain sterility and falsehood that can be confirmed in the poet's craft. Too sublime. Too elevated. Too noble. Overly spiritualized. Can I help it if Norwid fused for me with the faces of several people whom I knew then, who were marked by exaltation, as if they were feverish every day—people who perished and whom I think of with an aching heart? The poetry of Anna Swir, who was the author of whimsical, charming poetic miniatures before the war, demonstrates how great was the tension of that exaltation. I was astonished when she contributed a very good poem,

"The Year 1941," to my anthology, *The Invincible Song*. What was she doing writing such a hymn?

> *But though ever so many will perish*
> *perhaps I, perhaps you,*
> *the nation will not perish.*

SEPTEMBER 3, 1987

July 1944. Hot. Warsaw, after almost five years of occupation, wears a smile, as carefree as only it can be; the walls of its apartment houses are pocked where hostages were executed on street corners; its central districts no longer exist, transformed into the wasteland of the ghetto destroyed by the Germans. What a cheerful city, observing with a stifled giggle the hurried evacuation of the enemy's offices, the loading onto trucks of wardrobes, trunks, suitcases. Swallows in the pure blue sky, the women's flowered outfits, the laughter and shouts of boys in courtyards hosing each other down, leaping into improvised swimming pools. So, the end of the war is in sight. After so many deaths, let the living enjoy the sun, the greenery, straining their ears to catch the rumbling of the approaching front.

How many inhabitants of this city understand that this is not a victory, but rather the total, utter defeat of a country that resisted invasion and then continued the struggle for years, on land, on the sea, in the air, and here in the "underground state"? How many of them are capable of differentiating appearances from reality? That country, such as it was, will never exist again, even though it lasted until the moment when the heavy guns of the army from the East could be heard.

For his colleagues on the underground newspaper for which he wrote, Kroński played the role of an old-fashioned patriot, privately mocking the way they turned the fatherland into an absolute value. Their obtuseness prevented them from seeing clearly the decrees of history. Instead of drawing conclusions about guilt and punishment, they were taking refuge in the petty dramas of their own little bailiwick. In the meantime, the attempt at unifying Europe through Fascism had ended in a crime; it was a different conquest than that of Greece from the outside, by Philip of Macedon, because it was internal, and now it was the Persians who were going to scourge Greece–

Europe as a punishment. If that was the case, then the cults of local divinities were insignificant.

Tadeusz, called Tiger by his friends, the son of a Jewish father (Attorney Kroński), a philosopher, a friend of the Czech philosopher Jan Patočka, clearly derived his ideas from his private traumas and hatreds. In underground Warsaw he saw a continuation of the same mentality from before 1939 which had caused him so much pain. With the sadness or, rather, the melancholy of someone who knows without a doubt what others do not want to know, he prophesied the horrifying disasters that that mentality would, inevitably, lead to.

What attracted me to him? The breadth of his vision. In no one else did I find such a lively historical imagination as he rightly prided himself on. That imagination could only be tragic. They wanted to return to the pre-war state of affairs, as if the gas chambers and crematoria could be just an episode and did not cry out to the heavens for vengeance. Cry out so successfully that they brought on the invasion of the Persians.

Kroński forbade himself and others to speak or think about the Persians. I don't believe that he had any illusions about them, but it was forbidden to become agitated over the inevitable. That was where we disagreed. Depressed by pangs of conscience, because I had forced myself to entertain noble sentiments, I needed an iconoclastic, brutal act, but I would not have been capable of one were it not for his influence. I cut off the dead hand of the past that was restraining me, and my inner freedom—and, at the same time, the possibility of a poetry that was different from the endless lamentation over defeated honor—dates from that time, from 1943. As usual, however, I was inconsistent; I am not ashamed of that inconsistency, because it was good for my mind. Despite Kroński's injunctions, I did not forbid myself either to think or to speak about the Persians.

I could say a lot about the Hoser seed warehouse in Okęcie (Hoser was Warsaw's largest garden-supply company), especially about the company that gathered there by chance on September 13, 1944. Picture a large, unfinished building (those districts of Warsaw had a good many buildings like that virtually from the moment the war broke out; the city had been expanding, in other words), standing practically in an open field, towering over a lane lined with small houses at one end of the field. Either they hadn't had time to wall in the building, or they hadn't been in a hurry to finish the job; in any event, only open stories existed and we were lying on the highest one, amid sacks of seeds. We had come there across the fields with Zyg and Futa Poniatowski and others when the Germans started setting fire to the buildings and the fire was approaching the building in which the Poniatowskis' apartment was located—at 16 Kielecka Street, as I just discovered while reading Maria Dąbrowska's memoir. Janka and I were with Zyg and his wife because on the day the Uprising began, not suspecting anything, we had walked down our Independence Avenue toward the trolley stop on Rakowiecka Street. To pay a visit to the Krońskis. It began with German machine-gun fire from the bunkers on the corner of Rakowiecka. We had been walking along the lefthand sidewalk and we dashed into a side street, from where it was just a couple of steps to the Poniatowskis', our closest neighbors, but we managed to make it there only by dawn of the following day.

People say "Uprising" and they forget that it was not a single, unified whole but a collection of events; for example, the building at 16 Kielecka Street simply waited, from day to day, straining to hear when it would be over and the Soviet tanks would enter. In fact, that one small modern apartment house would supply plenty of material for observation if one could take each of its inhabitants, the men and women, and closely observe each one of them. But the seed warehouse fulfilled all the conditions necessary for a narrative or a screen play. Here's why. People thrown together by chance; the danger they were in, because the auxiliary Russian troops, eager for rape and murder, appeared outside the building from time to time; it was lucky that they weren't attracted by our apparently empty hangar, but were distracted by the goods of Western civilization (they were busy learning to ride bicycles); but had they looked in, it would have been a bad situation. In the midst of this danger, conflicts of temperament, character, and point of view, and also extraordinary human types whose presence in the city we had not even guessed; also, the unbelievable background, because since there were no walls there was a panoramic view of the white city in the sunlight, with flames and smoke from the fires, with the musical accompaniment of the sounds of battle, explosions, artillery shelling, the stuttering of small-arms fire. Of those comrades in misfortune the one who is inscribed most clearly in my memory is an acquaintance of the Poniatowskis', a Mr. Okulicz. As his name indicates, he was of gentry origin, from the Kresy—a minor official by profession. He said, "All my life, all I do is run from them. I remember, I was seven years old when I fled across the ice near Minsk, wrapped up in a quilted cape." Let us ponder this wonder of wonders, from which far-reaching conclusions can be drawn. The Germans are here; we are in immediate danger; but he (could it be because he was born over there, in the Grand Duchy?) knows one thing only: the Bolsheviks are coming.

September 4, 1987

The disappearance of a human being. His looks, his movements, habits, character are preserved in the memory of a few individuals who knew him fairly well, and I can now count those individuals on my fingers. Jerzy Andrzejewski—no longer among the living. Zygmunt Hertz—no longer among the living. Kot Jeleński—no longer among the living. A couple of friends are left. One after the other, those with whom one can speak about the absent die, and what remains is silence. A name evokes no image; disappearance is forever.

In a marriage, we inflict pain on one another, and the feeling of guilt when it is too late to fix anything will not disappear, even though it undergoes constant changes. Relief may come with the thought that everything that once was comes to an end with death, passes into eternity, that there is no responsibility, and he who remembers will also soon pass into eternity without a trace. But immediately, in opposition to that thought, an objection arises: let there be a judging, let there be the torment of self-knowledge, if only our belief in every moment of our life enduring somewhere, forever, can be proved true.

Since I am the only one who knows this much, do not I, who lived with her for so many years, have an obligation to speak about her? She never wanted me to speak; she kept aloof. Her jealous privacy, her acceptance of anonymity, expressed her aristocratic nature, though she was not of aristocratic or even intelligentsia lineage. She came from a Warsaw family with roots in the petty gentry. Her father, Ludwik Dłuski, slim and flaxen-haired, with the charm of a modest, soft-spoken man, was apprenticed in his youth to a master brazier. Then he worked two years in a metallurgical factory on the East Coast of the United States, but he returned home because he was lonely. Before the Second World War, he was a court usher. Her mother, Czesława Dłuska, née Szczerbińska, had a terrible temper and possibly exhibited some signs of psychological disturbance, but when the four of us lived together on what was then the end of Independence Avenue, there were only brief outbursts, and we spent the years from 1941 to 1944 harmoniously. When I was in Poland in 1981, Tony and I visited the village of Zuzela, which was Janka's birthplace and also the birthplace of her contemporary, Cardinal Wyszyński. She always suspected that he was one of those village lads who rocked and overturned their boat filled with little girls in their Sunday best.

Among Janka's virtues were the high, perhaps excessively high, expectations that she had of people, books, works of art. She had a rare sense of quality, which increased the number of her enemies. I would count as one of her faults the way she kept her distance from other people, especially from my literary colleagues, while I, according to Wikta (Józef Wittlin's half sister), was a child who always wanted to splash in the mud with the other children.

September 6, 1987

I ask myself if it is at all possible to describe a marriage, its various stages, both happy and unhappy. In my case, the difficulty is compounded by the ten years of her illness that separate me from her true self. That I, with my Manichaean tendencies, should have had to face that daily sight of undeserved suffering, terrible unhappiness, degrading physical humiliation. With an image of her former self in my mind—beautiful, laughing—I had to look at a pitiful human shell, observe its defenselessness, passivity, dependence on the hands that lift it, place it on the commode, bathe it. It is heartrending, unbearable, but one becomes desensitized by routine, and one's responses are blunted. The words "pity" and "empathy" do not apply to this situation; one would have to find something else, perhaps *misericordia* is closest, since it includes the sense of misfortune. How can one keep from hurling that word, invented by human beings, against the heavens? One would think that the cruelty of the twentieth century, if only imagination were capable of perceiving it in the sufferings of individual human beings —that those sufferings would suffice to destroy all faith in Providence. It is even worse when an individual human being under sentence by Providence is crushed before our very eyes. In the first phase of her illness, when the paralysis crept steadily upward past her legs, Janka's voice seemed to express a certain stupefaction: "Who is doing this? Who needs this?" Who is doing this, indeed? If we accept the idea that *someone* is doing it, we cannot avoid thinking that he is malicious. If we accept the notion that no one is responsible, we are left face-to-face with the mindless cold reptile of matter.

During one of her hospital stays, Janka shared a room with a Ukrainian woman who would enumerate the operations she had gone through, and describe the varieties of pain she had experienced, in the absolute conviction that God wanted it that way and that she was obliged to accept suffering from His hand. Janka's mind was struggling with the descending curtain of dissociation, but even had her mind been working properly, she would not have sought solace in a fervent faith like that. She was pious in her own way, but her own way tended to be agnostic.

A mind that is conscious of its own descent into darkness, of forgotten dates, names, events; a high intelligence that is still capable of serving her paranoid fears and her anxiety about the fate of her children. She had a gift for love, exclusive, blind love, one might say a love that matched her uncompromising character, always yes or no, and capable of determined acts of self-sacrifice. If those ten years had been only the misery of a body ravished by disease, but no, there was also the humiliation of the spirit that daily loses successive remnants of its power, until it is hidden away who knows where, perhaps in a tear, the sole sign of consciousness in the moment of death, while everything else appears to be proof of her reduction to the activity of her diseased brain cells.

The suffering of innocents. She was absolutely straightforward, pure. Writing this, I have no intention of rendering an idealized version of her, as is so common when we remember the dead; I know her faults, which were different from my faults, and her virtues, which I lacked. Her yes-no mind was the direct opposite of my dialectical, tortuous mind; her integrity exposed her to the accusation of refined irony and contempt for others. And perhaps it wasn't Alzheimer's disease, or schizophrenia, or "sclerosis of the brain," but a profound depression that developed out of her increasingly apprehensive or prideful self-isolation from people.

SEPTEMBER 7, 1987

The wild fennel (*Foeniculum vulgare*), taller than a man, is in bloom now along the road that I walk on in the mornings. For me, it is the recurring accent of autumn. The weather continues to be fine, but the sky is often clouded with the pall of smoke that hangs over California from the forest fires in the Sierras.

Milosz's wife. A writer's wife. I don't like the word "writer." A pathetic fraternity. Somewhere, I came across this image of the behavior of every type of artist: There's a meadow with a crowd of people in it; everyone is releasing his own balloon; the sky is full of balloons, and every one of these people is wishing that the other balloons would burst, is dreaming about pricking them, so that only one balloon might remain—his own. Writers gather in crowds, they have a need to, almost a herd instinct; if they didn't, the ritual of gossiping about each other and constructing hierarchies wouldn't exist. Also, everyone believes that his colleague is slightly lower than he is. And then the closely bonded association comes to an end, and out of five hundred or a thousand names, only one is preserved for posterity.

Janka was not one of those writers' wives who officiate, who light candles after supper and declare with adoring breathiness, "Kazio is going to read." She was too ironic for that, and that irony was good for me. She kept a disdainful distance from that "milieu," but she was able to be friends with a few of my colleagues. Before the war, that friend was Józef Czechowicz; we were an inseparable trio at Polish Radio on Dąbrowski Square. In Warsaw during the war, it was Jerzy Andrzejewski and also Stefan Kisielewski. She couldn't stand Jarosław Iwaszkiewicz; judging him by his pre-war books, which she and her friends had read in school, she thought of him as a corrupter of souls. She also never accompanied Andrzejewski and me when we would go to feast at the Iwaszkiewiczes' in Stawisko. But the three of us would take the suburban electric railway to visit the Wertenstein family, who were renting a cottage near Komorowo. What a sight in the middle of the occupation, while the inhabitants of the ghetto were being murdered! It is tea time and three generations of a Jewish family—grandmothers, aunts, cousins—sit down to the table as if they hadn't a care in the world; it was an idyll maintained with great effort in opposition to unremitting danger.

Janka loved to drink vodka with Andrzejewski; she was fond of him, but she had a poor opinion of his writing, and she was probably the only person from whom he could accept criticism. He was so dignified and haughty toward others that I envied him his self-assurance. For Janka the war was a time of opening up, of warmth and friendship; she didn't find alcohol offensive then, but later on she hated alcohol because of my need for literary talk-fests and the drinking that accompanied them, and also because I shamed her by flirting with women when I was drunk.

She valued my writing so much that I even accused her of approving of no other writers but me. When she found out in 1953 that the U.S. State Department would definitely not issue me a visa, she screamed at them in a rage, "You'll be sorry, because he is going to win the Nobel Prize." Nevertheless, beginning with our years in France, my profession as a writer was increasingly in conflict with her love for our children, despite the fact that for a long time it was our family's only means of support. The price one pays is the self-torment of a too active imagination, despondency, long hours of walling oneself off in the study from one's surroundings—all extremely damaging to family life. Loving me, Janka would have preferred me to be the most ordinary of men; a baker, for example. The Nobel Prize, when it came, was, for her, a tragedy.

SEPTEMBER 10, 1987

Spent two days on the coast, north of San Francisco. Almost all my visits to Mendocino take place under gray skies; this one was an exception, with sunshine and a blue ocean; the summer fogs must have passed. The splendor of the cliff cathedrals amid the spume, the roar, the ceaseless motion of the waves, constant and yet always varied. My time, and all human time, is insignificant. *"Je te salue, vieil océan!"* (Lautréamont). Yes, I am a writer, and watching a beautiful chain of pelicans stretched out across the evening sky, I think of Robinson Jeffers, who described them.

Cormorant colonies on the rocky outcroppings. Gulls. Brown pelicans, then a large flock of white pelicans viewed through binoculars near Bodega Bay. Several species of herons. Murres—I don't know if there is a word for them in Polish. Flocks of birds industriously wading in shallow lagoons.

The objective existence of the world as a form of relief. I propose not to probe too deeply into my feelings while writing this memoir, for fear of falsifying them, which is inevitable, because how can one stand onself without making cosmetic changes?

At night, right after returning from a screening of the Soviet film *Repentance* in Wheeler Hall, with the director present, the auditorium full, an audience of several thousand. An amazing film. Abuladze's answers to questions from the audience demonstrate his deftness as *homo sovieticus*.

$\mathcal{S}$EPTEMBER 12, 1987

The director Abuladze quoted some American's remark to the effect that such an honest and open film could not be made in America. This is nonsense, the usual American breast-beating. The truth is that such a film could not be made in America for entirely different reasons than a lack of honesty. I saw the capitalist financing of films in pre-war Poland by the owners of movie theaters, who dictated what should be in the films. That old Polish capitalism is to American capitalism as a street in Drohobycz, as described in Bruno Schulz's *Street of Crocodiles*, is to an American street. The American crocodiles who finance films make sure that they contain the appropriate dose of sex and violence and, if possible, of madness, illness, and perversion, too. Another factor is unconscious infection by a dehumanizing atmosphere which paralyzes the imagination independently of any financial concerns.

$\mathcal{S}$EPTEMBER 13, 1987

After a day at the annual pig roast that Allan organizes in his family's summer house near Big Sur. Between steep hills that are almost totally parched by the sun to a golden bronze, there is a gully formed by a stream; luxuriant grass, trees (mainly alders and sequoias), shade, bindweed, masses of lady's-smock near the water, almost the same magical greenery that suddenly appeared amid the dryness in the ravine near the ancient cloister in Nonza, on Corsica. A whole pig, stretched out on the coals, roasted from six in the morning to four in the afternoon. I followed the path beside the stream down to a small beach among the cliffs, but it was impossible to swim there; the surf was violent and the ocean too cold.

SEPTEMBER 14, 1987

What if one were to investigate the political tendencies of particular individuals, tracing them back to their innate features, their character? Then
my permanent aversion to capitalism would turn out to be more or less the
same as my aversion to nature. The reason is a feeling of menace, my
revulsion against brutality, pity, all mixed together, difficult to disentangle.
All my observations of cruelty in nature. "The cry of the hare as it is torn
to pieces fills the forest." And my consciousness, perhaps even exaggerated,
of the fate of the poor in America, their miserable neighborhoods, their hard
labor, their fear of unemployment, also the hell of the inner-city ghetto.
America does not threaten *me*. *I* experienced success in America, but so
what? It is not out of the question that, sufficiently protected by my industriousness and my ability to submit to discipline, I would not have perished
in America under any circumstances. Still, I could never assent to the state
of nature—that is, that each person should have to live as if he is constantly
endangered, as in the time of the cavemen. Of course, capitalism is *natural*;
whoever wants something different is going against the elementary right of
survival of the strong, and no one knows if attempts at escaping from that
right can be successful.

At a pig roast in a gully near Big Sur I am integrated into middle-class
America. Not necessarily as a man of letters; it is sufficient that I am a
professor emeritus. Afterward, on to Carmel to pay a visit to Robinson Jeffers's
Tor House, which is now owned and maintained by the Tor Foundation,
a society of Jeffers enthusiasts.

SEPTEMBER 15, 1987

I read two reviews of Andrzej Walicki's book, *Encounters with Milosz*, in
Arka [The Ark] and Walicki's response. He is right to raise questions about
the debates on the Stalin era by people who have no recollection of that
period but judge it according to their later experiences. For example, Michnik
and his *History of Honor in Poland*. Why be surprised at foreigners' incomprehension when even people who grew up in Poland are unable to appreciate
the intensity of the terror in those days? It was not just fear. Those attacks

on *The Captive Mind* implying that I had dreamed up some kind of abyss, while what was really involved was simply fear for one's own hide, are way off the mark. It was a terror born of the unexpected awareness that the worldwide triumph of Communism was on its way, and that dreams of an independent Poland would have to be placed in a museum. Is that insignificant? And that is why, looking back, I am mistrustful of the noble pronouncements in Jacek Trznadel's *Domestic Disgrace*. Certainly, if there should be a return to Poland-the-martyred-nation, the one from one hundred or two hundred years ago, then such distinctions (here, purity; there, ignominy) would be well founded. I myself have compared Wałęsa to Kościuszko. The emotional tracks are worn quite smooth. But to do this soberly? Objectively? One would have to prove that the Stalinist period was only a deviation, followed by a return to our normal condition—but what is the meaning of "normal" in our part of Europe?

September 16, 1987

Those who became Communists in 1945 had all the logical arguments on their side. As for the young writers, even their alternative option was not very plausible. The country was incorporated into the new Imperium forever; all one had to do was look at a map. So who could resist it? Those who didn't understand it, who were counting on a new war, on a miracle, and so forth. That's one category. The other was people who disagreed with the atheistic religion of Communism, which, however, assumed a greater familiarity with the Russian phenomenon and a better understanding of it than Polish writers possessed. Not many of them, most likely, had read Dostoevsky's prophetic novel *The Possessed*. Of course, the Catholic populace had an intuitive understanding and it was enough for them to see the marks of the devil's claws. Among intellectuals, those who were religious (Jerzy Turowicz, Hanna Malewska) remained constant in their faith, but that meant accepting the likelihood of martyrdom, which is something people forget about today.

My personal Ketman (in my book *The Captive Mind*) was related somehow to the Catholic refusal to serve (speaking metaphysically now) the forces of darkness. I don't know how I would have behaved under a direct threat; I managed to avoid that.

Most enigmatic was the behavior of the stoics, in contemporary guise, that is—people who understood the world to be devoid of ethical sanctions. Professor Henryk Elzenberg. Zbigniew Herbert. Though it may be that Herbert's stoicism is illusory. Reflecting on Anna Swir's poems, I found in them, side by side with her agnosticism or atheism, a blind attachment to one *imponderabilium*: the fatherland. Something similar is present in Herbert. One absolute.

September 17, 1987

Perfect weather all day long. Perhaps Elzenberg, too, should not be counted as a stoic, since he had Buddhist inclinations, and Buddhism, after all, is an a-theistic religion. But poets such as Herbert can point to an authentic, moralistic-patriotic current, concealed in Poland beneath appearances that are maintained by the collective with deep respect, a current that testifies to the fundamental non-metaphysical nature of Poles.

I think that my resistance to Communism had other sources, including my "metaphysical temperament" and also my understanding of the gravity of that movement which was truly preoccupied with one thing only: the dethronement of God. So my lecturing on Dostoevsky later on at Berkeley was totally consistent. And since I did not have a cult of Poland as a superior value, it would have been better not to digress in my poetry into public questions. Unfortunately, given the accidents of history, it was difficult to achieve such a degree of self-restraint.

Those of my poems in which I am a faithful chronicler of reality on the basis of "I see and I describe" and nothing more, however, are certainly honorable. No different than Leśmian's poetry. ("How in non-existence to establish our economic life?")

The author of a diary would be well advised to remember Simone Weil's aphorism: "All the good and all the evil that one thinks about oneself is false at the moment one thinks it. Therefore, one must think only ill of oneself. And one need not know that it is false" (from *La Connaissance surnaturelle*).

SEPTEMBER 18, 1987

The days of the Pope's visit to America and our West Coast. I preferred watching it all on television. Many people, very many, did the same, with the result that the crowds were smaller than expected. The newspapers were generally more favorable than the television commentators, whose progressive glibness in defense of dissent ought to shame dissenting Catholics. Public opinion is driven by the mass media in the direction of banality, and suddenly these Catholics can observe their opinions served up as banality while the Pope attempts to remind them that Christianity is a "sign of refusal." The Pope in Hollywood: he has come to the lions' den, and unaware that they are ready to rip him to pieces, he recommends that they start eating vegetable cutlets instead of their bloody cuisine. A marvelous text. It makes one think that it *is* possible to address the most spoiled community and to move or convince some members of it. The Pope in San Francisco: the same thing; the courage to proclaim the Word in the city of the loosest mores, in the capital of homosexuality, in a city that would be expected to turn a deaf ear. St. Paul in Corinth? The speech at the Dolores Mission was a masterpiece of balanced construction. About St. Francis, the patron saint of the city, and his spirit of love. Then a homily about the Prodigal Son and the Father's love for every sinful son. Followed by quotations from St. Paul, the enemy of homosexuals, but actually about something else, about his, Paul's, own transgressions that show he is the lowest of all sinners.

The greatness of John Paul II and his missionary journeys. For intellectuals it is repetition to the point of boredom of the same thing in a huge number of words. They forget, however, that millions of people are hearing the simplest truths for the first time. And John Paul II's mind embraced those millions like children who need him most in his role as teacher.

SEPTEMBER 19, 1987

That same day, when the Pope flew from San Francisco to Detroit, one of the participants in a television discussion, a Jesuit professor of theology from Berkeley, spoke out in clear opposition to the papal teachings. According to him, there is no right to deny participation in the Eucharist to people who have obtained divorces and entered into non-Catholic marriages. I am curious about what the bishop whose diocese includes Berkeley will do. In compliance with the papal admonition administered to the three hundred bishops in Los Angeles, he ought to apply sanctions. But that would mean publicity, notoriety. So most likely he will do nothing.

My strictness, my defense of discipline, amuses me. As if *I* conformed. Let's say this expresses my great need for a higher order. In this regard I am Italian or Polish, not American. We have a right to behave swinishly, but there should be that higher authority over us. Rules exist in order to exist, not in order not to be broken.

It seems to me at times that I am a character from a work of fiction. This is a serious intuition; it goes deep. For our imaginings about ourselves, whether written down or not, are a composition. Consciousness is like a law of form. My cat, Tiny, does not dream up any stories about himself.

September 20, 1987

Among the statesmen, the monarchs, the leaders of the twentieth century, other than Karol Wojtyła there is not a single figure who could fit our image of kingly majesty. Only he could truly play Shakespeare's kings.

Excitements. My life has been full of excitements, of rapture at the very existence of people or of works. Even now, when for the last couple of days an irritating virus has taken up residency in my chest and is making it difficult to breathe.

The dividing line between life and death is so fine. The unbelievable fragility of our organism, which suggests a vision: a fog of sorts condenses into human form, lasts for a moment, and is instantly dispelled.

September 21, 1987

Difficulty breathing and weakness. My main reading is *Congregation*, a book sent to me in page proofs by the publisher. American Jewish writers about the Bible, each writing about a different book. A beautiful idea, and some of the chapters are truly impassioned. I read it lying down in the afternoon and also when my coughing wakes me up at night.

September 22, 1987

Yesterday Robert Hass and I finished our work on my *Collected Poems*.

I have been looking at texts from around 1950; for example, Konstanty Gałczyński's translations of Shakespeare and also of Schiller ("Ode to Joy"), of Neruda and the Russian poets. What a topic: the triumphal Communism of the twentieth century after the victories of Stalin's armies in the years 1942–45. Aren't they exaggerating today with their hollering about the immorality of those who entered the service of Communism at that time? Also, expressing astonishment at their blindness, since millions were rotting to death in the gulags over there, while here there were odes to joy, enthusiasm for the new life, "the new man"? They ought, instead, to contemplate the fundamental duality of the written word and of things as they are. Who knows? It may well be that people need permanent duality, in ever changing degrees of intensity. All those poets on several continents—Vallejo, Neruda, Alberti, Aragon, Eluard, Quasimodo, Ritsos, Hikmet—*positive* that they are taking part in the colossal transformation of man into a new, radiant being; glorifying the youth of the planet, enraptured, because they have signed up with the right side, not the side of moribund capitalism. Translations of these poets filled the pages of Polish journals. Polish poets who, in my opinion, at a particular moment honestly believed, who were swept away by the fever of fraternity, of the common march of the best part of humanity: Mieczysław Jastrun, Konstanty Gałczyński. Gałczyński translated this Russian poem for us:

> *Let song upon song flow on,*
> *let songs echo in every deed*
> *where dream and reality meet . . .*

> *Let song after song flow on,*
> *praising the names of the brave;*
> *song swelling to praise that band*
> *of men who vanquished oppression—*

while over them now our Russia
extends her radiant hand.
                    —*Aleksandr Prokofev*

An example of the atmosphere of those days. Definitely incomprehensible
to the Polish activists in the anti-Hitler underground, who sat in their prison
cells after 1945 awaiting the execution of their sentence: a bullet in the back
of the head.

Neruda. I remember our meetings, including the last one at the PEN
Club Congress in New York in 1966, when I asked him why he had written
such disgusting things about me ("in the pay of the Americans," etc.), and
he replied, "Milosz, I was wrong, I apologize." I don't know what to think
about his fame and the possibility that it will endure. That eloquence, those
floods of words, practically logorrhea . . .

September 23, 1987

Autumn, Berkeley style. The fogs are different from the summer fogs. The
reddish color of the plane tree's leaves, but, then, they start turning red in
July, after the height of summer in May and June. Weakness and antibiotics;
apparently some virus is attacking my stomach and lungs.

Guillevic sent me two new volumes of his poems published by Gallimard.
The old satyr, subdued by age, writes about beetles, flowers, rivulets; in other
words, it seems that as we approach eighty we are inclined to pray to our
own divinity, some to God, others, like Guillevic, to nature.

Terrifying dreams. Escapes. The sensual details come from California (the
coast, tall pines, the needle-covered paths beneath them, the mountainsides).
The plot from the terror of the war years; the sensations (the heart thumping
while I run uphill) from my organism. What causes what? The second part
of the dream supplements an earlier one: about gluttony. Magnificent meat
sandwiches, lots of them, the taste of ham, pastrami, kielbasa. For a bard,
your dreams are utterly commonplace; or, as Zygmunt Hertz used to say,
"For a hunchback, you're quite handsome."

Almost every day, Public Television airs nature programs, mainly for young people. About spiders, fish, lizards, coyotes, animals of the desert or of alpine meadows, and so on. The technical excellence of the photography doesn't prevent me from considering these programs obscene. Because what they show offends our human, moral understanding—not only offends it, but subverts it, for the thesis of these programs is: You see, that's how it is in Nature; therefore, it is natural; and we, too, are a part of Nature, we belong to the evolutionary chain, and we have to accept the world as it is. If I turn off the television, horrified, disgusted by the images of mutual indifferent devouring, and also by the mind of the man who filmed it, is it because I am capable of picturing what this looks like when translated into the life of human society? But the children, those millions of young minds, are they able to watch this with impunity since they don't associate anything with the blind cruelty of Nature? Or, without realizing it, are they being slowly and systematically poisoned by those masters of photography who also do not know what they are doing?

September 25, 1987

The makers of those films have a scientific outlook and show the truth, nothing but the truth; furthermore, they appreciate the splendid photogeneity of nature. It is difficult to reproach them. Nonetheless, they are not only eyes that observe; their camera lenses are at the service of whatever occupies their heads—their theory. The story that they convey through their images is a moving illustration of the theory of evolution, of natural selection, and so on. Whether their theory is scientifically valid or not, it is what selects and composes their material.

Balzac lived during the reign of natural history; he didn't have to wait for Darwin. In the *Comédie humaine* he wanted to depict the species that make up human society. And he depicted them. During the German occupation we read Balzac passionately because the brutalized reality that surrounded us made a mockery of noble works and confirmed the brutalized France of the first half of the nineteenth century that we found in Balzac. Obviously, his writing is a model of the realistic novel, etc. Thanks to him, we are able to understand a lot about the day-to-day arrangements among people at that time. But, in fact, the *Comédie humaine* is a great fantasy, like Theodore Dreiser's America. True? Or false?

Is hunting and devouring each other the very essence of Nature? It is, and that is why I dislike Nature. Still, I try to keep a distance from our, from my, imaginings. I would prefer not to place an equals sign between our fantasies (even if they are scientific ones) and reality.

SEPTEMBER 26, 1987

A recurring nightmare about being late for a train. The city seems to be Paris. The tickets are for nine in the morning. My watch shows five minutes to nine as I ride in the taxi. The next train is at eleven at night. Many suitcases, Janka, our sons, mobilizing all this crowd to get there in time, and once again—too late.

I recall Soviet discussions about Darwinism from the era of the greatest ideological frenzies, when the inheritance of acquired traits (Lysenko) was opposed to natural selection through genetic mutations, and cooperation between animals (based on Kropotkin's theories) to the blind struggle for existence. It may well be that the main goals of that discussion were peda-gogical, to ensure a happy childhood (*schastlivoe detstvo*) for the new generation, thanks to the most cheering indoctrination, the furthest removed from reality. Darwinism is too gloomy for that.

I am afraid that I share the views of the most extreme behaviorists. To-talitarian education turned out to be, not only possible in this century, but productive. The Pioneers, the Komsomol, the Hitlerjugend, are amazingly similar in their uniforms, their ties, and their inculcation of a deep faith. I am not convinced by assertions that they will never succeed because eternal man will have the last word, because he requires truth, etc. Quite simply, this education responds to real needs of the youthful heart. Children require a harmonious world, one that is painted in bright colors; they love discipline and clearly given instructions on how to behave.

I am reading a short novel, *Arberon,* by the Lithuanian writer Vytautas Bubnys, which has been published in Warsaw in Polish translation. Reading it, I revisited my Wilno, now the realm of the girls and boys of a Soviet high-school class. The world in which they were born and grew up seems normal and obvious to them, no less so than it once did to me, even though it was so different then. And all the joys and dramas are played out just as they were then, between them and their teacher—nicknamed, let's say, Giraffe—their classmates, their grades, etc.

Higher, or written, culture and lower, or oral. I elaborate on this distinction, which I have borrowed from Gellner's paper at Castel Gandolfo, in the lecture on nationalism that I'm preparing for a conference in Ann Arbor. The impetus for this is Alain Finkelkraut's book *La Défaite de la pensée*, which I bought in Paris this year. I have also read Isaiah Berlin's essay on nationalism. Political romanticism as the moment of the transition of the masses from oral culture to a culture inculcated in school. The consumption of one's native literature as "national heritage." Confirmation of this in my own education. Professor Chrzanowski's textbook of Polish literature was the most ordinary nationalistic indoctrination.

What end do we who work in language serve? Is it inconceivable that an aircraft carrier be named *Pushkin*? Or a submarine *Dostoevsky*? Or a spaceship to conquer distant planets *Gogol*? Poor Gogol. He didn't want that. He didn't know. And do we know how we will be used?

SEPTEMBER 27, 1987

I read the following in a journal devoted to the humanities in the American high school (*The Humanities and the Nation*, an official publication of the National Endowment for the Humanities):

"The refusal to remember, as Nobel Laureate Czeslaw Milosz argues, is the principal characteristic of our age. There are certainly numerous examples demonstrating that it is the principal characteristic of our nation. We hear of students who do not know that George Washington led the American army in the War of Independence, that there was a Second World War, that Spanish and not Latin is the main language of Latin America. National surveys reveal shocking gaps in knowledge. According to studies conducted recently by the Hearst Corporation, 45% of those who responded to the survey believed that Marx's pronouncement, 'From each according to his ability, to each according to his needs,' can be found in the United States Constitution."

So, I have emerged as a reformer of the American educational system, or at least I am an inspiration for it. I, who have something to say about collective memory if only because my children began their study of history in Brie-Comte-Robert with the sentence *Nos ancêtres les Gaulois* . . . "Our ancestors, the Gauls, had blond hair and blue eyes." So, memory is structured in a particular fashion which is totally at odds with the French Revolution's slogan that one belongs to La Nation by choice.

And what if it were true that the less memory there is, the fewer the occasions for indoctrination; the more memory, the greater the temptation to arrange it in pre-selected patterns? Furthermore, a given collectivity's memory is linked with pain and humiliation. One remembers what hurt. The Jews remember. The Poles remember. Comparatively speaking, the historical knowledge of Polish youth is immense; it sustains national legends and is renewed by them. A question: How to preserve the most memory possible with the lowest possible dose of indoctrination?

September 28, 1987

According to the London-based Polish periodical *Puls* [Pulse], the 577th anniversary of the Battle of Grunwald is being celebrated in Poland. There was a "great patriotic demonstration" at the Grunwald battlefield.

"The ideas of Grunwald are inseparably linked today with the ideology of People's Poland, its *raison d'état*, emphasizing state sovereignty, a strong economy, defensive capability, political wisdom, lasting alliances."

In the past, this sort of arrant nonsense would infuriate me and send me into despair. Now I am detached from it, because in another year or two I will no longer be alive; there is a measure of relief in this fact. I belong to the realm inhabited by Janka, and Andrzejewski, and Jane, and Czechowicz, and Kot Jeleński, and Sadzik, and Zygmunt Hertz—where everything is contemporaneous. Did they lose so very much by dying earlier and not seeing these recent transformations; the "Grunwald celebration," for example? And will I lose so very much by not surviving until the year 2000?

But at the same time I'm reading a thick manuscript that was sent to me from Poland—the papers and discussion notes from an unofficial two-day seminar on Milan Kundera's writings. So much knowledge about the events of the twentieth century, and so many lively young minds; no, forty years ago it would not have been possible.

I have also read a book about Polish–Lithuanian relations in 1939–40. The author (Łossowski) writes about Lithuanian nationalists and Polish nationalists in the fashion of those times. What care I for your meadows, earth? Names, innumerable names, of people once known but deceased. Poor Juozas Keliuotis, the editor of *Naujoji Romuva* [Baltic News], later a long-term prisoner in the gulag.

SEPTEMBER 29, 1987

In Kundera's *The Unbearable Lightness of Being* (a weaker book, I agree, than *The Book of Laughter and Forgetting*), everyone is fascinated by the opposition between God and excrement. Because man defecates, God cannot exist. It is difficult to understand why this is so significant; the arrangement of the sexual organs and the grotesqueness of the act of copulation offer just as good an argument as the digestive system. We ought to be angels; what a pity that we're not. But, in addition to this reasoning, there's something else in Kundera: an obsession with the worst, most shameful side of corporeality, which recurs in one form or another in the literature of the twentieth century and determines its possibly atheistic, or at least Baroque-related, metaphysics. I have constantly circled around such themes in my poems, but only occasionally did something come of it. I have even been preparing myself throughout my life for a direct attack on this knotty question in a treatise, a poem, or a work in prose.

An autumn heat spell, oppressive because it begins early in the morning, no fog. The deer haven't put in an appearance in weeks. The heliotrope is growing almost literally before my eyes and it will soon come into flower once again. Dances of hummingbirds. Just as every year in this season, finches; more precisely, house finches, relatives of the Polish linnet.

For a long time I have carried the following rhyme in my memory; it's amusing, because it proves that we had no lack of homegrown philosophers back then, in our backwoods:

> In Lithuania,
> In Ruthenia, too,

Peepee and doodoo
Are what people must do.

Lithuania and Ruthenia were as far as our imaginations reached in those days; we weren't sure what things were like beyond them, but our horizons were sufficiently large for the observations we gathered to be applicable to all of humanity.

For me, this little rhyme conceals a deep content. First of all, "peepee" and "doodoo" are children's words and they refer to a phase of human life when these functions are accepted as absolutely natural, pre-reflexive, both by children and their adult environment. There's no shame in sitting on a potty chair, no shame in peeing while everyone is watching, and the ability to emit a swift stream from one's own hose can even unite boys in a fighting song, like the one Tony and his classmates used to sing in Brie-Comte-Robert:

Allons pisser sur le gazon
Pour ennuyer les coccinelles,
Allons pisser sur le gazon,
Pour ennuyer les papillons!

(Let's piss on the lawn / To bother the ladybugs, / Let's piss on the lawn / To bother the butterflies!)

Though there's a certain amount of nastiness in this song, to be sure, what lies behind it is a prohibition against peeing on a lawn. When does consciousness intrude and take the place of innocence? Consciousness is based on envisioning the people we see as *bifurcated beings*.

SEPTEMBER 30, 1987

People create their own society of spirits every day. Language, customs, rituals, the exchange of money and goods, politics, religion, art, and so forth—aren't these the work of spirits? But immediately a suspicion arises: they are only pretending to be spirits. They participate unceasingly in a theatrical spectacle, appear on stage in prescribed costumes (fashion), make prescribed gestures. Yet they have to rush to the toilet every minute to empty their bladder or take a crap; every so often, either their throat or their lungs or their stomach refuses to obey them because of illness; organisms age, and then suddenly they're gone, and other actors take their place. Neither costumes nor studied gestures can totally conceal the fact that the ethereal lady over there is built just like everyone else and that, alas, she stinks. Thanks to the increase in the number of bathrooms, we have a tendency to forget about stench, but stench is part of our nature, and if Beatrice remained a spirit for Dante, it was only because he was married not to Beatrice but to another woman, with whom he engaged in acts that used to be called by various inventive names in Parisian argot, including *mélanger ses urines*. It would seem that this duality of spirit and body is as obvious as can be, but if you think about it, it reveals its mysteriousness; it determines the exceptional place of the species and is located in the center of religion and art.

    The division into soul and body was only one of many attempts at naming this condition that eludes naming. This is where all the treatises on *ars moriendi* belong, on taking leave of the body and finding a haven in the soul, the dances of skeletons, the charnel houses of white bones that used to be one of the attractions of city strolls in Paris, and certainly the brothels on the ground floor of the Sorbonne's theological schools. Eros and Thanatos: lovely words, but their association simply proves that they both signified something terrifyingly elemental—birth and death. The question remains: To what extent can one think completely nakedly; that is, rejecting all imagination higher than physiology? One should ask prostitutes about this, since they have a great fund of knowledge about the comedy and misery of the simplest instincts, but that would be fruitless since in general they are people entangled in their own ambitions and dreams and often sentimental. Simone Weil considered their profession the equivalent of slavery and attributed it solely to poverty, which would certainly have fit London in 1862 as described by Dostoevsky: hordes of prostitutes, many of them minors, the cult of Baal on whose altar England was sacrificing her lower classes. Simone Weil's opinions, exaggerated though they are, still hit the mark when she speaks of the compensatory dreams that are peculiar to slaves; the slave's incessant search for imaginary solace shields him from reality.

    One way or another, consciousness of the body constructs its own fata morganas, and it is impossible to descend to an animal level. Nor is it possible to remain for long in the spiritual realm; the desire to spoil sublimity, to stick out one's tongue, has belonged to literature for a long time. My favorite scene from Sterne's *Tristram Shandy*: during a theological dispute at the dinner table, a hot potato drops into someone's codpiece.

Eros would not be present at all were thoughts about corporeality not in the background: to imagine a non-person, a visitor from other planets, who observes, scientifically and without passion, the women arousing me with their imagined shapes concealed beneath their dresses.

White fog since morning, though the rainy season is probably still a long way off. Yesterday, a visit from the gardener. Since Marek can't work now, the gardener digs up the feijoas and transplants them; they will have to be watered until the rains begin.

OCTOBER 1, 1987

Yesterday the fog lifted around noon; now it's hot again. Toward evening, a trip to San Jose to attend a seminar on the hundredth anniversary of the birth of Robinson Jeffers. A marshy, boring plain, no longer under cultivation; factories. An enormous new complex of Japanese–American automotive plants. Approaching San Jose, there's the hump of a mountain, almost unreal in the light of the setting sun, a pink-colored specter. I left the freeway to get a sandwich in Milpitas; many newly constructed streets, entire neighborhoods. The seminar is at San Jose State University. I don't quite realize that I have fallen into a lions' den, that is, into the company of "specialists on insect legs"—English professors for the most part who devour and digest Jeffers while dutifully idolizing him at the same time. I think my talk was closer to Jeffers's spirit, even though it was directed against his philosophy, because I refrain from oversophistication. Unfortunately, I have a feeling that no one understands what I want to say. I read my poem "To Robinson Jeffers," where my opposition is clearly demonstrated, I think. But I, who defended Jeffers's greatness when no one in the universities studied him, appear to be only his enemy, or envious of him. This performance doesn't reflect badly on me; it is only a tactical error; what I thought was obvious, the audience perceived as abracadabra. It is curious, after all, that Jeffers, who was held in contempt until recently, is now making a comeback as the representative of a Nature that deserves to awaken ecological passions. Staś and his daughter drove up from Los Gatos for the lecture. Staś begs me not to die yet, because so few of us from our class at the Zygmunt August High School are still alive. Returned to Berkeley around midnight.

I return to the theme of corporeality. It is not unrelated to my thinking about people as children who have grown up for a moment, become somewhat mangy, as it were, while the condition of childhood is natural for them, with its stupidity, ignorance, and innocent attitude toward the excretory functions. Then all of a sudden there's the shame that comes with the discovery of sex, and even the discovery that there is pleasure in doing something bad, like Proust's Mlle Vinteuil, who would have had no pleasure were it not for her feeling that it was sinful.

There are two distinct varieties of sex—sex of the upper and of the lower story, to coin a phrase, for want of better definitions. The first is *pudique*, somehow, modest or even birdlike, a total experience, separate from thoughts of the specific, physical arrangement of the organs. The second variety is based on mutual pleasurable descent into a repulsive, alluring sphere. Montaigne in his *Essays*:

> And considering often the ridiculous titillation of this pleasure, the absurd, witless, and giddy motions with which it stirs up Zeno and Cratippus, that reckless frenzy, that face inflamed with fury and cruelty in the sweetest act of love, and then that grave, severe, and ecstatic countenance in so silly an action; and that our delights and our excrements have been lodged together pell-mell, and that the supreme sensual pleasure is attended, like pain, with faintness and moaning; I believe what Plato says is true, that man is the plaything of the gods:
>   What savage jest this is! —Claudian
> and that it was in mockery that nature left us the most confused of our actions to be the most common, in order thereby to make us all equal and to put on the same level the fools and the wise, and us and the beasts. The most contemplative and wisest of men, when I imagine him in that position, seems to me an impostor to put on wise and contemplative airs . . .

Zbigniew Uniłowski, whom I knew briefly in Warsaw (although I never wrote about him), used to sing a song that I remember to this day which says just about the same thing.

I have noticed that Americans, with rare exceptions, have enormous difficulty in comprehending the physiological-spiritual duality of man, and that therefore a certain kind of humor is inaccessible to them. I have no idea how they read Baudelaire, for example, whose entire idea circles around the consciousness-body opposition. I also do not understand how it has come to pass that in a country based in Protestantism there is a joyous acceptance of everything that is "natural," for example, sex as a form of calisthenics. (Aldous Huxley was a fine observer of the twentieth century in his *Brave New World.*)

OCTOBER 3, 1987

Aboard a plane from Oakland to Detroit via Chicago. It's early in the morning, but my sleepiness and weakness come from my slowly ebbing illness. Uniłowski leads me to thoughts about the two decades between the world wars. It's said he was the only realistic prose writer of his time. Today, that entire period seems like an astonishingly brief pause. But a fruitful one for the state of literature. Just think how much was achieved. I have frequently brooded over Uniłowski, asking myself why there wasn't a single prose writer among us in Wilno, because Jerzy Putrament doesn't count, after all. I suspect the causes are similar to those that contributed to the weakness of the nineteenth-century Polish novel. To plumb those causes, however, I would have to delve deep into myself, down to barely accessible layers. It seems to me that my childhood and youth in Wilno must have been quite a nihilistic experience. I received a patriotic indoctrination: school, the ladies' auxiliary of the Polish Military Organization, parades, the Polish School Association, the Tomasz Zan Library, all the Wilno Polishness of "the dear city," the enmity toward those who threaten it; i.e., the Bolsheviks, the Lithuanian "Klausiuks," the Jews (because they welcome the Bolsheviks and hang red flags from the telegraph wires on the first of May). But I suspected immediately that that wasn't the way it was at all, that the Polish argument was not the only one, that "our people" could mean Lithuanians, Jews, that *they* might look upon Poles as outsiders. It's just that a given individual's membership in a linguistic or ethnic group always occupied first place. To be conscious simultaneously of Polish arrogance, Polish anti-Semitism, Lithuanian fanaticism (which during World War II led to the beating of the faithful in church for singing in Polish), the Jews' pro-Russian tendencies; it most likely meant doubting the fundamental principle of group ties in general. Something like when I hear of fights between Flemings and Walloons today over the language of the Mass. A plague on both their houses. Nonetheless, the individual did not exist outside his group; he was inaccessible. And he did not enter into relations with other people directly, but only through his membership in a group. Descriptive prose requires a focus on the individual, and the individual was weak.

Wilno had patriotic exaltations and, in addition, one more basis for stratification: class divisions. None of the members of Żagary, our literary group, was of plebeian origins. Everyone was gentry—middle or petty gentry. Henryk Dembiński was a machinist's son, but his gentry mother had entered into a *mésalliance*; anyway, his surname was a gentry name. Only Jędrychowski, on his mother's side, was descended from German burghers. *Gentry Poland.* It certainly was gentry. How to observe that Wilno and write prose fiction about it? It might be possible with the degree of consciousness I have today, but even that is insufficient. What courage it would take to make of that city what Joyce made of Dublin!

Uniłowski at least had his childhood in the Warsaw proletarian district on the Vistula River. He wrote about individual people, profiting from his brief liberation from patriotic pathos; perhaps, through those popular sources, his work is related in some way to the poetry of Miron Białoszewski.

OCTOBER 4, 1987

Ann Arbor, the Campus Inn. Yesterday Marysia met me at the airport; in the evening, I drank and talked with Father Tischner and Krzysztof Michalski; afterward, dinner with a group of Polish-speaking people, including Zbigniew Brzeziński.

Fascination with the duality of spirit and body, the metaphysical side of twentieth-century poetry. The torment, the bitter remorse expressed in it are most interesting; that is why it has outraced theology and philosophy, which have lost the gift of touching on ultimate things. Within this circle of poetry is meditation on time, the mystery of time—the greatest of all mysteries, according to Simone Weil. Everything, probably, that makes poetry similar to pre-Socratic "naïve" seeking belongs here.

I am uncertain whether I can include Robinson Jeffers, even though he wanted to be a poet-philosopher. It's easy to criticize his system of *inhumanism*, or naturalism taken to the extreme (Darwin plus Nietzsche), but that is not the point. The insignificance of all human affairs in comparison with the enormity and perfection of the universe is a given in Jeffers: Three million years of life on earth—what does that amount to? The universe equals God, magnificent, indifferent to our petty good and evil. Beauty is a metaphor for his unnamed energy. Just as wind-borne dust in sunlight allows us to see the force of the wind. But does Jeffers confront Nature or the theory of Nature? He was troubled by science and he observed Earth and the galaxies with the eyes of a scientist. Like the makers of television nature films. Like a scientist, he places himself *outside*, or apart from, the universe. Which may well explain the excess of macro-dimension and the dearth of micro-dimension in his work, and also the unjustified generalizations instead of a grainy, human-historical tapestry. His worst political poems in opposition to America's participation in the Second World War, in which Roosevelt and Hitler are condemned together (though in the company of other "seducers"—Christ, Joan of Arc, Napoleon, Marx), are examples of this. I once read a poem by some American poet (I haven't been able to find the title and I don't remember the author's name); I would oppose this poem to Jeffers's philosophy, for it expresses sympathy for the human condition and a "naïve" engagement with commonplace things. It tells of a cheap hotel room with no bathroom, just a washbasin. Two people, the poet and a girl. They make love, fall asleep; he wakes up in the middle of the night and sees her quietly, careful not to wake him, urinating in the washbasin. And that is all. But in Jeffers: "The destruction that brings an eagle from heaven is better than mercy" (from "Fire on the Hills"). Our normal reflex is to say: "Not so, mercy is better than destruction, no matter how magnificent that destruction may be." If we thereby offer proof of our demagogic and sentimental tastes, so be it. Only people. Tiny. Little insects.

OCTOBER 5, 1987

Ann Arbor. The Campus Inn. Pleasant autumn weather; the trees are greener than in Berkeley. I'm not satisfied with the lecture I delivered last night at this three-day seminar on contemporary religious movements in Central Europe. If I don't write out my text but only dictate it, as I did this one, it always turns out badly. But I didn't feel like writing; I was sick, after all. Besides which, the question of nationalism really doesn't interest me; it is scholastic, contrived—especially its history. There will always be these so-called constructs. Does the "nation" have its origins in the Enlightenment, the French Revolution, Romanticism? Who cares? My personal interest: the consumption of the writer by the nation. That's the only thing that was of value in my lecture.

OCTOBER 7, 1987

En route from Detroit to Oakland, with a change of planes in Denver, I faced up to my exhaustion and continuing illness. In Berkeley I learn that I have missed a heat wave, a record high of 102°, which lasted for exactly the two days of my absence. I found the feijoas transplanted; *Leptospermium* shrubs were planted where the feijoas had been. The transplanted bougain-villea is beginning to flower. I lie down on the sofa and can't move an arm or a leg. This trip was too much for me.

If we picture the work of the lesser devils gathered around the bed of a dying man, as I describe them in *The Issa Valley*, or, in general, what they do when some poor guy's vitality is diminished, as has been happening to me these past few weeks, it is based on the unveiling of his soul's evil. To make him assent to his demonism from which there is no salvation. A definition of demonism: confessing to oneself the feelings or lack of feelings that one *truly* has toward person X or Y, not the ones we ought to have if we are to maintain our self-image as a moral and good person, but those that horrify us because they seem so monstrous. Then all our good instincts can be suspected of theatricality for the sake of self-love, and there is no salvation for us, because the hook of Heaven, if I may put it that way, will have nothing inside us to bite into, and will be unable to pull us upward.

In my lifetime I have accumulated many experiences of duty fulfilled with clenched teeth. Particularly in the face of illness. Which might qualify me to write a treatise on nurses. Among their numerous abilities and temper-aments there is certainly room for empathy and love of one's fellow man. But let us posit conditions in which neither *agape* nor *storge* figure. What remains is duty, and also revulsion, anger perhaps, pity, but not empathy.

For example, the nurses who took care of my old friend in that terrifying home for the aged and the terminally ill in Oakland. A lot has been written about the hells people have organized in the twentieth century for the purpose of torturing people. But here, right next door to us, these "homes" with lovely names operate every day; they're expensive, but families prefer to pay, just so long as they can get rid of their mothers, fathers, wives, the deformed, the paralyzed, the no longer needed but still living. Or they hand over their loved ones because it takes two or three people to lift a paralyzed man. My visits to that unindicted hell of broken dolls . . . No one is responsible other than the pitiless order of the world. At least I didn't hand over Janka to that misery of consciousness; the residents of those institutions see others who are just like themselves and they must know that the end is near. But is that always true? One of the participants in my seminar at Harvard spoke of her work with the terminally ill in the hospital where she was doing her internship as a student of theology (being in the presence of the dying). The majority, despite the obvious, believed in their recovery, that they would return home, and so on, and the student, pitying them, was angry at Simone Weil for her unyielding severity toward the imagination that serves up deceptive comforts (slaves, the sick). Be that as it may, Artur was aware that this was the end, and his screams of protest could be heard from several doors away as I walked down the hall to his room. It is a duty to visit the sick, but isn't it true that I wanted to get away as fast as possible, to leave that abyss, that horror, behind me? And the nurses? Doesn't the sight of the humiliated human body or, worse yet, the spirit (because it puts in its appearance reduced to the simplest egoistic reflexes) exert a numbing effect, so that only indifference and cynicism are left?

OCTOBER 9, 1987

I could write a treatise on the provisional. Every day new topics crop up, but I don't feel like elaborating them into essays as I used to.

In Warsaw, at the beginning of the German occupation, a café was established opposite the Main Railway Station; it was called The Temporary. Everyone who passed it smiled. The Germans are here temporarily. It took five years, however. But I want to reach beyond these commonplaces. We accept a particular period of our life, the conditions and people who surround us, as provisional, because we gamble that our *true* life, for which the present life is but a substitute, does exist somewhere. I examine my conscience and I see one phase after another which *in its time* I considered temporary but which has acquired a certain consistency in my memory. I should think it would be possible to construct a hierarchy of the ways of experiencing time. At the very bottom would be those almost pathological states when reality appears to be colorless, empty, hollowed out, engendering a feeling akin to nausea. Higher up would be assorted varieties of dissent from what is in the name of some kind of change that will resolve everything. I experienced such states in Wilno when the solution had to be individual; I experienced them in wartime Warsaw, waiting for the end of the war; I experienced them later in France, in America. *The present* is always rendered powerless, deprived of value; only an imaginary turning point acquires full weight. However, since we live among people, we accumulate temporary friends, temporary women, and we cannot rule out the possibility that those others—not the ones we have received by mere chance—will never exist.

Would it be possible to live every minute attentively? Not running ahead, but at a complete standstill in the present?

OCTOBER 10, 1987

Under the influence of an excruciating cough and difficulty in breathing, I thought that my gratitude to God is well grounded. In order to write so many books, one needs good health above all. An incredible amount of pent-up energy is contained in one page of good prose, in one line of poetry; one measure of this is the number of cigarettes smoked. I stopped smoking— when? about fifteen years ago—but I have smoked thousands and thousands of cigarettes. I might yet pay for that.

In the spring of 1936, however, "the present" did exist for me; my poem "Slow River" is proof that it did. It begins, after all, with words of ecstasy: "There has not been for a long time / A spring as beautiful as this one."

My attention was focused, however, on sensual detail, while the Wilno of the people of those days was no denser than fog. At that time, in 1936, I very much wanted to be capable of love and friendship, although I doubted that I had that capacity and was even in despair because of it. Today I have no desire to explore the psychological sources of this tendency; I accept a certain coldness or detachment as a kind of occupational disease. Which is closely linked to the sense of the provisional, perhaps simply of life as a provisional state—because that other, true, life is *elsewhere*. I am not thinking of religious faith; this is something much more elementary, which can incline one to religious faith, but need not do so. Could it be that this *elsewhere* is revealed in poetry, in painting, in music? Here, in life, there is a kind of passivity, a submission to whatever social relations fate provides, rather than searching them out; there is even, and this is unpleasant, a distracted absence:

> *Tender, faithful animals, short-lived humans,*
> *tear in vain at my hands, which are clasped in adoration.*
> —*From my poem "Elegy," in* Three Winters, 1936

Artur prompted those thoughts. His remains are buried some fifteen meters from Janka's, in that hillside cemetery in Berkeley where I go to place flowers—usually everlastings—on her grave. The view from there is one of the most spectacular views of the bay below, the islands, the bridges, San Francisco's skyscrapers, all the way to the ocean. My friendship with Artur was extremely provisional and lasted more than twenty years. First Artur visited us in Montgeron; later, when we moved to Berkeley in 1960, we found Artur and Rose there and it was easier for us to be close with them than with Americans or non-Jewish Poles. Artur grew up in Bielsko; his culture was German—the German Gymnasium in Bielsko and economics at the University of Berlin. Rose was born in Czaniec, a hamlet in the vicinity of Żywiec. They spoke German to each other, but Polish with us. America, Poland, anti-Semitism, Judaism, Christianity, socialism, Thomas Mann and the other Manns, the German colony in Berkeley—these were the subjects of our conversations.

OCTOBER 11, 1987

Yesterday, in the journal *Chrysalis*, I studied a portrait of the young Swedenborg from around the year 1700, when he was a student in Uppsala. One of the loveliest faces produced by the portrait art of that time, which was, to tell the truth, inclined to beautification. A sensual-whimsical-spiritual face, a face that one would want to label *sensuel et spirituel*. I think about his patron, Charles XII, and the Battle of Poltava.

Aggravation: today's (Sunday's) *New York Times Book Review* contains a chapter from *Conversations with Czeslaw Milosz*, naturally without the changes that I requested, and, even worse, under an altered title. Instead of "The Image of the Poet," the idiotic "Separate Nations: Poetry and the People." In other words, yet another twisting of my words. I have never stated that poetry and the people are two different nations.

Artur. Talking with him was difficult because he was full of passionate furies and complexes and would just explode, so that one had to temper one's opinions in order to avoid an eruption. He hated Judaism because of his childhood experiences in cheder, but at the same time he was a one-hundred-percent Jew, was interested only in Jews, and every conversation with him eventually focused on Jews. He hated Christianity, especially St. Paul, a Jew who was superbly well educated in Scripture and was the founder of Christianity. Yet he knew the Gospels very well, practically by heart. He hated socialism, the religion of his youth, but he was still guided by the emotions and reflexes of a rebel against the established order, which was particularly apparent during the Free Speech Movement and the whole Berkeley "revolution" of the sixties. I probably had more sympathy for that movement than Aleksander Wat, who was in Berkeley at the beginning of the movement. Those fanatic girls (Bettina Aptheker, the daughter of a prominent New York Communist, was their leader) reminded him of the girls who used to collect money for the International Organization for Aid to Revolutionaries in Warsaw in the twenties. Artur, however, would give his hatred of authority free rein. Once, he literally spat at the police, which upset me. What were *they* guilty of? *Nota bene*: Artur was acquainted with Wat but was hostile to him as a deserter from Judaism, because, though a Jew has a right to be an atheist, flirtations with Christianity are bad.

In short, Artur was a difficult man, difficult even for Rose, who loved him. Largely out of consideration for her, I would bite my tongue, not wanting to drive him into one of those rages that were bad for his health. Rose was warmer, more Polish than German, aching in her Polishness, because her childhood in Czaniec, in the only Jewish family, had left a memory of daily persecutions and exclusion from the village community, by which she was forbidden to become a Pole. Janka's and my tact in dealing with Artur was well worth the effort. We took many car trips with them throughout California; also, even though Artur considered me well informed about Jewish matters, I learned a lot from him, especially about Jakub Frank and the Frankists, whose history he had studied. He knew a great deal and had even written a book about them.

Artur and Rose were devoted friends on whom one could count in times of need. True, I, too, demonstrated real devotion when I attempted once to draw Artur out of his depression with the help of a commission from my German publisher: the translation of my book *The History of Polish Literature*. This went partly against my own interests, because I had some doubts about his style. Here I enter an arena of dangerous questions: How should we behave toward friends who are engaged in the same work as we are— writing, painting, medicine, etc.—but whom we don't consider to be among the best in their profession? Artur was a journalist in his youth, and then a professor. In America he tried to publish a couple of books and received generally negative responses from publishers. Unfortunately, I know they were justified. It would appear that confidence in one's own judgment is necessary wherever a strict hierarchy of achievement applies, but such confidence borders on pride and arrogance, which are especially common among writers and artists. Speaking frankly, however, isn't it true that I considered myself, at least potentially, better than my Wilno colleagues?

October 12, 1987

Despite my weakness and coughing, I have begun rereading Kot Jeleński's letters to me; I read through an entire packet in one evening. They make a fascinating book. Kot appears more uniform in his likes and judgments than one would have expected. Logical, honest, loyal, wise. I realized just how much space he had occupied in my life and how much he deserved my gratitude. For years I had only one reader, him. My prose had found Polish and non-Polish readers, but as a poet I was taken on faith even by those who recognized my talent. For example, I didn't expect opinions about my poetry from Zygmunt Hertz. He thought *The Issa Valley* was my best book, and advised me, "Czeslaw, write for people." Poems were not especially for people, not to mention essays. In my émigré isolation there were months when I toyed with the idea of writing myself letters so I would find something in my mailbox. The sole confirmation of the value of what I was doing was in Jeleński's letters. One reader—but what a reader!—is probably enough. True, suspicious Lithuanian that I am, when I received his praises I would deduct something for his goodness, since he knew about my isolation and might have wanted to cheer me up. Besides which, some of his intellectual constructs struck me as too Parisian; for example, when he spoke of my a-humanism (I was an a-humanist attempting to be a humanist; Gombrowicz was a humanist attempting to be an a-humanist), I interpreted that as the extraordinary sensitivity of his antennae to alternating currents. Now, however, reading his letters, I hold a different opinion. In his evaluations he was his honest self; he did not shrink from criticism but at the same time he had an unusual capacity for enthusiasm. And that is what links us: a sustained moment of enthusiasm. So much so that he ascribed to my poems the capacity to revive the fabric of his memory about his own childhood, which, for reasons he was aware of, had atrophied.

OCTOBER 13, 1987

Yesterday, at the invitation of Leonard Nathan, I took part in a Department of Rhetoric seminar on the work of Czeslaw Milosz, which Nathan team-teaches with Arthur Quinn. Intelligent students, a successful discussion; we didn't even notice that two hours had passed without a coffee break. A seminar in the Department of Rhetoric devoted exclusively to texts in translation. Maybe in twenty years the Department of Slavic Languages and Literatures will offer such a seminar.

Kot's letters evoke a portrait of the Paris circles of *Kultura* and Editions du Dialogue. Future historians and literary scholars will immerse themselves in these materials. I would say the most intense period was between 1960 and 1980; the main participants during that time were Jerzy Giedroyc, Zygmunt Hertz, Zofia Hertz, Father Józef Sadzik, Jaś Lebenstein, Olga Scherer, Danuta Szumska, and, later, Ola Wat. The correspondence of Kot, Zygmunt, Sadzik, along with the issues of *Kultura*, *Preuves*, etc., reveal the temperature of those times. Still, it would be better to wait a while before publishing Kot's letters to me; there are too many drastic comments in them.

The years of my absence from Paris, and yet of my presence. It seems that just as in the fifties I was still strongly embedded in the Warsaw or Cracow "scene," later on I became all the more integrated into this Paris, between rue Surcouf (Editions du Dialogue), rue des Ecouffes (Jaś Lebenstein's studio), Maisons-Laffitte (*Kultura*), corresponding with people, making at least one visit a year. I think that the people who were active then had a much weaker sense of the provisional than I did (even immediately after the war, when the fate of Western Europe was uncertain, even doomed,

if one believed Hostowiec). Somehow or other I participated in the strengthening of the provisional, and the friends given to me provisionally became
my lifelong friends. Such a one was Zygmunt Hertz, whom I discovered on
Avenue Corneille in 1951 when I sought shelter in Maisons-Laffitte. Zygmunt was not an intellectual and we had few things in common. I was
gradually enveloped by his goodness, his warmth, his devotion, and our
shared brand of humor. With Kot, too, our friendship was not instantaneous.
We called each other "Mister" for a long time. My meeting with Józef Sadzik
was probably my closest encounter from the very beginning, from the first
glance. I was aware that he was a thoroughly exceptional priest and this
probably influenced my response to him. Stendhal's theory of "crystalliza-
tion" applies not only to love but to friendship, too.

An erotic background does exist in friendships between men, but it would
be ridiculous to immediately start talking about homoeroticism. It is a physical joy, the eyes' joy at the sight of a friend, the same as at the sight of a
woman whom we love, a kind of affirmation of being. Like my poem "Esse"
about the girl who sat opposite me in the metro, the object of my love for
a couple of minutes.

Reading Kot's letters, I realized that it was thanks to him that I was teamed
up with Gombrowicz, that the three of us were teamed up. In the same way
that, like it or not, I also represent the last literature of the rural manor. Not
directly, as in Orzeszkowa, Rodziewiczówna, Weyssenhoff, or various memoirs, but in a roundabout way; still, it's a curious fact that the manor has
been preserved, but not by those who were most called to it—the relatively
healthy ones, firmly settled in their old-fashioned loyalties. Jeleński understood perfectly well Gombrowicz's fundamental incapacity for life, his isolation from reality as if he was walled off by a pane of glass, and his surrogate
self-construction through his work, in which the manor is described by an
outsider, a cripple. According to Kot, I was the exact opposite—vitality itself,
and passion; but in my opinion I was even more internally entangled than
Gombrowicz, or so it seemed to me. And a not insignificant factor in this
was my *shame of origins*, my class shame. Kot himself was something of a
young master of the manor, but what a Polish master he was! Italian on his
father's side, he had invented an unusual formula of both total Polishness
and total cosmopolitanism. He judged his Polishness soberly and yet he was
always faithful to it; he was dual in everything, for he liked both women and
boys, but at the same time he was also all of a piece. What could he have
in common with a character from a respectable gentry novel? Although the

argument could be made that, whenever we take a closer look, "normality" will turn out to be thoroughly crooked, just as when we look for a Christmas tree we become convinced that there are no ideal trees.

OCTOBER 14, 1987

In the new issue of *Kultura* I read Kisielewski's farewell to Zygmunt Mycielski. One of his best texts; marvelous concision and a breathless wealth of details from his friend's biography. Mycielski was my friend, too, but a distant one ("distant" as in "distant cousin"). But more than just a colleague. I first heard of him in the autumn of 1934, I think, when I was living in a dormitory for scholarship students on rue Lamandé, and went one day to a concert hall for the premiere performance of one or two songs by Mycielski, who was a student of Nadia Boulanger at the time. I can still remember: "The room was dancing, the table, / Four horses, the fifth ox"; that's from Bruno Jasieński's *Song about Jakub Szela*. (Bruno Jasieński, 1901–39, was a Polish Communist poet who emigrated to the Soviet Union, where he wrote the first Socialist Realist novel, *Man Changes His Skin*, published in 1933. He perished in the gulag in 1939.) Imagine, a Galician count choosing that poem in particular . . . Later, in Wilno, we spent many hours in conversation during the winter of 1935–36. Then there were meetings, mainly in Paris, and correspondence, and finally my visit with him in Ojai, California, where he had come on vacation, to do some composing. The house belonged to some elderly, wealthy French ladies; one of them had once been his girlfriend in Paris, which explains her tender attentiveness to him.

An unusual man, magnificent in his *detachment*; I have never encountered such a degree of detachment in anyone else. It was as if he hovered beside himself, indulgently observing his own fortunes in the same way that he indulgently observed other people, the history of his century, the war. He was usually pessimistic, but that didn't deter him from acting.

OCTOBER 14 (CONT.)

Stoicism used to recommend engagement in human affairs, but only as if one were not engaged; in other words, it recommends prior acquiescence in the unfortunate decrees of fate. There was nothing stoical about Mycielski, probably because the coldness or stoniness that we usually associate with stoicism was alien to him. I imagine that one can find sages like him only among the masters of Zen Buddhism. He was capable of being here, beside me, and at the same time he resided in another realm from which his own "I" appeared quite small, as if viewed through the wrong end of a telescope. When, on rare occasions, he spoke of his participation in the war, you might believe that then, too, just as in his telling of it, he had experienced what was happening to him as comic. A gay man, constantly tormented by the "urgings of the body," I think he maintained the same amused superiority of mind in his erotic pursuits. I detected a metaphysical experience in him that elevated him almost to the level of sainthood. Could it not be that his last composition, the *Liturgia Sacra*, points in the same direction?

OCTOBER 15, 1987

Well, it's almost a month now that I've had this bronchitis, asthma, or whatever it is, and I have hardly taken advantage of the sunny weather. When we lived in Montgeron, the French children used to say of such people, "*p.p.h.*" (*ne passera pas l'hiver*—he won't survive the winter).

There wasn't a trace of arrogance, presumptuousness, or snobbery in Mycielski. He was an aristocrat, but a real one; that is, he behaved absolutely naturally. Like Jeleński, he contradicted the not very nice model of the upper classes in Poland "strutting around for all they're worth."

One other member of the gentry comes to mind: Stanisław Ignacy Witkiewicz, "Witkacy," from Sołgudyszki in Samogitia. Mycielski could have been a character in one of his novels or plays, because he had all the appropriate attributes: he was a count, but a "degenerate" one, a composer, a homosexual—Putrycydes Tenger himself in Witkiewicz's novel *Insatiability*. Witkacy would have demonized him, however, taken away his modesty, his nonchalant, diffident manner. Besides which, Witkacy's characters lacked distance from his own "I"; their "metaphysical sense of the strangeness of existence" did not liberate them, but, on the contrary, strengthened their egos and thus locked them up in the prison of an isolated monad.

My generation did not experience the orgies that took place in Zakopane in the 1920s and the very beginning of the thirties. Witkacy, Karol Szymanowski and his *Harnasie*, Iwaszkiewicz, Jerzy Rytard, Leon Chwistek. In the final analysis, Zakopane, which in a sense had already become the artistic capital before World War I, supplied Witkacy with a good many models. Zbigniew Uniłowski was the only one of the younger writers who had rubbed shoulders with that society. I don't know if Mycielski, who was four years older than me, spent any time in Zakopane, and if he did, when he might have done so. I was acquainted with Iwaszkiewicz, Szymanowski, Rytard, but that was all; he, on the other hand, was a member of their clan. Judging by what I have read about artistic-literary London during more or less the same period, about Virginia Woolf, for example, erotic freedom was very advanced there. In Zakopane, they went in for heavy drinking with the highlanders to the accompaniment of highland music; there were also plenty of love affairs, both homosexual and heterosexual. Apparently for the participants it was a time of Dionysian intoxication with no presentiment of dread. In other words, Witkacy, with his black vision, was an exception.

OCTOBER 16, 1987

In a plane from Oakland to Iowa City via Denver. Despite feeling weak from my bronchitis, I decided to go because the organizers are counting on me; it is the twentieth anniversary of the International Writing Program directed by Paul Engle and his Chinese wife. My seat on the plane is in row 13. The seats in the other rows are all occupied; this row is practically empty. So people are still superstitious.

This happened in the summer of 1939. A sunny Sunday at the Legia swimming pool. The loudspeaker was playing hit songs, *Paloma*, of course, and others, with Polish words fitted to the imported melodies. A *Thief in Love* was played over and over again; I can still hear it. The sunburnt bodies of young men and women. And those nobly patriotic (rabidly nationalistic) Polish youths an instant before the onset of a horror that no one could imagine, preoccupied with sports and flirtation, marked for sacrifice, for dying from a bullet, in prison, in a camp, for a sum total of unimaginable sufferings. Suddenly, a commotion, something's happened, people are diving, searching. A boy has jumped in and hasn't surfaced. They find him, perform artificial respiration, but it doesn't help. Apparently he died of a heart attack. Then everything calms down; once again, A Thief in Love comes out of the loudspeaker.

Chance. Or maybe Providence didn't want him to die slowly from a bullet in the belly or to be kicked by boots in Auschwitz. We have the habit of attributing everything to chance. But this is only the top layer; it proves to be true when we think about *others*, but we arm ourselves with amulets and commend ourselves to the particular care of the Mother of God. What is more, it is perfectly justified to delve below what appears to be obvious. It is difficult to think about this, because nothing here yields to intellectual efforts. Are we afraid? Providence in Christianity extends into the predestination of the saved and the damned (in Catholicism, too). The damned in Dante's Hell had to be sinners before their birth. Who can find that appealing?

OCTOBER 17, 1987

Yesterday, right after my arrival and the drive from the airport in Cedar Rapids to Iowa City, Paul Engle moderated a discussion with Seamus Heaney, Levitas of The New York Times, the poet Coleman McCarthy, and me. Many people I know are in the hall: Ivar and Astrid Ivask, Janusz Głowacki and Jan Józef Szczepański from Cracow. Afterward, cocktails in the Museum of Art. I feel so weak that after one glass of wine my head is spinning; I leave after half an hour, lie down in my room in the Iowa Union, and skip the banquet. I read a philosopher of the Kyoto School, Keiji Nishitani; so my mind must still be working, because it's a difficult text.

One more of my disguises. In discussing literature, I pretend that I care about it, instead of proclaiming that it is a frivolous, godless occupation. Frivolous because, although it is supposed to turn reality into words, very little reality penetrates it. *Exemplum:* the extent to which the twentieth century has been captured in it. Yesterday, Paul Engle spoke about his grandfather who fought in the Civil War. He covered thousands of miles as a cavalry soldier in the Union Army, and when his grandson asked him what it was like, this veteran of the bloodiest of all nineteenth-century wars replied, "Paul, there are no words to describe it," and he never told what it was like.

A godless occupation—what else could it be in these times when literature and art have separated from religion, which hasn't, by the way, helped them worm their way into the embrace of science? Neither here nor there, somewhere between religion and science, primarily exploring various forms of atheism.

But if not to literature, then where should one go? To philosophy? Keiji Nishitani, in *Religion and Nothingness* (translated from the Japanese), makes every effort to embrace two heritages, the Western and the Eastern; however, his citations from literature (Dostoevsky, Nietzsche, the Zen Buddhists' haiku) are more eloquent than the pages of his supposedly rigorous arguments. Whatever else it may do, literature gives expression to the agitated struggling of men trapped by the power of science but for whom science is insufficient. And occasionally a poem or two by some hermetic poet . . .

A Polish Pope, Solidarity, etc., have universalized the Polish problematic, so that my colleagues can be Polonocentric without encountering any great resistance. Nonetheless, the religiosity of that country has held despite the movement of Europe as a whole, including Russia, with the sole difference that here God is killed by indifference and over there by declaring Him an enemy. Were it not for Poland's role since the beginning of the nineteenth century as the romantic model of Central and East European nationalisms, the Polish Church would have declined to a significantly more modest position. In other words, anyone who attempts to draw conclusions from Poland will be prone to an excessively optimistic evaluation of the vitality of Christianity. In the King Zygmunt August High School in Wilno I discovered the contradiction between physics and biology classes on the one hand and religion classes on the other; that contradiction gave a direction to my poetry, and my profound experience of it distinguished me from my contemporaries who had either skipped it or had declared themselves atheists. Nonetheless, appeasement and pretense are not fitting. The essence of the twentieth century is the triumph of science, and religion's efforts to escape from the clutches of science have not yet been successful. There is no reason to delude ourselves: the methodology of science carries atheism with it and it defines the context of philosophy as well as of literature and art. Popular pilgrimages and the religiosity of the masses can be balanced against this, but they are not sufficient.

OCTOBER 18, 1987

Yesterday, Jan Józef Szczepański gave me his book *Kadencja* [Term of Office], which was published in the semi-legal press; it is a report on his activities as president of the Writers' Union just before Solidarity, during Solidarity, and afterward, up until the dissolution of the Union. I read it in the plane from Cedar Rapids to Chicago and then to Oakland. There's also something about me in it. Here's a passage about my visit to Poland in 1981:

Milosz arrived on June 5. I was anxious about meeting him. Our relations were not good. We first met many years ago at the estate of Mrs. Jerzy Turowicz, where we spent the last weeks of the war under the same roof—he as a refugee from Warsaw, I as a "fence" on leave from the woods. In one of my early stories I described our last wartime New Year's Eve celebration in this rural home. One of the characters in the story was modeled on Czeslaw Milosz. The poet was deeply offended by the resemblance. He refused to meet with me during a number of my stays abroad, and when we finally did meet, in Berkeley in 1979, he did, in fact, assure me that that ancient business no longer had any significance, but I felt that he still harbored resentment.

When I met him now in Iowa City, I didn't think about New Year's Eve in Goszyce. I don't know if I refused to meet with him. I only know that once, when he and his wife were in Berkeley—it might have been in 1969—I regretted that we missed each other; Janka and I were traveling at the time. But of course it was interpreted as a refusal to see him; a system of clues, as in Gombrowicz's *Cosmos*, that has to form a logical whole.

The truth is, he personified for me the painful and shameful past preserved in that unfortunate story, although it's clear he never understood why I felt offended. That New Year's Eve was a descent into hell, into the bottom of a historical nightmare; I drank and behaved like a buffoon in order to extinguish thought, but in vain; my consciousness was clear and, unable to cope with such a grotesque situation, turned it into a tormenting nightmare. Eternal Polishness, the Polish manor, Nawłoć* one minute before the day

---

* In Stefan Żeromski's novel *Przedwiośnie* [Early Spring, 1925], Nawłoć is a manor, presented satirically as the epitome of the gentry's carefree life, in contrast to the miserable life of the peasants.

of reckoning, before its disappearance forever, and I, with my shame and my ambition to escape from the manor, thrust back into it once again as a sign that, like it or not, here is where I belong, that I had tried in vain to escape from the traditionalism that I disliked and the religion of absolutized values. A Dante of Sarmatia was needed to portray a scene from this *Finis Poloniae*. That's what I told myself, but that experience, which was far too traumatic, never made it into my prose; rather, the "Spirit of History" section in my long poem *Treatise on Poetry* is rooted in that experience, and that experience only. My experience not just of a few hours at a New Year's Eve party but also of what my imagination suggested to me right then, at that very moment, as being inevitable, and also my experience of what actually did happen a few days later, following the pattern of the 1918–19 dress rehearsal: "Bolsheviks in the Polish manor." The rounding up of cattle, horses, sheep from the barns and stables; the catching and slaughtering of chickens, ducks, geese; a green light to looting, the end of the good life. One of the Warsaw refugees was Helena Bilińska, a teacher, a spinster faithful to her fiancé who had died fighting the Bolsheviks in 1920. She, too, felt that something was taking place that cried out for witnesses; many years later, when I was teaching at Harvard, I had a chance to read her journals, with their day-by-day entries. After the war, thanks to her knowledge of English, Bilińska worked in the Washington embassy with me; later, she became a teacher in New England. Her memoir does a very good job of conveying the Polish dread in the face of this invasion by an alien, incomprehensible civilization or, rather, by a continent that had spawned a vast number of tribes on the march and was rolling westward with tanks, artillery, and, above all, on millions of infantrymen's feet. I returned Bilińska's memoir, telling her that no one in America would publish it; she would be accused of racism. In essence, she perceived the incursion of the Soviet Army as an invasion by a race different from the human race, or at least from white people; as an invasion of Mongols, which suggests the survival of atavistic fears stretching all the way back to the Tartar raids that once laid waste the Polish lands. Of course there were many Asians among the soldiers; somehow, she scarcely noticed anyone else.

I was repelled by Szczepański's story—not by what it contains, but by what is missing from it. It is possible to strip events of their apocalyptic dimensions, but doesn't one then diminish the tragedy of countries and societies by tailoring them to an excessively local pattern? Once upon a time there existed a vast sovereign state; it went into decline and was divided up by its neighbors, but it survived some one hundred years as Nawłoć. And even if Stefan Żeromski's novels haven't aged very well, that diagnosis from *Early Spring* still holds. So, the end of Nawłoć, like the end of Poland, unmistakably, in that January 1945, engulfed by the Imperium forever. A most paradoxical tragedy—gentry Poland as the essential, true Poland; her submersion as the opening of a school for slaves. Szczepański does not write about this because the story form could not handle it; there's also censorship to consider. But you can't even sense the author's consciousness in the background. Michnik was able to find enough material in this story to include a discussion of it in his *History of Honor in Poland,* because the contrast between those moral positions is clearly outlined in it. Actually, since the argument is about the final battle of the Warsaw Uprising, the debate is really about how to behave in a defeated country: honor or collaboration. It is always painful to see one's own internal complexities reduced to a type, like Szczepański's fictional character, the poet Wielgosz, who, it is true, proved to be right. If I am supposed to be Wielgosz, I can applaud Michnik's book, but only because I live safely in America. Observed more closely, the book reveals the abstractness of divisions into black and white; the particular cases of Henryk Elzenberg or Hanna Malewska are related, to be sure, but when elevated to the rank of a Catonian principle they share the weakness of all moralizing by preachers. Wielgosz, had he gone on living in Poland, would probably have collaborated one way or another. Milosz, however, became a "relative ermine," a term he himself coined, only because he broke with the Polish People's Republic in time.

My poetry reading yesterday was a success. To hold the attention of a hall of some six hundred people and to be applauded even for individual poems, while reading in a foreign language, is honey for one's self-esteem.

OCTOBER 19, 1987

In Iowa City I talked with a Polish poet, Joanna Salamon, who lives in Holland now. She attacked me for *The Land of Ulro.* I readily accepted her opinion that no one in Poland dares to write about the book, since it introduces esoterica that are unknown there. Other than Barańczak's review, there were no Polish commentaries, though I was comforted by Sadzik's and Jeleński's high opinion of it.

It may have been a mistake to introduce Gombrowicz into *The Land of Ulro*. Or, in general, to indulge myself by writing such a capricious book, a book that isolates me from Poles, who are fundamentally an anti-metaphysical people. For example, Kisiel, whom I am very fond of, is speaking in the voice of the people when he dismissively refers to *The Land of Ulro* and my other religious idiosyncrasies.

My basic assumption was that the book would find five Polish readers, no more. It found a few more, but mainly because of what I have to say in it about Mickiewicz, Słowacki, Gombrowicz—not because of my ideas on esoterica that no one needs. For me, it was a continuation of *The Captive Mind*, a deepening of questions raised in that book, and it was met by something similar: *oratio obliqua* was received as *oratio recta*. That is, I, as an opponent of materialistic science, a "spiritualist," was said to be opposing the spirit to matter, etc. My goal was to make a diagnosis, not to deliver a sermon, but people wanted to take literally the leapings of my dialectical mind. One order of beefsteak, please.

My colleagues, immersing themselves in Marxism after World War II, had only a feeble grasp of the genesis of revolutionary thought; they were not conscious of the reasons why the dogmas of "scientific socialism" over-whelmed their minds with their *obviousness*. It may well be that that ob-viousness has now been dispelled in Poland, but that doesn't mean it has been dispelled in the rest of the world. In the course of the nineteenth and twentieth centuries, the mind has grown accustomed to certain methods of understanding that have become as natural as air. The thinking subject approaches the world as an object that has to be sorted out in order to be understood, that has to be rationalized in order that it may be mastered. It is virtually inevitable that the position of the subject in science will be transferred into the social and political realm. A member of the nineteenth-century Russian intelligentsia, an American laboratory scientist who is my contemporary, an elementary-school teacher in Honduras or El Salvador—all belong to the same intellectual family, and no matter what their political views may be, anything that bears the stamp of science or that appears to be scientific is marked with a plus in their eyes, because it combats chaos—the chaos of the free market, for example—with the orderliness of edicts. That is why, if we must look for practical justifications, it makes sense to consider the premises of scientific thinking themselves.

OCTOBER 20, 1987

To look back and recall the titles of one's books, which fill many shelves in their translations into various languages. Thus a miser, often in an agitated state, counts and recounts his thalers. Although, to be sure, "no one knows the paths to posterity" and one must include one's mistakes in the reckoning. Voltaire valued his poetry above everything he wrote, but who today connects his name with poetry? And Boetius, for example, writing his *De Consolatione* in prison, did not know that he would be remembered centuries later because of this writing that he did for himself alone. I do not know what will "remain" after me, as the saying goes. For over thirty years I have been watching the development of *The Captive Mind* into the status of a "classic," helped, to be sure, by Jane's splendid English translation. For me, it was a peripheral product, rather like the theological treatise of a Reformation poet. The same with *The Land of Ulro*. Whether it will last or not is a matter of complete indifference to me, although on one point—this critical test—I am not indifferent: Were we really struggling against resistance or succumbing to a flabby dream? See Jeanne Hersch's *L'Etre et la forme*. Aside from that, the only important thing is the extent to which a person has "acted up" in his field; I did a lot of splashing, I think. "To yearn, to act, and to pass on; the rest is night."

The Captive Mind, painful, written out of an inner compulsion, was conceived in prayer. Were it not for my piety as a child raised in Catholicism and my capacity to pray as an adult, I would not have known what to do, I would have perished ten times over. On the boundary of prayer, in intense concentration, that is, I was visited on rare occasions, at important moments in my life, with a kind of intuitive clairvoyance when my future would appear to me for an instant. According to Sartre, whoever postulates that the universe is interested in his existence, i.e., that his personal existence has a metaphysical foundation, is a swine (*salaud*). Thus, we are obliged to accept that our foundation is nothingness, the condition of our absolute freedom. Because I believed that I do have a place in the divine plan and prayed for the ability to fulfill the tasks before me, I was a typical *salaud*.

A knight invisibly commissioned to do battle against liars? In *The Land of Ulro* there is a gallery of figures, each of whom assigned himself a place as prophet: Swedenborg, Blake, Dostoevsky, Oscar Milosz. And my disheartened tolerance: So what if human weakness is so great that we are unable to achieve anything without pumping ourselves up with faith in our exceptional importance for mankind?

It is an incontrovertible fact that science and technology transform man from within, changing his imagination. Why should we shut our eyes and pretend, rejecting the obvious, that Ancient Rome is again in decline, and this time it's not pagan Rome under the blows of Christianity, but the Rome of the monotheists' God? Since this, and nothing else, is the undeclared theme of contemporary poetry in various languages, obviously this conflict has already crossed the threshold of universal consciousness. We do not know if those who were the opponents of the Land of Ulro, who prophesied a new era of reborn Imagination, were right. Perhaps what will remain will be the one Church of Science and after transitional hesitations it will return to a fundamentally mechanistic orthodoxy. Or new perspectives will open up that are in no way similar to the prophecies of those prophets. But a poet who writes in the language of a country in which the churches are full is not supposed to think about such things.

OCTOBER 21, 1987

The recently planted gardenia has flowered. The heliotrope recovered after the deer devoured it, but it's growing slowly. It's sunny all right, but it's still the end of October.

No doubt Oscar Milosz will be a bone of contention for readers of *The Land of Ulro*—my tendency, that is, to (often) adopt his views as my own. Especially in everything that he has to say about motion and space. I take Simone Weil's *Selected Writings* in my Polish translation down from the shelf and find an entry that could serve as a bridge between her and Oscar Milosz:

> To unite the rhythm in which the body lives with the rhythm of the world, to continually feel that bond and to feel also the continual transformation of matter thanks to which the human being is immersed in the world.
> Which nothing can take away from the human being so long as he lives: as movement, breathing, where volition manifests itself, as per-

ception, space (even in a dungeon, even with gouged-out eyes and broken eardrums, one recognizes space).

Very likely I went beyond the pale of decency by mentioning in *The Land of Ulro* Oscar Milosz's prophecy about a new order of the united planet Earth and by seeming to agree with him when I accept the possibility that it would be a theocratic order going hand in hand with radical decentralization. Terror. Kot Jeleński, an earnest and enthusiastic reader of this book, bridled at the thought, and rightly so, because of Khomeini in Iran and the quiet aspirations of the Catholic clergy here and there that emit the odor of the fires of the Inquisition. I probably should have crossed out that sentence, but does theocracy have to mean government by a priestly caste? Perhaps in the twenty-second century it will mean something different, even piety in relation to the principle that orders the rhythm of the universe but is inaccessible to our understanding today.

I consider Oscar Milosz's influence on me to have been both positive and damaging. Damaging because Caliban is not supposed to want to soar like Ariel; man imprisoned in his flesh, *l'homme sensuel*, is not supposed to be carried away into excessively romantic registers or to seek an impossible love, a brotherhood of souls. As if there weren't enough Polish romantic poets, I had to go and treat myself to yet another one just like those others, with his Beatrice and his eschatology, with the expectation of the fulfillment of History.

OCTOBER 22, 1987

Either the sadness of a defeated life or the sadness of achievement? Or perhaps both the one and the other? I am besieged by the excess of what I would like to confess, not knowing how or to whom, a need for silent confession, as if remorse for my sins would itself suffice. It is more than a little strange that when I take stock of my conscience my social anti-talent occupies such a prominent place that I find it impossible to comprehend how I managed to make it through so many years without having had any childhood training. Which is demonstrated obliquely by my failure to notice people, my boredom with people who appear to me as the magma of mask-faces, not as specific individuals. It began with my torments at the dinner table in Krasnogruda, torments of timidity, and heralded the anxieties of a snob: that no one pays any attention to me, that I make an effort to appear intelligent, but nothing comes of it.

At 6 a.m. I was awakened by a phone call from a journalist in Oslo; Joseph Brodsky has received the Nobel Prize. My heartfelt, instinctive decision to write him a consoling letter (Remember, the beginning of exile is the hardest) when he found himself in the West has paid off handsomely in a friendship that has lasted many years. He is a faithful friend despite his towering arrogance, to which I have been witness on many occasions. I envied him his haughtiness and arrogance that put pompous fools in their place and assured him a superior position. That's something I lack. Most of the time I was polite (timid), but barely conscious, walled off behind a pane of glass. But then at times I would have outbursts of contemptuous rage. If my life story, the triumph of the foolish son over his wiser brothers, is replete with moral instruction, Joseph's story is all the more so—and the moral came much more swiftly than in my case.

As I followed the fortunes of the Russian, Polish, Czech, and Lithuanian "dissidents" who, beginning in the 1970s, went into emigration either voluntarily or because they were forced out, I felt somewhat envious of them. Because I had the hardest time staying afloat. I was on the very bottom in Paris from 1951 to 1953; Zygmunt Hertz often had to treat me to cigarettes. The Prix Littéraire Européen, Geneva 1953, was the breakthrough that allowed me to bring my family over from America, but our life—first in Bon on Lake Leman, then in Brie-Comte-Robert, and later in Montgeron —was always on the edge. It wasn't until 1960 that Berkeley guaranteed our stability. They, however, the dissidents, received honors, fellowships; most important, they were accepted, not treated as lepers like me.

Singer started the series of Nobel Prizes for émigrés. But when I learned of my friends' efforts (Jeleński, Kołakowski), I didn't take it all too seriously, because in the past émigrés didn't stand a chance. (Just once, long ago, Bunin.) Nonetheless, the awards have been raining down: Milosz, Canetti, now Brodsky.

The pleasure that I derive from this memoir: along with my old inclination to extract the essence (great events, currents, ideas), this time I am yielding to a fabric woven of specific people, of old and new events, which is, perhaps for this very reason, closer to the tonalities (to fragments) of poetry.

I have figured out why it makes sense to read the Japanese philosopher Nishitani (*Religion and Nothingness*) and Proust at the same time. This professor from Kyoto carries out a superb critique of Western philosophy, beginning with Plato and Aristotle, but I doubt that the remedy he proposes for contemporary Western nihilism can penetrate Western minds, since it would be the equivalent of a suprarational and supralinguistic Buddhist enlightenment. Nonetheless, modern physics appears to be predisposed to that kind of thinking, and Proust could well serve as an illustration—his reality is almost the same as Nishitani's, with life being simultaneously non-life, a phosphorescent, changing sea wave that is *sunyata* or absolute noth-ingness, a vacuum, and every moment achieves clarity thanks to its identical nothingness.

OCTOBER 23, 1987

A brief rain, the first after months of drought, but it cleared up instantly. Chardin's albums, selecting a still life for the jacket. An income-tax con-ference with Mrs. Fujie. I enjoy going to her office because I have a fondness for Asians; they seem to me to be a more attractive race than whites. Mrs. Fujie has been preparing my tax returns for such a long time that I have been able to follow the changes in her face from year to year; but the Japanese somehow age well and my attraction to her continues to have an aesthetic basis.

OCTOBER 24, 1987

The city below looks scrubbed. Sunshine, summer.

Here and now—over there and some other time, later. And what if there is no more "there" and "later"? I include among my faults my having lived too little in the "now"; therefore, I must look around me carefully in order to gather up (to what end?) the memory of details, or, above and beyond any "collecting" (because that, too, is a future-directed movement), in order to reinforce the moment itself. My household, for example, the four young women whose presence warms me: Carol; Ewa, who is putting my library in order; Mary, who organizes my correspondence; Ania, with her daughter, Natalia, and her husband, Marek, in the cottage in the garden. A temporary circle, but weeks and months pass and you hardly notice how one year passes and then another. These people figure prominently in my field of consciousness; I imagine things about them, and would like to submit their images to artistic reworking, but I probably won't have time, because that usually occurs much later. Here I should add that the inattentive experiencing, in passing, of a particular "now" does not at all mean that it hasn't made a deep impression beneath the surface inattention, which is something I could verify empirically.

Moments of intense suffering in love. That I should still wish to revive those moments by reading Proust. Swann's torments of jealousy, so very much my own. This is comforting because repressed, forgotten, they return, they are real for a moment, and they prove that I must really have loved.

OCTOBER 25, 1987

Only a slow improvement in my asthma, which I have never before experienced in my life. I would like to lie out on the patio for a while looking at the blossoms, looking at the flowers, but I don't want to let the sun mollify me.

Memory. Our attitude toward memory changes during the course of our life. In July 1980 I came to Geneva from Paris, where Józef Sadzik and I had been working on my translation of *The Book of Job*. (He died a month later, right after taking the edited manuscript to the printer's.) My discovery, while I was still a schoolboy—influenced by Mickiewicz's *Forefather's Eve, Part IV* (Gustaw's story about his return to his family home) and Słowacki's *An Hour of Thought*—was grounded in imagining the sweet melancholy with which I would one day remember what was happening now. Actually, to be accurate, I made this discovery prior to my readings in romantic poetry, since I had an innate talent for the melancholy that Edgar Allan Poe considered to be poetry's most fitting tone. Walking to school in the morning, I would look at the hills beyond the Wilia and in my thoughts I would journey to my lost paradise, Szetejnie; in other words, already then—but who would have thought it?—I was oriented toward the past, unaware that its bulk was gradually increasing in size.

And now the past that used to be so incomprehensible. I came to Geneva to mark Jeanne's seventieth birthday with her friends. It ought to have been a melancholy return to the spring of 1953, across decades, to the time when I accepted the Prix Littéraire Européen in this city and she introduced me to her circle and we traveled around Switzerland together. I walked along the lakeshore, looked at the plume of water from the very same fountain. Nothing had changed here. Then I took a taxi and found myself at a garden party where I encountered familiar-unfamiliar faces: How can that be, is that old man Robert Hainard, and that old woman Mrs. Naëf's daughter? To tell the truth, I didn't feel very much, although I was conscious of a certain exoticism in the situation. Swiss society, for me, a poor cousin from the wrong Europe, could evoke echoes of some of my former cosmopolitan longings, but now the differences dividing us fell away in the face of our common aging. Perhaps I would have felt differently had I come to this birthday celebration from back there, from the land of misfortunes, but I appeared as a professor from across the ocean, an American tourist.

Just as the boy walking to school in the morning in Wilno could not discern the future that was awaiting him, so that summer in Geneva I could not anticipate many events that would take me into a new dimension, although I did half consciously perceive that a new turning point was being readied. And now once again, after yet another phase, I find in myself very little appreciation for the gentle sadness of ephemerality; rather, as always, its mysteriousness makes me uneasy.

October 26, 1987

Marvelous poems by Zagajewski in *Zeszyty Literackie* [Literary Notebooks] #20. At the same time I read all of Czapski's *Souvenirs de Starobielsk* (published by the Swiss house Noir sur Blanc). What a lasting blossoming this man has had, how much he has achieved! And this testimony of his about the murdered and in the name of the murdered will endure forever, not the way some works of art "will last," but as an unflinching documentation of a hideous truth. Together with the names and personalities of his colleagues and fellow prisoners who, were it not for him, would never have appeared in human memory. For as long as Russia exists, this crime will disgrace her and cry out to the heavens for vengeance. A few days ago I was at the Yakushevs' at a dinner with Alexander Zinoviev. He casually mentioned that in 1943 the officers in his detachment knew who committed the crime at Katyń.* "But we saw it in a positive light." Horror.

Forty-seven years after that grave, the poetry of Zagajewski. It is truly amazing how resilient and surprising life can be. I am thinking of the poets who lie there, frozen in their pre–World War II style—Władysław Sebyła and Lech Piwowar. At the same time, it is horrifying that Poland's one weapon continues to be martyrdom.

OCTOBER 27, 1987

In a plane from Oakland to Denver.

Those moments when one has an acute sensation of the particularities of a given phase which is unlike any others, as today, during the drive to the airport across the hill by way of Grizzly, Fish Ranch Road, and the tunnel. Every time it seems that if one were to live indefinitely there would be no end to the continual succession of newer and newer phases. Or to the new (always from a different aspect) formation of what we experienced once upon a time and are barely conscious of. I can picture the paper, the typeface, of the issue of Kwadryga [Quadriga] I purchased by chance in Wilno in 1929, I believe. It contained some poems by Gałczyński, whom I encountered there for the first time, and also some poems by Włodzimierz Słobodnik, about the countryside, of course, and I didn't understand the word gar; the word I knew for "pot" was garnek. Later, rumors or a legend about Kwadryga

---

* Katyń, a locality near Smolensk, the place where in April 1940 several thousand Polish officers were executed by order of the Soviet authorities. They had been interned in 1939 when, in fulfillment of the Hitler–Stalin pact, the Soviet Army entered the eastern part of the Polish state. They were kept in three P.O.W. camps.

On October 14, 1992, a special messenger of the Russian government, the chief archivist of the Russian Federation, Professor Rudolf Pichoya, personally transmitted to the president of Poland, Lech Wałęsa, complete documentation on the Katyń massacre. By decision of the Soviet Politburo of March 5, 1940, countersigned by Stalin, Polish citizens, both interned officers and arrested civilians, were to be sentenced without a hearing to death. Altogether there were 21,857 Poles. Of that number, 4,421 were executed in Katyń, 3,620 in Kharkov, 6,311 near Tver, 7,305 in other camps and prisons.

The Soviet Union stubbornly insisted on a concocted version of the crime, ascribing it to the Germans, who, after attacking Russia in June 1941, had entered the territory where Katyń is located and discovered mass graves. (Other sites of the crime were unknown at that time.) The Western governments were reluctant to offend their Soviet wartime ally and pretended to believe the Soviet version.

surfaced and then disappeared, chiefly in the person of S. Ryszard Dobro-wolski, who, if I'm not mistaken, was doing his military service in Wilno; but individual *Kwadryga* poets appeared on my horizon separately, not at all as a group, and it seems they never were a group. Stefan Flukowski and the run-down apartment of his father, a tailor on Złota Street in Warsaw; my visits there and our lengthy conversations. Lucjan Szenwald and the secret meetings of leftist, predominantly Jewish, youths, their faces recorded in memory: Magda, the daughter of Benedykt Hertz, the author of fairy tales, and her boyfriend Salman; later, both of them were in America and then once again in Poland, he as the journalist "Arski." It was then, too, that I saw Leszek Raabe, probably for the first time; he should be discussed in connection with the German occupation and the socialist organization Freedom. Radiant, handsome, noble, heroic—handed over to the Germans by whom? Some people said by the Communists. Zbigniew Uniłowski, allied with *Kwadryga* at some juncture in those regions of time. Finally, Władysław Sebyła, who was connected with the Miciński family, although I don't remember in what chronological sequence, and who was associated with my unsettled state, my lack of self-assurance in Warsaw. Permanent inhabitants of that city, like Bolesław Miciński, who moved about in it normally, having their own daily routine, their own social circle with whom they attended concerts, went to exhibitions, university seminars—for me, they moved about in a zone of supernatural beings. I never, though I tried to, learned to believe in the reality of Warsaw—neither the city before its destruction nor the city after its destruction—and its inhabitants lost that aura only when one socialized with them in another city or another country (for example, Nela Micińska). That, too, is the source of my special relations with Bolek and Nela—short-lived with him, lasting for most of his sister's life, but already abroad. How Bolek viewed me, I don't know. I used their apartment in Saska Kępa when Halina and he were in Grenoble on a fellowship; afterward, I recommended him to Sosnowska and got him into Polish Radio. I think I was overawed by his philosophical education. The seminar would keep coming up in our conversations, Apcio (short for Apollo, as Bolek and Kroński called Professor Tatarkiewicz), the anti-Semitic scandals at the university, his seminar colleagues. His *Journeys to Hells* appeared in 1937 as a *Prosto z mostu* [Straight Talking] publication, which made no sense, since Bolek, during the months when he was teaching philosophy in the Warsaw lyceums, was in despair over the nationalism of the youth. He was friends with Jerzy Stempowski and had a Cassandra streak, reacting with revulsion to various arcane points of right-wing ideology. I received his essays rather worshipfully, not too intelligently, since their basis was rather poetic, and I think that the essays I wrote then show his influence, because there was no other model then in Polish. Today I think that the essay should be a lucid, unambiguous genre, should not suggest through indirection, but should develop a train of thought. At that time, the essay was new in Polish letters, and even my wartime essays still delighted in lyric transpositions; in other words, they lacked the virtue of solid prose. That characteristic of Miciński's essays, and of my own, I consider to be a sign of the murkiness of those times.

Miciński introduced me to his philosopher colleagues. Juliusz Tadeusz Kroński gave a lecture in Miciński's mother's apartment after his year-long stay in Prague. I don't remember a thing; the lecture was highly technical, about phenomenology, and the name Patočka was mentioned.

The same face, gestures, pipe, the many Russian words and sentences injected for the sake of humor—straight out of Witkacy. Truthfully, though, despite my affection for him, there was something indefinite about Miciński's personality; many areas were beyond my reach, including his fiancée and later wife, Halina Krauze, her depressions, her psychoanalysis, which Bolek was very interested in, his friendship with Witkacy, etc. I would say that a certain interwar Warsaw was fulfilled in Miciński, while this same domain somehow passed me by, perhaps even the entire domain of interwar Poland, which was barely known in Wilno. I was also in awe of Nela, who worked in the library of the Ministry of Foreign Affairs at that time; that is the beginning of my warm, non-erotic ties with the Miciński family—with her, and later with Dunka, Bolek's daughter. I think I met Władysław Sebyła at Nela's. They were friends and he dedicated several poems to her. Evidently, since I deliberately went to Praga to visit him, he must have attracted me with his attempts at going beyond the poetry of Skamander and beyond the avant-garde toward a philosophical poetry. A very easygoing person, thoughtful, with a sad smile, a slow talker. Very self-sufficient after his early socially minded poems, and necessary to the economy of Polish poetry. "And suddenly the dawn drips blood / through all the columns of the heavens— / like the poems of Sebyła, / like the murdered family of Tsar Nicholas," Gałczyński sneered in his poem "Zabawa ludowa" [Popular Entertainment].

But not the *Kwadryga* circle; Józef Czechowicz and his apartment on Smulikowski Street were much more real to me. I will confine myself to just a few names, because, in the final analysis, so much went on in that short interlude of interwar Poland that it is almost unbelievable. What do ten, twenty, years mean in the history of countries, languages, societies?

OCTOBER 29, 1987

Yesterday and the day before yesterday, an experience from yet another phase. I flew to Denver, where I was met by two professors and taken by car to the campus of the University of Northern Colorado in Greeley. A small town fifty miles from Denver, fifty miles from Boulder, fifty miles from Cheyenne, a five-thousand-foot plateau, but warm, sunny. On the horizon, the Rocky Mountains. Agriculture: corn, sugar beets; irrigation canals with water from the mountains extend this far; to the east the so-called dry crops begin, wheat.

Our conversation in the car and the interview that Professor R. conducts afterward let me form an impression of him. No European will admit that he doesn't understand something; he will pretend that he understands. Professor R., when he speaks of Sartre, says that he tried on several occasions to read *L'Etre et le Néant* but after seven pages he still hadn't understood a thing and put the book aside. Perhaps there is humility in this confession, but, at any rate, there is something natural and a total lack of arrogance, which is not unconnected to the universal breast-beating of American liberals, their pacifism (because the enemy is a person, too), and their firmly rooted habit of evenhandedness in evaluating Russia and America.

I handle his interview questions quite well; later, in the hotel, I read and rest up. The reading in a filled auditorium is successful, although the audience is more timid than in Iowa City and only rarely applauds individual poems. There is also a group of Poles from the new Solidarity emigration. The next morning, an hour-long session with professors and students, to their satisfaction and mine, because they engage me in a lively exchange of questions and answers.

The appearance, then, of wonderfully friendly relations with my Europeanness only enhancing the flavor of an almost American poet and professor. Much of this is the result of my adroitness, however, my knowledge of what is off-limits. After all, the range of topics that interests professors of English in particular is so wide that it is easy to avoid overstepping a certain limit. Nonetheless, I am conscious every moment that I make things easier for myself and, at the same time, that if I didn't make things easier I wouldn't accomplish anything, either. It is a great pleasure to be able to associate with kindly people who wish others well, who seek truth and want to do good. If one were to attempt to explain to them, however, that the Devil, or pure evil, exists, they would be offended by the reactionary character of such a supposition. No matter whether they are secular humanists or members of

AMERICANS

one or another denomination, their religion manages perfectly well without the Devil. Those two days in Colorado were an experience of my doubleness—one more doubleness, though not a new one. Furthermore, reflections on the influence of such professors on students. The endless renewal of the figure of the naïve American.

OCTOBER 31, 1987

"The eye does not see itself." "Fire does not burn fire." These maxims (Nishitani) reach deep, aimed against Western understanding which always begins from the subject, from the Cartesian *cogito*. This subject, the opposite of objects, or substances, is itself understood as substance. But the eye does not see itself, it sees what is beyond itself; consciousness does not grasp its self, which eludes categories, definitions, form. I know neither who I was nor who I am. From which, most likely, the probability arises that that nothingness, *sunyata*, is our own background. Meister Eckhart's divine emptiness.

Tolerance and patience. I ascribe these virtues to myself, although it may well be that they have appeared because I am old. (I can't get used to applying this category to myself: old.) I regret my former fanatical demands, rages, bad moods. True, they passed quickly, unlike Janka's bad moods and depressions; she could "punish" me with a ten-day silence. But they did occur and they troubled me. Now, when I am capable of restraining myself and shrugging off "what ought to be," I sometimes have a suspicion that the passionate intensity of my demands, which was painful both for those who were close to me and for other people—for others because it wounded their professional ambitions, for instance—was an indispensable condition of my industriousness. And also that tolerance is not without a measure of contempt for oneself and for others: Why should I upset myself? How much time do I have left, anyway?

I am writing this in a plane from San Francisco to Honolulu, en route to a week's vacation, supposedly to convalesce after my asthma. Also, no doubt, as a concession. An American on vacation. A hound's-tooth jacket. To be demanding. After all, one of the causes of inequality among people is that only a minority are conscientious and competent. Painstaking artisans, farmers attentive to custom and the soil's needs, proofreaders who never let a single error slip by, musicians who practice endlessly in pursuit of perfection. The majority pretend that they are capable, that they are doing something, and they sneak past. Their ideal is doing nothing, vacations. For me, a vacation for vacation's sake was always a little indecent. Even when I traveled to Martinique and Guadeloupe in December 1984 to meet Jeanne, the pretext was a public appearance. I found the French provinces there from, for example, the Bordeaux region, with a color-based social hierarchy: white colonialists, a mulatto bourgeoisie, and below them, the blacks.

I have committed an offense against my grandfather, Zygmunt Kunat, who was a model of competence. He ran a productive farm in Szetejnie, on an estate that, because of his efforts, was not divided under the Lithuanian land reform. He was a professional agronomist, had graduated from Warsaw's Central School, and was brought up in the late-nineteenth-century tradition of "organic work."* I don't claim that Szetejnie could not have been a wealthy manor (it was not), but factors other than his incompetence were at work here. Yet, in one of my conversations with Aleksander Fiut, I said that he really did nothing at all. Why did I say that? I don't know. That's how little we should rely on verbal utterances. It's true that he didn't engage in physical labor, but the fields and barns would have looked miserable were it not for his eye and mind. And don't I owe him a considerable debt of gratitude for that trait of diligence and reliability in my own character?

* "Organic work" was a program of adaptation in the 1870s to the Russian occupation of Poland through intensive work at improving the country's economic situation.

November 1, 1987

The Kahala Hilton. On the principle of "In the final analysis, why not?" My pretext is a good one because yesterday afternoon I went swimming and I am really beginning to get my health back. I think about the shrinking of the planet Earth in my lifetime. In the plane the person sitting next to me was a young Swiss who had just graduated from high school and was traveling to see the world. From Honolulu he would be flying on to Australia. When did traveling begin? First through Europe. My great-grandfather Syruć died in a railroad accident (!) near Baden-Baden in 1870. One of the Kunats, Stanisław, who was in the emigration after 1831,* was a professor in the Ecole des Batignolles in Paris. Władysław Miłosz's father, also an émigré, lived in Italy. His son went everywhere; he also set foot in northern Africa, apparently. And his son, Oscar, was a cosmopolitan. That's the sort of family they were. My father was in Siberia and in Brazil; his granddaughter, my niece Joanna, lives in Melbourne and has visited us in Berkeley with her daughter Natalia. Janka's father worked for two years in a metallurgical plant somewhere in New Jersey or Pennsylvania. What about the fashion for travel before World War I? I know from Ela herself about the experiences of "blossoming young girls" as they encountered the ocean at Biarritz.

This is the second time I have been in Hawaii. Prepared for it since childhood by the literary legend of an earthly paradise scarred by Protestant missionaries. Thinking bitterly about the countries that have been swallowed

---

* The uprising against Russia in November 1830 and war with Russia lasting through 1831 were followed by a mass migration to the West, mostly to Paris.

whole and digested by enormous monsters. Unable to trust any historical testimonies, since they were written by the conquerors. Centuries of the Polynesians' existence on these islands, without whites. The epic tale of their foray from Tahiti into unknown regions of the ocean, following the will and command of their leaders; then the long history of the newcomers' autocratic, feudal (what else can it be called?) society, employing religious taboos as the guardian of their civilization. Those lovely waitresses in the hotel restaurant know nothing, remember nothing, have lost the language of their ancestors.

November 2, 1987

I really cannot understand life as anything other than preparation. And this is the cause of my present crisis. Because I am like a bellowing mute who knows that he will never really speak. Up until now, I have believed that I would speak, and my poems are the trace of this belief. Of course I have known lengthy periods of muteness, which later turned out to be a slow inner ripening. Now, however, reflection over what is happening inside me does not lead to any productive conclusions. I feel closest to the short poems I wrote in 1985, but I don't think I will manage to write like that again. Fragments of unfinished poems: "I did not think the Berkeley hills would be the last." "I live shallowly. My breath is too short." "There wasn't much. A few days and nights / Between one date and another on a stone."

Bits of history of the Hawaiian Islands. Fantasies; I don't probe their accuracy. An absolute caste system: kings, princes, leaders, priests, the people, among whom there is an assortment of warriors, and at the bottom, a caste of slaves. A large number of prohibitions in a cruel religion. The absence of social injustice as we understand it. Complicated diplomatic games, efforts at attaining power through marriage, and the scandalmongering of the royal families, accompanied by murders if necessary. Continuous bloody warfare conducted by the kings of some islands against other islands; invasions, defeats, battles on the beaches. Then unification into a single state. This was achieved by King Kamehameha, who deployed a force of a thousand pirogues and forced the other island states to submit to his state on the island of Hawaii. But this was finally achieved with the use of artillery, coinciding with the arrival of the missionaries. In the memoir of the last queen of this dynasty, Liliuokalani, I read how she was sent in 1842 to a missionary

boarding school exclusively for children from royal families. There the principles of the Christian religion were instilled in them along with an attachment to the English language, but the missionaries were stingy, the children
were not well fed, so they stole from the neighboring gardens and, as the
queen tells it, since they had the inherited ability to make fire by rubbing
two sticks together, they cooked their own meals. In any case, the missionaries
soon grew bored with religion, went into business, and established the foundation of the plantation owners' wealth.

There was no conquest. It was a gradual swallowing, with the preservation (almost) of the appearances of democracy. The royal dynasty reigned
throughout almost the entire nineteenth century; there was a functioning
parliament—but always with the silent presence of force in the form of the
American ships anchored outside the harbor. How to judge what is better
for the population? For which one, the native population or the Chinese–
Japanese–white population? What would I feel were I a Hawaiian? Would
I be interested in everything else, only not that, like those waitresses in the
hotel?

I shed bitter tears when I read about the sufferings of the inhabitants of
Milan when it was destroyed by Frederick Barbarossa. It was a novel for
young people from the time when my reading was provided by the annuals
Kłosy [Ears of Corn], Biesiada Literacka [Literary Feast], and Przyjaciel Dzieci
[The Children's Friend], borrowed from the library in Szetejnie, I believe,
but enjoyed during a winter spent in Podkomorzynek—where it was warm,
but where the rooms rustled with large black cockroaches. By candlelight.
Milan comes to mind now, but I could just as well be visited by other stories,
an entire collection of motifs from nineteenth-century literature, translated,
reworked, abridged for immediate consumption.

On the beach I read an internal German discussion about the history of
Germany and its responsibility for the crimes of 1933–45. They are incapable
of seeing themselves from the outside, through the eyes of non-Germans.
Thus, the eternal question: How could it be possible? But if they turned into
Poles or Russians for even a moment (which they are prevented from doing
by a lack of imagination), they would understand a great deal. For Hitlerism
was not such an obvious caesura. Both before and after Hitler they have
been ruled by contrasts: clean–dirty, respectable–not respectable, light–dark,
high–low, cultured–barbaric. The second half of these contrasting pairs began
at Germany's eastern border. And even the "final solution" must have orig-
inated in their revulsion at Polish, or Eastern, Jews.

November 3, 1987

"Because we know only the passions of other people, and whatever we learn of our own, we were able to learn only from them" (*Du Côté de chez Swann, I*).

In order to access one's own snobberies, one has to peel off layers, one after the other, as if peeling an onion. One has to defeat one's own reluctance to admit that we yearned to find ourselves in the company of certain people since that gave us a higher status. We call the grapes sour because they are too high. "What do I care about being at X's or Y's?" But what joy if they invite us.

Tracking down one's own unconfessed passions. Alas, they were not spectacular, rather like the subject of an ordinary human comedy.

November 4, 1987

I shall return to this; meanwhile, about truth. What happens if we are faced with the choice: the truth or our life? There are entire areas in the histories of individual human beings and of whole societies that are assiduously bypassed every day, and others that we approach cautiously, on tiptoe. And usually even a glimpse of the truth ends with our stepping back, because one has somehow to get organized internally. Complete acceptance of the truth leads to suicide. For example, someone discovers the truth about his love, his mistress's unfaithfulness, say, and shoots himself. Is truth good and compromise paltry? But let us assume that that someone survives and later he is astounded by the banality of the cause. Then a question arises as to the relative weight of two truths—the first and the second. "Life triumphed." That is not a convincing argument. Lev Shestov's aphorism:

Perhaps truth is by nature such that its communication between men is impossible, at least the usual communication by means of language. Everyone may know it in himself, but in order to enter into communication with his neighbor he must renounce the truth and accept some conventional lie.

Spring 1945 in Cracow. We were living with the Brezas on St. Thomas Street at that time. Theatrical premieres, government receptions, and the like, were taking place side by side with the depressing spectacle of the migrations of nations. And still it was important who received an invitation and who didn't. It ought to have meant nothing to me, but here Breza was invited and I was not, and, frankly, I must confess that I suffered. I commend this useful detail as an aid in comprehending the connections between governments and literature.

Before her death by suicide, Dr. Wikta Winnicka burned an enormous archive of Tuwim's letters to her, because she believed that they compromised the poet, who suffered from an exaggerated love for Moscow. She told me that once Tuwim spoke proudly and emotionally about receiving an invitation from President Bierut. To which Wikta replied, "You should be ashamed, Julek. What kind of a president is he? A two-bit agent. And you—a great poet. You're doing him a favor, not the other way around."

I can proudly say of myself that I was concerned with the estate of Polish poetry and in that sense I was a patriot. But just let someone neutral, from the outside, attempt to get a feel for the mental state of a poet who, in 1945, is acutely conscious of what is happening to his country and also, potentially, to his language. Two-bit agents like Bierut, appointed from outside—although it's true that that territory has been ripe for agents from outside since the eighteenth century.

Mandelstam was no longer among the living in 1945. An example of a poet who was fanatically concerned with the estate of Russian poetry. Mandelstam wrote many poems about his predecessors, who were deserving, who opened up new paths. Also, his imperial patriotism extended beyond Russia. "When children throughout the world will learn to speak Russian," he wrote in one of his essays. And wasn't he so offended in 1914 by the *strelki*, as he called Pilsudki's legionnaires, with their stupid idea of severing Poland from Russia, that he dedicated a poem to this issue?

Nations make use of us poets. Even after they kill us or condemn us to exile. But what a difference between a poet of a small language and a small nation (Polish) and a Russian poet! What could I do, what can I do, what will I be able to do?

ℵOVEMBER 5, 1987

Yesterday, a drive around Oahu Island. Some of these out-of-the-way places, enchanting, festooned with tropical lushness, remind me of Guadeloupe. The botanical gardens near the waterfall are a joy to look at. I contemplate the polite crowd of tourists, blond and white-skinned, among whom I find myself for some unknown reason. This park is part botanical garden, part ethnographic museum. Hula-hula dances performed awkwardly by local young people. For forty years, I hear, the hula-hula was forbidden, and I can understand why: these are danced recitations of rhymed sagas and tribal legends. Or perhaps because the only thing the white men saw in them was the grinding of hips. I asked the performers if they speak Hawaiian. No, only enough to be able to recite while dancing. From the old woman who "runs" this museum and who speaks, writes, and reads Hawaiian, I learned that there are six hundred people like her on the islands. But now the language is being taught in the schools. In Provence, probably up until the Second World War, children were punished if they spoke Provençal among themselves.

Consciousness is employed against the manipulations of seductive magic. This, more or less, is how it works: I am conscious of my old age and my location in the line of fire, since people my age are dying one after the other. However, *just because* I am conscious, my turn will be skipped. Logically, this makes no sense, but it demonstrates the mind's reflexive resistance to the laws of inescapable repetition.

Richard has his own theory of long life. In his opinion, it is a matter of justice that people such as he and I, with the enthusiasm of gluttons and gourmands, should enjoy long lives, and that people who don't derive much pleasure from life should have short lives. Such a theory seems reasonable, but only as long as our organism functions without complaint. The touchstones are tobacco and alcohol. When I smoked, the slightest indisposition—a cold, for example—would take away my desire for cigarettes as well as my desire to write. Alcohol is less normative, but it's true that only a healthy organism can enjoy the taste of chilled vodka.

Drinking, often to the mirror, has been too important for me to ignore it in this memoir. Apparently I drank less than Jerzy Andrzejewski, who developed cirrhosis of the liver quite early in his life, while my liver is fine. As if this were a victory: score one for me. Like the petty victories of outliving one's friends by a year or a couple of years.

Unfortunately, the chief utility of these notes is negative. That is, they allow me to convince myself that the truth does not reside in them. Cézanne said, *"Le monde, c'est terrible,"* but my attitude toward the world contains even more horror, revulsion, pity. At the same time, I have always laughed uproariously, because the human spectacle was a preposterous fairy tale and a grotesque. Language did not provide the means to express those extremes, just as it did not provide words for true rapture.

November 7, 1987

Back in Berkeley, I found a letter from Czapski, a reply to my telephone call in which I thanked him for commemorating the murdered in his *Souvenirs de Starobielsk*. A long letter. Written in a great scrawling script by a man who is almost blind:

Perhaps this is the only way to react: to speak it, to write it down *immediately*. You said I did an important thing, that I brought back to life people about whom little is known; but I, too, know little about them. That old man from Lwów, he wanted so little—to die in Lwów. Every day he was ready for departure, in his cap and coat, with a small package of his treasures on his knees. Every day he waited, until they took him away . . . not to Lwów. That young teacher, who begged us before our departure to defend the Polish *language*, our entire fortune. And I have bad (?) thoughts—what will our words profit them? Will eternal life be resurrected? Amen. After my mother died, my father married a middle-aged Russian woman and lived with her for another fifteen years or so. The day after his burial in the cemetery near our house, she and I went to visit my father's grave. A rainy, chilly summer, slippery mud, a little bench near the mound of the grave . . . She cried the whole time, and then suddenly she asked me: "Do you believe he is alive? That he exists somewhere?" Almost shrieking: *"Net, net! Eto liudi vydumali! Potomu chto slishkom trudno zhit'!* [No, no! People made that up! Because it's too hard to live!]"

I still remember that half moan, half scream. The fragile old man and the young teacher each lived to get a bullet in the back of the skull and an *already* full, slippery pit. We have recorded their deaths, described their deaths so many times, and argued about *how many* corpses, *where*, and it seemed to me that we had forgotten about them behind the piles of written and printed documents. One crime among millions of others . . . [illegible] why am I writing to you, you know this as well as I do, you know the "devil's vaudeville."

When Bierut (or Berman?) or his successor reminded the Father of Nations about *his* five Communists who had perished; when *each time* the Father of Nations sighed, pretended to be making a phone call, said "We shall smash" the prison directors for not releasing them—Beria, who was showing him out after his final farewell, could not control himself: "Go fuck yourselves with your Communists!" he said.

Czapski encloses a copy of his article in *Tygodnik Powszechny* [The Universal Weekly], where I find the following: ". . . that I did not succeed, as did Goya, Soutine, and so many other painters on this earth, to move people with my painting and to express the darkest side of existence: this is an unceasing, ever present torment."

In the part of his letter that he dictated to his secretary:

I was always interested in the topic of the scream in literature, and even the people closest to me here, such as Wojtek Karpiński and a couple of others, are such classicists that they cannot tolerate screams and are convinced that screams must be bad literature. I am convinced that even the loudest scream can be literature, if a man is capable of it, and that is why I consider my painting to be a semi-failure.

And what about my poetry? I wanted to scream, but at the same time I knew that a scream is futile. While feeling guilty that I was not screaming.

November 8, 1987

I would like to read a novel about the twentieth century; not one of those allegories in which human affairs are depicted metaphorically, but a novel, a report about many characters and their actions. It would have to be an international novel, since the century is international, despite the rise of all sorts of nationalisms. I cannot find such a novel, so it would be necessary to write it—and I am curious as to whether there is someone, somewhere, who feels capable of creating it. The currently fashionable narrative techniques—in the first person and about oneself—are an obstacle. It would have to be a panorama employing representative characters, as in Thomas Mann's *The Magic Mountain*. And the heroes should not be ordinary, gray; on the contrary, they would be modeled on colorful, exceptional personalities—there is no lack of such people. I would choose Rome as the setting, or a monastery such as Our Lady of Gethsemane in Kentucky, for example, which people of all professions and outlooks used to come to in order to visit with Thomas Merton. Thomas Merton himself, with his conflicting desires, might appear in the novel, not only debating the philosophy of Duns Scotus with Maritain (who was one of those who visited Merton), but also thrashing about politically. In Rome, a model of considerable stature would be Cardinal Poupard. His views on the state of faith of Catholics, especially of the clergy, which I heard him express in company, were so bleak that they made me uncomfortable. For a philosopher, someone modeled on Leszek Kołakowski could appear in Rome or Gethsemane. A famous writer would also make an appearance, presumably glued together from several famous names and treated not too kindly—for who, if not writers, allowed themselves to be deceived by stupid ideologues and then excelled in seducing minds?

The book would not be limited to clashes of views and positions, although the Naphta–Settembrini quarrel in Thomas Mann would be reborn in a new shape. It would not leave out romance; that is, women would have to be brought in. This creates a problem: Why should the female half of the protagonists be good only for bed? But where are those exceptional intellectual women of the century who are capable of stirring the chronicler's imagination? There is no doubt that the most famous among them, Simone de Beauvoir, is no credit to the amazons of feminism, and the sooner she is forgotten, the better. She is not suitable as a model because she is of too low a caliber, and we're not talking about a satire. When she published her novel *The Mandarins*, a gossipy *roman à clef* tailored to the dimensions of provincial Paris, I asked Albert Camus if he intended to respond to it. He shrugged his shoulders: "One does not respond to the gutter." He was right.

Two exceptional women, both philosophers: Hannah Arendt and Jeanne Hersch. They would deserve to be introduced along with the master they both admired, Karl Jaspers, and in the background, perhaps, the not at all ideologically innocent Heidegger. I met Hannah Arendt through Jeanne in Paris; we had dinner together. But they would have to be described by a contemporary pen, and Hannah Arendt is dead, while I have never even tried to sketch a portrait of Jeanne.

So, a novel of the life of the higher intellectual spheres, of international congresses like the Rencontres de Genève, the papal seminars to which non-Catholics like Jeanne and Leszek are also invited, or of Vatican circles. One way or another, I consider it my privilege that I am able to spin such fantasies, because in this century I have met quite a few famous people, including a number of individuals whom I think of as wise and noble.

November 9, 1987

Thomas Mann's *The Magic Mountain* entered my realm of imagination early, in my student years, and that is probably why it has defined the direction of my thinking about the novel in general. It has also become overgrown with numerous associations. I identified myself with Hans Castorp; I pictured Claudia Chauchat as J.W.; later, not immediately, I learned that the young Georg Lukacs is partially represented in the figure of Naphta, and Hauptmann in the figure of Peeperkorn.

It also happened that California became the family home of the Manns in emigration. Thomas Mann's widow lived here until recently, just a couple of miles from me, and Michael Mann, Thomas's son, a professor in the German Department, was my colleague. In other words, there was a German colony in Berkeley, with which I had some contacts through Artur. Mrs. Mann entrusted Artur with the task of preparing the notes for the published edition of Thomas's correspondence. A member of the German colony, Dr. Zwang, played an important role in my family life. The first diagnosis of Janka's illness was amyotropic lateral sclerosis (ALS)—an incurable disease, a paralysis of the motor nerves that progressively affects the entire body. A couple of months after this diagnosis and the total paralysis of her legs, Dr. Zwang was called in at Artur's suggestion. He declared the diagnosis to be nonsense, which was confirmed by tests in the university hospital in San Francisco, and an operation was performed immediately. My medical malpractice lawsuit against the Kaiser doctors (ALS, instead of a tumor in the spine) took about two years, but ended in victory for us. Finally, in order to mix literature and life appropriately, I must mention the gradual erosion of identification with the protagonists of *The Magic Mountain* as one grows older. How can I identify with that youngster Hans! But my fanatical rages have long since dissipated, so I don't feel an affinity with Naphta, either. What remains for me, perhaps, is the old, rich Dutchman, Peeperkorn, who from time to time visits his lover Claudia in the sanatorium (and perhaps spirits her away to tropical islands?). Independent of any actors, however, duration exhibits what I would call the shaping of space between characters, and I myself, perhaps, would similarly shape my hypothetical novel about the twentieth century.

November 11, 1987

For years I was sustained by my engagement with the estate, not only of Polish poetry, but of all Polish writing; that is, I followed the intellectual changes that were taking place over the course of decades. Reading widely in several languages, I gave primacy to Polish readings because they were the most interesting. What had seemed impossible theoretically had actually taken place. An enslaved country was flowering more abundantly in a cultural sense than many first-rank countries; smarter and smarter generations succeeded each other, and the active interdependence of motherland and emigration overcame the closing off of the country. Rare energies, talents, receptivity, ability to improvise—against the background of the well-known misery of daily life, nationalistic fevers, and police degradation, a race of sorts between uphill and downhill forces. A fragile existence, continually on the edge of ultimate collapse. And always I held stubbornly to the opinion that we, we from the other Europe—that is, what people are finally beginning to define as Central Europe—are livelier than the West, and livelier, too, than the Eastern monolith.

Polish poets. Probably the most difficult to lecture on is Gałczyński. He is untranslatable, so I hardly even tried. Most likely, however, he is the most difficult because he raises many unanswerable questions. What hidden resources does a country need in order to produce such an ingenious poet? Such a multicolored upstart from subterranean caverns, a juggler, a kobold?

Wikta Winnicka, who worked for a very long time in the World Health Organization in Geneva, told me that she once entered the office of one of the high-ranking bureaucrats there, an English aristocrat (Burton?), and saw a photograph on his desk, and she could not believe that she knew that face, because how could Gałczyński be on an Englishman's desk? He confirmed that it was Gałczyński. He had been in a P.O.W. camp with him in Germany. "The most unusual man I have ever met."

I have written about Gałczyński, but I have an additional hypothesis now which is not too closely related to the generally accepted hypothesis about his amorality—that is, a pen for sale to anyone. Gałczyński was one of those Polish literati who had had some experience of Russia in their youth and who read Russian poets in the original. Like Iwaszkiewicz, Witkiewicz, Kazimierz Wierzyński. Or later, among the younger writers, Tadeusz Borowski. But Gałczyński, despite his fondness for the poetry of Alexander Blok, despite his having spent the years of the First World War in Moscow—years that were so conducive to becoming infected with Russianness—was fundamentally non-Russian, non-apocalyptic, non-historiosophically-tragic. At the same time, he wasn't at all affected by the twentieth-century ethos that prescribed negation for poets. Various types of negation—the insufficiency of the world, loathing for the bourgeoisie, rebellion against the rules of language, etc.—can be found in the numerous incarnations of modernism, including the Polish avant-garde movements, but they were alien to Gałczyński. This could be explained by the joy that many people felt at "recovering our own rubbish heap"—i.e., the independent Polish state— when he was a young man. Or it could be explained just as easily by a conscious rebellion against the fashion of modern art, as if he had sworn to himself that he would never be a revolutionary poet. He was only loosely connected with *Kwadryga* in 1929–30. I doubt that he was among the *Kwadryga* poets who paid a visit to Iwaszkiewicz in Stawisko to revile him for his "bourgeoisiosity" (even Sebyła was still on the left at that time). I consider "Cherubim's Song" from 1930 the key to all of Gałczyński's work. Its affirmation of reality is the same as the affirmation in his later poems in praise of People's Poland, and is expressed in almost the same words.

For twentieth-century poetry, Communism was a dream fulfilled about shedding the grimace of fallen angels and passing into a realm of complete affirmation—or of kitsch, as Milan Kundera, who gave this word its particular significance, would say. But not for Gałczyński, because he always affirmed. Quite simply, there was a splendid convergence of his most personal inclinations and of the state's boastfulness, which he exploited masterfully. It seems to me that Gałczyński really believed, although not like those who turned against themselves in order to be liberated from their past selves on an earth presumably cleansed now of alienation. The rhetoric of that earth, sacrificed by the new order, was consistent with the style that he had chosen earlier. In other words, Mohammed didn't go to the mountain; the mountain came to Mohammed. Of course he loved money, but it is hard to imagine him writing while laughing diabolically at his deceitful little tricks.

True, there is one poem in which one can suspect more consciousness than the author discloses. "Poem for a Traitor" (1951), which is about my escape, undoubtedly gives free expression to the moods of that whole Warsaw literary Party circle, its total consternation, since this was the first defection. Another soon followed: Borowski's suicide. But the poem also testifies that Gałczyński was truly shaken:

> *Oof, I ached from this matter,*
> *as though I'd been hit with a stick,*
> *I swear on my mother and Warsaw,*
> *that it still is making me sick.*

"Poem for a Traitor" is an exorcism. It also employs all sorts of devices of patriotic demagoguery: the hell with those foreign Palermos and Taorminas, it's lovely here, the Vistula and oak trees, titmice and woodpeckers; a traitor who "exchanged Poland for a suitcase" will be punished because only in Poland can one write poems, and whoever emigrates condemns himself to sterility.

> *That's our*
> *Chopinesque thought—*
> *that's our*
> *Stalinist watchword.*
> *Truman will never*
> *Extinguish our lights.*

"But why, Czeslaw," Stanisław Vincenz asked me after reading this poem, "why does he place you in Ravenna?"

> *With a traitor's eye you look at Ravenna,*
> *at the mosaics' radiant stones . . .*

"Ravenna is Dante, after all, and Dante is the patron of poet-exiles. It appears that he's winking at you."

Vincenz knew that the exorcism, even though it was full of kitsch, was having an effect on me, and he wanted to comfort me. Nevertheless, there *is* something to that Ravenna. Although I don't interpret it as a wink. The verse develops a certain line of argument to support the curse hurled at the fugitive. To whom is a fugitive a traitor? To his country or to governments imposed from outside? To strengthen the argument, the sixteenth-century poet Jan Kochanowski is introduced (he went abroad, but he returned). Gałczyński's intelligence suddenly slips him a thought about Dante: After all, one of the greatest European poets was an exile, and he did not recognize the government of Florence. Perhaps Milosz will manage to profit from the freedom that doesn't exist in Poland? No, that's impossible, he won't succeed:

> And you thought it would be better for you,
> and you thought that the lute is a little peddler's box
> with which one can wander the highways.

In other words, in the meantime it's necessary to exorcize one's own doubts.

I deduce from this that Gałczyński attached a certain weight to my poetry and that is why this incident concerned him, although we don't know how deeply. We also do not know if he experienced a sudden shock at some point that made him aware of how far afield he had floundered. The story that I heard in Paris must remain a puzzle.

The sculptor Karny told me that immediately after Gałczyński's sudden death in December 1953 he was summoned to make a death mask. He observed a black welt on the neck that, in his opinion, could only have come from a rope. The fact that Gałczyński had hanged himself was carefully and successfully concealed, and the cause of death was given as a heart attack. I don't think Karny had any reason to concoct such a piece of information. Gałczyński's treason, though, might have inclined patriotic opinion toward a scheme of guilt and punishment. Since he was apparently the only witness, and since none of the family would have benefited by revealing the secret, Karny's version cannot be substantiated; perhaps some kind of testimony will turn up eventually. I really don't know what to think of it, although, if it turned out to be true, it would confirm the Englishman's opinion about the "most unusual man" he had ever had the occasion to meet. I must add that Gałczyński was exceptionally complex and secretive, so that any analysis of his personality, including my own, will be misleading. For example, he concealed his enormous erudition. Only rarely would he reveal some part of it; for example, that he knew by heart many poems in various languages—Horace, Rilke, the English poets, the Russians.

Gałczyński's post-war poetry uses two main devices: praise of the quotidian and catalogues of the names of artists "who are with us," and who will certainly not raise any objections—Horace, Virgil, Bach, Beethoven, Brahms, Chopin, Kochanowski, Stoss, etc. Together they affirm: Life is beautiful, joyous, and cultured. But that joyous tone is curious in its total exclusion of Gałczyński's inner struggles, which did exist and which are noticeable in his 1946 *Notes from Unsuccessful Paris Retreats*; after that, they no longer appear on the surface. He must, however, have remembered his prayer:

> *Forgive me, Lord,*
> *the wind is too strong for my fleece;*
> *ah, withdraw your terrifying abundance,*
> *restrain the waves in the ocean.*

A poet is measured by what is best in him, not by what is worst. I do not accept the rebuke that I belittle Gałczyński. I have written elsewhere about the beauty of his poetry, placing it higher than all the avant-gardes of his day. One of his peak achievements, the pre-war *Ball at Salomon's*, assimilates the apocalyptic moods of the time (in contrast to Tuwim's *Ball at the Opera*), transporting them into the realm of dream.

I have received a letter from J.W. in which she writes:

Theodore was a person who was close to you, but he was a man of small caliber, he didn't understand that the time of pleasant hominess, of local games, of the backwater, as you called it, had passed; he ought to have understood that it was time to make a manly decision and take his stand on the losing side; after all, he had several roads to choose from, and he chose the worst. Perhaps I am unjust toward him? I can't imagine you, however, writing such awful things.

At that time—in other words, in 1940.

Nearly half a century later an old woman and an old man are still thinking about their city and the people-shades of those times. In order to avoid making a choice like Theodore's, I escaped by crossing borders illegally, and today I remember the discussions of those times. To go or not to go; the risk was enormous. Leszek B. and his wife claimed that the risk was too great. They stayed. He took a position as a lecturer in Marxism in a school for workers, and when the Germans arrived, he declared himself a Belorussian and got back his estate, somewhere in the vicinity of Dzisna. He walked around with a plaited whip and threatened the peasants, "Now I'll show you Communism." The partisans killed him, shooting him through the window as he was eating his supper.

There is no reason to conceal that my motivation, and the secret of my energy, was love. I would characterize my condition over many months as not overly conscious, as "medium-like." If I confess to not understanding many of my poems that were dictated by some daimonion, then I should also recognize his undivided mastery of entire periods of my life which reveal their strange logic only *ex post*, while what was really driving me to act one way or another was often unclear.

I was troubled for a long time by the question: When did the bells fall silent in Wilno? I asked J.W. She didn't know. She, in turn, asked many residents of Wilno, orally and in letters. No one could provide an answer. Maybe they fell silent gradually? Maybe instead of forty churches playing, fewer and fewer played? Or did they all fall silent one day in response to an order? Did someone's hands remove them, and whose?

Some streets preserve their color and tone, the cream of the walls, the oblique lines of shadow. Thus, a street that I often walked on, which led from Port Street to Mickiewicz Street and the Łukiszki district. It tormented me that I was unable to recall its name. And then in Zahorski's *Guide to Wilno*, from 1928, I think, I found it on a city map: Styczniowa, January Street.

𝒩OVEMBER 14, 1987

The past. But the past is the present, or rather, what was experienced decades ago and what was experienced just yesterday appear simultaneously. Images in the mind of a drowning man.

It has always been the case that I would think of people one day as being incomparably wiser than I am, and the next day, as incomparably more stupid. And it was hard to decide what they were really like. At any rate, my isolation in Berkeley was rooted in my negative evaluation of American liberals, and the people who might have become my friends all had those slogans encoded in their minds. This does not mean that I would have found understanding among the conservatives. Simply put, whether I gave the people who lived in Berkeley high grades or low, I felt superior to them in one thing—in experience that cannot be encapsulated in words.

For the same reason I put forward the idea that the center of civilization is moving eastward. To Sochaczew? To Wilno? To Kiev? I don't know. It could take a very long time. For example, fifty years after my death. And just as I vacillate between considering people incomparably wiser or incomparably more stupid, one day I don't regret at all that it won't be granted to me to witness history's future contractions and distensions, and the next day I do regret it.

Yesterday, a visit from a sweet couple from Poland and an interview for *The Mazovian Weekly*. It's only during such encounters that I learn that I am a bard. Which is to say, on one level I am aware that that's how I'm thought of over there, but it's a theoretical awareness which dissipates in the face of my different way of life over here; nothing here nourishes it. Which is probably to the good. My interlocutors ask me if I am aware of who I am over there and how I respond to that role. I reply that they must understand my duality. When I read my poems in English on American campuses and command an audience of six hundred or a thousand people, they are not the same poems that crown me as a bard over there, considering the differences in language and content. The Polish public, after all, is looking primarily for an ideological message. I am not complaining; historical pressures have extracted a lot of voices from me and I could put together a collection of poems for the public over there that wouldn't be half bad artistically, but I think that my most difficult poems in terms of their content (for example, alluding to the debate about universals) have more admirers over here. Perhaps I am mistaken. The inequality of different groups' intellectual development—cities, provinces, generations, too—complicates any judgment. My experiences: poems that in 1937, for example, were understood by five people, because the reader's sensitivity reacted to older models, seem now, with the passage of time, to be as simple as readings for school children. It appears, too, that the younger generations over there are becoming cleverer and cleverer, although why this is so and how it can be happening given the low social position of teachers, I do not understand.

My contemporaries insist that this applies to Lithuanian youth, too, and also to Russians. And they are optimistic because slowly, from year to year, despite the wishes of the rulers, "the new is coming."

November 15, 1987

The rains have stopped; the days are clear again, but not cool. I read novelist William Gass's description of how some American writers traveled to Vilnius for a meeting with Soviet writers. As a matter of fact, I'd already heard about this meeting from Arthur Miller and Allen Ginsberg. The Americans walked around the city unaware of the other city that once was there but that now has vanished, has been replaced, despite the same architecture, by a new city. Tolerant as they are, they were thoroughly disgusted by the Russians' lifeless speech, especially since they were able to compare it with the liveliness and freedom of Chinese writers during two American–Chinese meetings. On the other hand, the Lithuanian theater wowed them. And I, learning the name of the company from Gass, was infused with patriotic pride, because they are still our people, either Polish-speaking like their parents, most likely, or Lithuanian-speaking. For Gass, the director Nekrošius was never Niekrasz, as he was for me. Mr. Czesław Niekrasz was in love with my mother; I was named for him. Cześ Niekrasz shot himself after World War I. For Gass, the set designer Kanovičius and the scenographer Jackovskis did not retain their duality as Kanowicz and Jackowski.

I am thinking of Irena Byrska's Theater Studio in Wilno and the names of her students. What if they had survived and stayed in Wilno? But I don't know where Mrongovius, probably the most talented among them, wound up. Szabłowska had tuberculosis. Bulsiewicz was killed at Monte Cassino.

Probably the greatest difficulty for an émigré writer from our part of Europe is his readers' lack of any connection to its geography and history. Danilo

Kiš, himself Hungaro–Serbian, has noted that the Russians—Nabokov, for example—are in a much better position because everyone knows the great Russian literature, so they are seen in context; similarly, their geographical range and their past do not have to be constructed from the ground up.

Were it only a matter of Poland, it wouldn't be so bad. But then there's Wilno and all those nationality complications! I have rowed stubbornly against the current, and my books, such as *Native Realm* and *Beginning with My Streets*, or *Conversations with Czeslaw Milosz* and even *The Issa Valley*, translated into other languages, have to a certain extent demarcated a territory that until now has been missing from the maps of world literature.

I just found out about the death of Ludwik Śliwiński. It is unbelievable that that death can be an abstraction. We were inseparable in the lower grades at Zygmunt August High School. We would walk each other home, unable to part. He lived near Zakret; from school, we'd walk up Mała Pohulanka Street, then from his house to mine downhill along Sierakowski Street to Podgórna. Later on, he was kept back for a year and I lost track of him. Anyway, our interests had diverged. I didn't see him either right after the war or during my visit to Poland in 1981. He had married, had children, lived in Toruń, apparently, or in the vicinity of Toruń, like so many repatriates from Wilno. But for me he exists absolutely clearly, in every physical detail, as a twelve- and thirteen-year-old boy.

November 16, 1987

I receive publications about Lithuania from Poland and I read about Lithuania in the Polish press. Why this mania, this mythologizing? Obviously, it's proof of how powerfully—more powerfully than in other countries—literature affects the imagination: the Romantics' Wilno, Mickiewicz's ballads, his *Grażyna*, *Konrad Wallenrod*, *Pan Tadeusz*; later, Milosz and others, Konwicki. Most likely, every geographic region can acquire legendary dimensions as long as attention is concentrated on it, or, more precisely, as long as places appear which the imagination can latch on to. But it has to be a delineated region, with clear contours. Ukraine, despite Malczewski and Słowacki, was too vast. "Lithuania" became narrower; in general, it was not identical with the Grand Duchy, since it did not encompass Połock, Minsk, Pinsk, Słonim, although it took in Nowogródek and Tuhanowicze.

The boundaries for fantasy were ample enough, since the rite of the "fore-fathers" is Belorussian, not Lithuanian; the same can be said of the Uniate priest; and yet, imaginary "Lithuania" virtually excluded Belorussian culture. The publications that I read beautify and romanticize Lithuania. Whatever else it may be, Lithuania is a country with a northern, melancholy nature. It may be prettier than the Mazovian plain, but that's an easy accomplishment. It's amusing to think that my type of imagination, so strongly spatial, drove me to draw maps of nonexistent countries—that that characteristic contributed to my transposing Lithuania into mythic dimensions. Not that I wasn't aware that literature is never faithful to real proportions.

A couple of kilometers from Krasnogruda, the end of large Lake Gaładuś was (as it is today) on the Polish side of the border, while the rest of the lake was in Lithuania. Walking around there as an adolescent, shooting at grebes (the memory of this torments me with a burning shame), I did not think of those districts as part of Lithuania, despite the fact that the village at the end of the lake, Żegary, was pure Lithuanian. Why not? Because the wind, which was fierce and cold even in summer, as was characteristic of the entire Suwałki region as a result of the clear-cutting of the forests, conflicted with my notion of Lithuania as a snug place nestled into the valleys carved by friendly rivers. And yet a significant portion of Lithuania is made up of bare post-glacial hills, lakes, and cold wind. I note this for purposes that have something in common with self-irony and humor.

NOVEMBER 17, 1987

I try to read contemporary American poetry conscientiously. It's understandable that where there are thousands of poets the overwhelming majority cannot be worth very much, though they provide an incentive and nourishment for the few, just a handful; it's the same everywhere. Something similar is happening in modern painting and the results are similar, too, because the paintings afford little pleasure.

One can say about these poets that their technique is first-rate but that they have nothing to write about. Their "life experience" shows through every line of verse; it is the life of lecturers on university campuses or in high schools and what they describe most frequently is their family-life complications, their own or heard about in the neighborhood bar. It is a

AMERICAN POETRY

common, monotonous reality, free of historical earthquakes; at most, it includes one or two earthquakes, in a literal sense. Nothing drives them to leap like salmon confronting an obstacle. Precisely that, this "having nothing to write about," is, in my opinion, quite a universal problem to be studied. But in the meantime I'll turn to something else.

Oscar Milosz trained me to dislike contemporary French poetry in 1934–35, accusing it of noting down skin-deep impressions; that is, of a passivity of perception. Half a century later, I think he was right. I may once have mentioned, unfairly, my sensitivity to Paul Valéry, when it is Blaise Cendrars and Guillaume Apollinaire who deserve my homage. But there's little to be gained from the later writers. Either there's a leap or there isn't; that great poem of compassion for the modern metropolis, Cendrars's "Easter in New York," was a leap. It dates from 1912.

Our timidity in the face of incomprehensible sentences and violated syntax gets in the way of evaluation. Many incomprehensible poems and paintings turned out to be exceptional works of art; that's why people are afraid. For my own use, I simply say, "I don't understand," and I don't worry about a given poet's rating on the literary stock exchange. He doesn't speak to me, I don't understand, he bores me, and that's the end of it. I don't have time to dig deep. I assume that there are many levels of incomprehension and that mine is sufficiently refined. Somehow, rejecting a great many poems because of their incomprehensibility has not hurt me, although it's a delicate matter and our profession does not like to admit aloud to such simple criteria, so as not to embolden ordinary people.

Who can guess what convoluted nonsense may be brewing in the minds of our fellow men, sometimes along with deep intuitions? In poetry, various hallucinations have earned the right of citizenship ever since the control of logic disappeared; that is the price paid for novelty, but also, because of it, it is difficult to draw the boundary between exceptional and inferior poetry.

NOVEMBER 18, 1987

A clear morning; surveying the damage after a deer's visit. Raccoons struggled with the lock on the garbage can; they didn't manage to open it, but made off with a rope, as if they needed it for something.

The poetry of a given civilization is, whatever may be said against it, a true reflection of its revealed or hidden essence. American poetry equals an enormous collection of snapshots from which we divine the things observed and the mind of the observer. In his mind we may discover the conviction that "there is nothing to write about" and that others, who have been buffeted by historical accidents (we, for instance), are privileged, because the reality of impressions (childhood, family, loving unions, illness, old age, death) does not really offer an occasion for interpretation other than changing impressions into words. Also, a question inevitably arises about the legitimacy of language: Is it a poetry of epistemological oversophistication or—I loathe foreign phrases, but what can I do?—as Tolstoy would say, *uton'chenie*? And this can be asked not only of American poetry but also of world poetry. What is the yearned-for domain in which "something happens"? Society, the system. Allen Ginsberg's *Howl* was a leap, but only owing to its somewhat hysterical American apocalypse and rage. Here I am approaching something important. Let's not forget that Samuel Beckett expresses the convictions of twentieth-century poets: human life suffers from a fundamental lack of meaning. Other than the absurd, nothing can be extracted from it. It can be deduced from this that something interesting begins only with the plural. Protests, atomic weapons, Latin America, and so forth. Aren't all intellectuals of this century characterized by an escape from the singular to the plural? And with all their concern about the salvation of the collective, aren't the clergy of the various denominations escaping from meditations on the human condition that threaten to end in nihilism?

November 19, 1987

I had just finished writing this yesterday when I found in the bulletin of the American Academy of Arts and Sciences:

> In current epistemology, in current theories of knowledge, as well as in poetics, in literary theory, there is, *in a literal sense*, a commanding nihilism. I do not use the word "nihilism" in any pejorative, in any adjectival sense. I want to use it etymologically throughout my remarks. There is nothingness. The cardinal notion, the center (it is paradoxical to speak of a center) is absence. The concept of absence commands the present prevailing energies of investigation and argument. There is ab-

sence of the subject, of the *ego*, absence of the Cartesian first person singular. There is an absence of veritable truth functions in respect of meaning. There is no longer a correspondence theory, a correspondence logic between speech and verity. There is absence of value in any objective or universal sense, absence of the absolute, absence of the canonic, absence of the dogmatic hierarchy of observed authorities.

The subject is no longer trusted, the subject is no longer seen as stable, central, inviolate.

—George Steiner, lecture to the Academy, April 15, 1987

It may well be that acceptance of such an *episteme* and of such poetry signifies the end of poetry—and we, a number of us, are distinguished by our vigor because we are behind the times; that is, our philosophical thinking continues to preserve the remnants of a relation to objective truth, to God.

A letter from Jerzy Turowicz, from Rome, dated November 1. I shall copy it.

Dear Czeslaw,
I have been in Rome (with Anna) for a month in connection with the Synod of Bishops; we return to Poland in two days. I tried to find out here if by chance you might be prowling about Europe. It seems you will be in Paris in November; it's a shame that we won't see each other this time. Yesterday morning we were at Mass with the Pope and had breakfast with him. He told us that he is reading poetry now more than ever! (But that since he became Pope he himself no longer writes any.) He read your *Three Winters* awhile ago (in the new edition with commentaries) and he liked it very much. He also said that he got to know you better recently at Castel Gandolfo where you read your poetry in Polish and English, and where you were the only one to remind those present of the rights of the peoples of Eastern Europe!

I picked up your *Chronicles* here, which gave me a great deal of satisfaction, and I am proud that you immortalized me in "Caffè Greco." Among the poems that I did not know before, I especially liked "Powers" and "But books."

We were enormously gratified that Joseph Brodsky has become your Nobel colleague. I would even have written to him, but I don't know his address, and then I doubt he would remember me, although we met at Alexander Schenker's.

I have always thought that consciousness is therapeutic. That is, that it avoids repetition of what has once been assimilated, even to the extent that it is possible to ward off death, since we are conscious of the repetitive nature of death. This proves that my mind was mythologizing and childlike. How many printed pages have been devoted, for example, to human vanity! It has been analyzed this way and that, and to no avail; those who are most conscious of its subterfuges yield to it and lay themselves open to the mockery of their fellows who are clever at tracking down the faults of others, but not their own.

Vanity is one of the chief comic seasonings of the human spectacle; if one were to take away vanity and take away sex, not much would be left of natural, so to speak, humor. Maybe Eros is vain, and all vanity is erotic? Now my imagination suggests a treatise on mirrors. On a vast number, thousands, of mirrors, and on the faces that have looked at themselves in those mirrors. Teenage girls and mature women, the combing of hair, hour-long sessions thinking about noses, chins, curls, necklaces, and earrings, how I look today, how he will see me today, whether this dress is sufficiently flattering. Mirrors ought to retain at least a storehouse of glances left behind by all those beings, but there is not a trace. And the men! Predatory—conquering nostrils, overpowering sideburns, a look of irresistible male power, the preening of roosters. It is easy to laugh; only we ourselves were once him and her.

Other types of vanity; for example, authorial vanity. As if I consider myself devoid of it, but I can remember my numerous visits to bookstores when I would grab the opportunity to look into the poetry or essay section and, not finding my books, would feel a slight disappointment, and then immediately tell myself: This is ridiculous. Once I found *The Captive Mind* in the psychology section. And the reverse: now, when I go to a bookstore, to Cody's or Black Oak Books, I am pleased that my books are displayed in such numbers.

In old age, vanity seeks confirmation of our existence. That is, an intelligent essay or a book about our poetry reminds us that we did exist; after all, we did write—the consciousness of which, despite what one might think, is definitely not present at all times.

Literature is a great vanity fair; just the sight of it evokes empty laughter and dread. The ranks of people who write poems, novels, plays grow with every year, but the hopes of those who aspire to the profession are mostly deceptive, and among those who are published, the majority strut about in vain. What do they want? To be liked. Eros, just as in front of the mirror?

November 20, 1987

I have been thinking a lot about quite an important topic—about an examination of my stay in America from 1946 through 1950. More precisely, what America meant to me in those years. It was not what it is today, nor, I think, what it is for almost all my contemporaries. Were I to try to ascertain this on the basis of my verse and prose writing from that period, I would not come to any unambiguous conclusions. I would characterize my situation as backbreaking, unbelievable, illogical, immoral, indescribable. After the passage of so many years, what I have managed to achieve in literature is projected backward; that is, the false game of those days is grounded *ex post*. At the same time, that historical phase loses it sharpness, and its most important features, perhaps, sink into oblivion.

Consciousness is often immoral only because it is consciousness. It has various levels on which we live simultaneously, deceiving ourselves, settling down temporarily, accommodating to our surroundings, but there exists one deepest fundamental level. Before 1939 I did not give the existing conditions much of a chance and I ought to have become a Communist, but what could I do if my consciousness of what Stalinist Russia was like would not allow that? Or perhaps it was simply because that system wasn't mine. I appraised the Polish patriotic mentality fatalistically, however; I believed it was doomed. Had I lived in a Western country, I would not have had to choose, I would not have had my back against the wall. But we had either Hitler or Stalin; between them, a few illusions appraised as illusions.

And then came the year 1945: Hitler is finished off at the cost of countless sacrifices and victims; the victorious army occupies Poland; there is no choice; the inhabitants of the country are spoken of as "our woods, our hares," and about other countries the Russians say *Evropa nasha* (Europe is ours). The Polish "creative intelligentsia" quarrels, temporizes, but in the end accepts the inevitable. Some are even quick-witted; they leave to take up posts. "Listen to a wise old Jew," said Antoni Słonimski. "Stay abroad as long as possible." Shortly afterward, Słonimski, who was trying to maneuver by occupying a position in the Polish Institute in London, was transferred to Warsaw, and made a fool of himself out of fear by writing a servile article attacking me. For which I and others forgave him later on.

I left for America under the protection of Jerzy Putrament and Jerzy Borejsza. Putrament warned me: "Remember that you are signing a pact with the devil." And it was, no doubt about it, a pact with the devil, considering my consciousness of what had happened. No ignorance protected me. The millions in the gulags, the deportations after 1939, Katyń, the Warsaw uprising, the terror in Poland—I was aware of everything. And at the same time the existence of a legitimate Polish Army in the West, just recently demobilized, and the legitimate government in London. And I against them, with the crowning argument that they had lost and could not possibly win. Should I break the pact, side with them because they are noble, faithful to imponderabilia? It's only today, after several decades of the People's Republic, that the steadfastness of the emigration is being glorified. But it looked very different then. Janusz Minkiewicz wrote a little poem right after the war (or was it during?), in which he said of the London government, "With the devil, not with you," and many of us writers thought the same thing, or thought that there was no one to be with. I suffered and accused myself of prostitution, although if émigré opinion was inclined to suspect people like me of direct profit, it didn't hit the mark; there were worse things, ideological things. Nevertheless, they were right in the sense that only later, as an émigré myself, did I understand the torment to which thousands of Poles voluntarily condemned themselves in the name of their principles, getting to know England and America from the bottom, through heavy physical labor.

So, ideology. Hegel? Historical necessity? An unbelievably difficult knot to untie, but something or other can be explained, beginning with America. Janka and I arrived in New York on a small half-cargo ship in the stormy winter of 1945–46. Behind us was Poland, crushed; if, in comparison, even despondent London had seemed a realm of peace and well-being, then what did America seem like? Our needs and our desires were modest, however, and today that modesty strikes me as downright funny. We accepted the wealth of Fifth Avenue as something that *is*, no questions asked; truly, that side of America did not impress us. My indifference to capitalist temptations was appropriately noted down and that's the main reason why I was assumed to be reliable. Another reason as well: the intensity of my experiences in Poland had erected something like an armored wall around me. What was here was unreal, and the minds of Americans were unreal; I belonged to another planet, and I could only observe their planet while shrugging my shoulders, wishing them well or not.

$\mathcal{N}$OVEMBER 21, 1987

In trying to rediscover several years of my life, I shall not avoid simplifications; one month was one way, a second was different, an evolution was taking place inside me. Only the tone was the same: leftist. I did not belong to any party; I had not joined the officially sanctioned Polish Socialist Party; they probably knew about the socialist Freedom organization during the Occupation, but that wasn't an obstacle. One of the first volumes of poetry in Poland after the war was my *Rescue*, which also included poems from the time of the German occupation. My entire system of references was there; in America there was nothing at all. In addition, I was sufficiently intelligent not to confine my observations to the smoothly oiled machinery of democracy but to make myself aware of the violence of the struggle for existence, the urban poverty, the loneliness of the individual, the fundamental anti-intellectualism of the system. I read a great deal, including Louis Adamic, who had emigrated from his native Lubljana at age thirteen and became in America a writer of the insulted and the injured, workers of Slavic origin. Apparently, alone among Poles at the time, I devoted myself to discriminating reading in English: Henry Miller, *The Partisan Review*, and the least orthodox journal of the New York intellectuals, *Politics*, which Dwight Macdonald bankrolled with his wife's money. That's also when I met Dwight. Later, in 1955, we took part in a convention organized in Milan by the Congrès pour la Liberté de la Culture. It is he who figures in my poem "In Milan." "Long into the night we were walking on the Piazza del Duomo." Mary McCarthy also participated in this convention. As a result of this reading, at least one sector of America became understandable and close to me: the New York left intellectuals of an anti-totalitarian bent. I came across the name of Simone Weil for the first time in *Politics*. Nicola Chiaromonte's articles in *Partisan Review* spoke right to me, although I didn't know who he was. I was pretty well oriented in current politics, both internal American and international. My dilemma, or ours, I defined in this way: "Which is better: to be locked in a cage with an intelligent bandit or with a kindhearted imbecile?" Which testifies to my not very high, and certainly traumatic, assessment of the politics of the co-creators of Yalta.

One incident in particular is worth noting here. I met Margaret Storm Jameson, a novelist and active PEN member, in 1945, when she came to Cracow from London (the first foreign writer!) with Ksawery Pruszyński and Antoni Słonimski. Later on, she invited us to dinner in London—she and her husband, Guy Chapman, a professor of history in Cambridge and a taciturn fellow who always let his wife take the lead, as if his own past as a heroic officer in the trenches in World War I were nonexistent. It was some time before I found out about that. Margaret, who is no longer remembered as a novelist, could have been a model human being, a model of Anglo-Saxon courage and righteousness, the worthy daughter of several generations of sailors, of captains who sailed the high seas. Her youth pre-dated 1914, and she once said to me, "Milosz, you have no idea what my generation's youth was like, what boundless hope we had for a better world; then suddenly everything that was fine among us vanished in the blood and mud of the trenches."

Margaret came to Washington, in 1948, I think, and stayed in Georgetown with some American friends—an admiral and his wife. Invited to join them for dinner, Janka and I had a taste of the America of wealthy homes. One of the invited guests was the editor of *Reader's Digest*, a man apparently "from where everyone comes from," with a trace of a Russian accent. I got into a discussion with him and he, smoking a fat cigar, said with disdain, "You intellectuals, you've lost. Your intentions of changing people are worthless. We won: we give them what they want, they read us in print runs that are way up in the millions, they do not want you and they never will."

It was then, I think, that I realized that I am a promethean romantic who has been inoculated with a belief in his special vocation, who attempts to "remake bread-eaters into angels"; the coarse laughter of his excellency with the cigar touched me to the quick, because he arrogated to himself both common sense and sober judgment. I also realized that, alas, their romantic lineage links intellectuals and Communists and that that man's America was not for me.

I became friendly with the sociologist Aleksander Hertz, with whom I had once worked at Polish Radio under Halina Sosnowska. Hertz adored America, which had given him freedom and saved him from pre-war Polish anti-Semitism. I could not go as far as he did in praising the American Constitution and the safeguards built into the division of power among the legislative, executive, and judicial branches, and privately I reproached him

EARLY IN AMERICA

for his enthusiastic decency, his "vegetarianism," because his sociology over-looked tragic conflicts. Which is to say, Hertz judged America too optimis-tically for my taste, but exactly the way Janka did.

America almost destroyed the loving closeness between us that had weath-ered years of war. After Tony was born, Janka changed, or perhaps it was I who became jealous; whatever the cause, we argued repeatedly, mainly about America. She was an intelligent and loving person, and not the first woman who had to cope with a husband afflicted with philosophical or ideological madness, although my case was a particularly drastic one. My "no" to capitalism suggested a "yes" to Communism. Nothing of the sort. What do you want, then, if neither is acceptable? Janka was terrified of the Russians. This was rooted in her childhood experiences during World War I; she had a recurrent dream from that period and it was the background against which she experienced January 1945 in Goszyce. For her, America was not first and foremost a land of well-being and wealth; rather, it signified security and a homeland for the children. An ironist, but utterly lacking in cynicism, she wanted to believe, and from the moment when all values broke down over there, in Europe, she believed in American democracy. That's why she found it so difficult to move to France—to move from a country that had already become her home, her children's country, to a land of foreignness. Much later, Kennedy's assassination was a terrible shock to her—not, as it was for me, just one of those dramas in which history abounds.

NOVEMBER 22, 1987

Still, when I look out my window at dawn, I rejoice at the colors of the bay below and the San Francisco skyscrapers in the translucent air. There aren't many views like that on earth, and I value it.

To descend deep into one's shame. Not only my own, of course. The first staffs of the embassy and consulates were more or less accidental, somewhat in line with the parties that made up the coalition government: the Polish Workers' Party (the Communists), the Polish Socialist Party, the Peasant Party, a few people under private protection, a few straight from the UB (the security organs), although we could only conjecture who was an agent and informer; as I later discovered, my guesses were none too accurate. They were all painfully experienced people, devoid of any illusions about Big

Brother. How, for example, could the consul have any illusions if, as a socialist, he had spent time first in a Soviet prison in Lwów and then among prisoners who were mowed down by machine-gun fire as the Germans approached in 1941? He survived; he fell down in time and was buried under the bodies of the murdered.

The overwhelming majority of such diplomats looked upon their presence in America as their chance to defect, especially once the comedy of the coalition government came to an end and the Polish Socialist Party was forcibly merged into the Polish United Workers' Party. Only a few returned to Poland; they fell away one by one. You could scarcely find a Communist among them; if there were any, they were from a very fresh batch. Oskar Lange, who was ambassador for a time, came out of the socialist left; Józef Winiewicz (from Poznań and a right-winger) hadn't the faintest notion of what Marxism was all about; Grzegorz and I, both of us, for better or worse, quite well versed in these matters, used to make fun of him for this. Winiewicz was one of those who spent the war in London and then bet on Warsaw. He didn't make a mistake; he had a good career. Ksawery Pruszyński placed the same bet: a short stay in the embassy, then (or the reverse?) in the Polish UN delegation. In New York I met a group of my Wilno colleagues who had made their way to America via Japan, and were brought over to this country by Oskar Lange. They were trying to decide what to do; in the end, some of them followed Lange back to Poland; the most farsighted among them, Władysław Malinowski, got himself a permanent position in New York with the United Nations.

The year 1950 was not the same as 1946. "What to do?" had grown into a tormenting nightmare, day and night. To return to Stalinist Poland would have been the most blatant nonsense. And yet, though it sounds ridiculous to say this, good little Czeslaw simply could not renounce his loyalty. In the final analysis, the Polish Communists hadn't done me any harm; they had even tolerated my hardly orthodox views. I, in turn, had not been playing a double game. If I made no use of the letter to the leading American Freemasons that Stanisław Stempowski gave me, it was because I was afraid of entanglements. This does not mean that I didn't speak frankly with people whom I included in my own, that is, my intellectual, circle—Thornton Wilder, for example. I think that the last performance Janka and I saw in Warsaw was Wilder's *Our Town* and now the kindness and even friendship of a writer I valued had great weight for me. Wilder thought that I ought to remain in America and he promised to set us up on a farm where I could write in peace. I also spoke frankly with Albert Einstein, whom I contacted through a friend of Oscar Milosz's in Princeton. (Not Christian Gauss; at that time, I didn't know about his friendship with Oscar Milosz. I certainly could have spoken with him then, since he died in 1951. Only much later, in the seventies, I tracked down Oscar's correspondence with Gauss among the latter's papers collected in the Princeton University Library.) Einstein advised me not to emigrate.

A great deal can be deduced from my poems written in America. Even had it been translated into English, "Child of Europe" (1946) would have been incomprehensible to Americans at that time, just like "Two in Rome" (1946), "The Spirit of the Laws" (1947), and "Treatise on Morality" (1947). The poem "Without sight" (1949), about Detroit, is openly unfriendly toward America. My rage—because doesn't this state of affairs lead to rage?—was directed against people's physiological life, against *l'homme moyen sensuel.* They eat, they drink, they multiply, and are content—but why?

> *This new Jerusalem of old Puritans,*
> *Their dream fulfilled, though in reverse,*
> *Is for me an oppressive, empty stage set.*
> *As when asleep I want to scream and cannot.*
>
> *I learned, however, to reject. This is*
> *A privilege long ago granted to us poets*
> *That wages, weddings, baptisms and burials*
> *Are not our true theme. They are no more*
> *Than glitter, a flight of reflections*
> *On huge black waters. As through a glass garden*
> *We walk, and see with sorrow more than is permitted.*
> *Are we really enemies of the species*
> *Yearning to change by force people into angels*
> *Of pure intellect? To tear out of the depths a spark,*
> *A hated spark of Promethean torture?*
>   —*"To Albert Einstein,"* 1948
>   *Translated by the author*

The fanatic Naphta from *The Magic Mountain* makes his bow. Now I am trying to pronounce judgment as objectively as possible, and it certainly does not come easy.

November 23, 1987

Literature and art as a rejection of bovine existence, which is also sometimes called revulsion against the bourgeoisie. It is doubtful that the revolt of the French bohemians against nineteenth-century society derived from their hunger for justice; rather, it was aimed against the cud-chewing existence of the philistines. Baudelaire, Flaubert, Rimbaud. Then the Symbolists contemptuously turning their backs on the public. In Russia, the moral-revolutionary impulse was stronger, but it also cannot be separated from rejection of physiological duration. Literature and art—wherever, in whatever country—are hereditarily freighted with opposition, and their adepts, like it or not, are marked. This may have been most cruelly depicted in Krasiński's *Un-Divine Comedy* of 1833. An apparently happily married couple, a cozy home, a child, and suddenly a drama. What can the sensitive, kind wife do to save the family nest if her husband is bored with well-being and peace, dreaming of a Maiden (poetry) who summons him to fly into the unknown, to dangerous adventures? The Maiden, after all, combines both intellectual and erotic arousal in her being; she can be, simultaneously, a Muse, a friend, a lover, an activist comrade. She is the dangerous rival of the despairing wife, and superior to her in every way, until the poor woman, striving to equal her and to receive the gift of poetic inspiration, becomes mentally ill. She believes that her husband will love her only if she becomes a poetess, and also that, alien as he is to ordinary (small) human feelings, he will love their child only if it is a genius. The wife's prayers are heard and Orcio the son receives the mark of a bard and prophet: blindness. The Maiden, on the other hand, who has managed to lead her admirer out of the house to the edge of an abyss, reveals herself there as a hideous corpse, a demonic phantom. It appears that the misfortune he has brought upon his family and his disenchantment with his lover have not cured the husband; his actions in Part Two demonstrate that he chases this same phantom in the shape of History and an eschatological politics, as befits a romantic man of letters, always tempted equally by deed and by word.

It is usually men who are ill with the insufficiency of existence itself; ideas, art, revolutionary projects appeal to them. Occasionally, however, a rebel dreamer is a woman; isn't Emma Bovary one of them?

November 24, 1987

The colors of autumn in Berkeley where, not long ago, before the first rains, there was gray and tan; now, the intensive green of the lawns on the hillsides. The rusty gold of the sycamore leaves, the unchanged color of the eucalyptus and the conifers. Splashes of bright cinnabar red: those are the cotoneaster bushes, covered with ripe berries.

    I am not enthusiastic about romantic habits. Their satirical exaggeration allows us to become conscious of how deeply rooted they are among us. I return to such ruminations only because they were implicated in the delicate chemistry of our marriage. Common sense and decency were on Janka's side; we ought to have stayed in America. For me, however, to stay would have meant choosing birth, copulation, and death, and nothing more. Because I could not imagine any activity involving language here. Not only was I no one here, which is humiliating enough, but I would have had to become someone outside my true estate—Polish poetry. In other words, quite simply, and rather than singling out particular motives, it would be best to refer to the voice I heard clearly, which was summoning me to fulfill my destiny. Evidently, it could not have been otherwise; at any rate, that is what I think now. I am opposed to mixing biography and poetry; unfortunately, at times it is difficult to avoid doing so. I shall not try to guess what might have been had I stayed in America instead of returning there ten years later, but I know it would have been different.

    Putrament watched over me from afar, undoubtedly admiring my talent and concerned about preserving me for our Communist-ruled fatherland. Later, he wrote that he had tried to channel that geyser into a (socialist) pipe. When, after serving as ambassador in Paris, he became secretary of the Writers' Union in Warsaw in 1950, he understood like a good fisherman that it wasn't a good idea to remove me abruptly from America, so he offered me Paris. This was a deft maneuver psychologically, because it left me the hope of waiting it out abroad. And a thaw really did take place, only not for another six years. I suspected a trap and was prepared to accept the worst, but only for myself, without endangering Janka, who was pregnant with our second child. She didn't want me to travel into the dragon's maw, leaving her alone, but she was afraid that if I remained in the States for her sake, I would hold it against her. That's the game that was played by a trio who knew each other very well, although Putrament apparently did not know that before the war, when Polish Radio wanted to fire him as a Communist (he was the so-called programming controller), Janka went straight to the director himself, made a scene, and the decision was retracted.

In the autumn of 1950 I sailed to Europe, which was much farther away then than it is today. I was afraid, but what was even worse were the doubts I harbored about the health of my mental faculties. Though praise and expressions of gratitude for one or another aspect of our books bring us pleasure, very often what is concealed behind them and what may even have made them possible continues to be a source of embarrassment.

November 25, 1987

The fabric of time. A shifting network of interdependent phenomena that have nothing in common other than that they are contemporaneous. Barely perceptible changes in fashion as well as changes in language, such that certain behaviors and certain word combinations are dated and could not possibly have appeared either earlier or later. This does not mean that divisions into high and low, bad and good, are abolished, but that when we look back from our position in a different moment of that fabric, in different loops of the net, we find it very difficult to re-create many of the interconnections of those times.

Or could it be that people are summoned in some chronologically defined intersection of warp and woof, parallel with this but not that style, language, color of events? For example, can I picture Ksawery Pruszyński beyond the day on which the Fates, deciding that his time was up, made use of their scissors?

Baloven' sud'by. I remember how Pruszyński leaned over toward Jerzy Wyszomirski at a Żagary poetry reading in Wilno and said those words —in Russian—about me. I was hurt, although all it means is "fate's spoiled child," with a hint of "fate's plaything." Twenty years old, talented—no doubt that's all Pruszyński meant to say—but at the time I didn't expect fate to play with me as it did, and I bristled at the apt prophecy. Pruszyński had come to Wilno because he was an associate of the conservative newspaper *The Word.* Wyszomirski contributed feuilletons to *The Word* regularly. He was the first to appreciate our talents.

He himself was the author of a couple of volumes of weak poems. A small man who wore a pince-nez, melancholy, very Russian (his father was a career officer in the tsarist army), a lonely figure in Wilno's drunken night life. Many years later, in occupied Warsaw, I bought his autobiographical novel about childhood in a garrison town (Zambrów?) for Władysław Ryńca. I don't know if it came out after the war. Wyszomirski committed suicide in 1955; he'd had enough, he didn't live to see the Thaw.

It was Pruszyński who could really be called "fate's spoiled child." He was born into a well-to-do family; he was a talented journalist, and his masculine good looks swept women off their feet. Spiteful people said that his prominent cheekbones, green eyes, and slanting eyebrows were much too Cossack and that one of the Ukrainian servants must have taken up with his mother or his grandmother. Be that as it may, his aristocratic origins were a help to him and he situated himself well, not on the foolish right, but with the conservatives from *Time* and *The Word*. His dispatches from red Spain were a sensation. He went there accredited to the Franco government, but changed his mind en route and remained in loyalist Spain.

Pruszyński's life is sufficiently well known and I don't have to repeat it. He served his country as a soldier, fighting near Narvik, Norway, and in Normandy; with his pen, as the author of war stories; and with his knowledge of languages as councillor or attaché in the London government's— the Polish government-in-exile's—embassy in Russia. A tumultuous life, chivalric, romantic (he himself must have been amazed that his generation had such a stroke of good luck when it seemed that the time of the Polish legions of 1796* was gone forever), and always on the path of honor. Many of his comrades-in-arms believed that he stained his honor by going over to the side of satellite Poland in 1945. It is true that consciously to choose collaboration on the model of the nineteenth-century Margrave Wielopolski required quite a bit of civil courage. He was an unusually valuable acquisition for Warsaw, and no one understood this better than the sovereign ruler of the press and literature, Jerzy Borejsza, who had created his own state within a state, and who ruled over it in collaboration with Zosia Dembińska, the widow of our Wilno Henryk.

So, Pruszyński showed up in Cracow in 1945, with Słonimski and Margaret Storm Jameson. The next time we met was in America. Our relations were

---

* After the last partition of Poland in 1795, the hopes of the Poles turned to Napoleon and Polish forces took part in his Italian Campaign.

cordial, but would not deserve to be called friendship. At times we carried on perfectly frank conversations, which were limited, however, to politics. One dimension that interested me was of no concern to Ksawery; the spark that flies between the words of people who know the same books and are tormented by the same philosophical or religious problems could never have caught fire between us. I could envy Pruszyński, because in a sense he was a king of life, but I made sure to conceal the sphere that was inaccessible to him, since, unfortunately, I already had the college of complications behind me.

But wasn't Pruszyński my colleague as a man of letters? His stories were nicely written, moving, and very sentimental. Were it not for their patriotic teardrops, he might have been more than an excellent journalist. Jane, however, didn't take any of his writing seriously. She appears in these jottings because I still think of her, many years after her death, as a person who combined extraordinary kindness with a vast intelligence, which is rare. Also, one could have meaningful conversations with her, and her slightly cynical sense of humor and openness added spice to those conversations. Jane and Pruszyński were lovers for a while and later she spoke of him warmly, although laughing a lot. It seems she was amused (as many women are) by the contrast between her partner's masculine vigor and what he had in his head, which, in her opinion, deserved indulgent tolerance. It's not that she considered him a stupid person, for he was a good deal wiser than the intransigent men who attacked him. Rather, if I may offer my own interpretation, she was amused by his particular case of Polish fantasizing or panache. Of course, it may well be that her laughter masked real engagement. In any event, for many years she tried to gather evidence that might reveal clues to the circumstances in which he died.

NOVEMBER 26, 1987

Jane was from Philadelphia, from the lower classes, the Polish immigrant laborer community. Her father was a priest of the Polish National Church, but the title meant nothing; it was still a ghetto. From her home she acquired a knowledge of the Polish language, but her mind was thoroughly American. She performed exceptionally well in school and at college, fulfilling the requirements for a master's degree in English at Columbia University so satisfactorily that the first job she landed was at Smith College in Northampton, a first-rate institution. Her relationship with Ksawery dates from the period (before and after) when he was traveling between New York and Rome, trying to arrange an agreement between the Polish People's Republic and the Vatican. There was such an attempt; I don't remember in which year, but it could be checked.

As far as I can remember, Ksawery hoped that Jane would translate his stories, and her resistance stemmed from her unfavorable evaluation of their contents, for, after all, they are based on the author's patriotic understanding with his reader; that is, taken out of that context, read by a non-Pole, they cease to be comprehensible.

Jane received a Fulbright Fellowship and left for Paris in 1948 or early 1949. And as soon as she arrived, she fell seriously ill. Sleeping sickness, transmitted by a tse-tse fly or mosquito, can take one of two forms: the patient either sleeps all the time or suffers from chronic insomnia, and Jane had the latter form. Most likely, she had brought it from the States, where some cases of it had been reported. This disease is usually fatal, or else it causes such great changes in the brain that one comes out of it with reduced mental functioning. In the summer of 1949, on the way to Poland, I stopped over in Paris and visited Jane in the Cité Universitaire, where she was convalescing. She had been saved and cared for by a young French doctor who gradually became emotionally involved and wanted to marry her. As it turned out, his pragmatic mother absolutely vetoed his marrying a foreigner, and a sick one to boot. The loving son left on a scientific expedition to Greenland.

I could speak frankly with Jane about everything, about politics and literature, and I had a great need of this in the trap I was then caught in. At the very least, she was a reliable person who would not go running to report on me to the Poles or to the Americans; furthermore, she could read me in Polish. Her brand of humor suited me, and in general we understood each other, despite some slight interference from her Americanness. The inhabitants of my part of Europe have always idealized America, especially after the misfortunes that befell them after 1939. Was that the reason why, several days after the Red Army marched into Cracow in 1945, a detachment of Polish red soldiers paraded through the streets of that city, singing a song that seemed to me, at that time and in those circumstances, a malicious joke?

This is America
The famous USA

This is our beloved land,
Where heaven reigns on earth.

It was a dubious heaven, however, for someone who had been born in a big American city of slums, poverty, unemployment, and racial conflicts, especially if her childhood coincided with the Depression. Jane was marked by the social radicalism of the late thirties and early forties, which meant that naïve images of the benefactions of a free-market economy didn't have much appeal for her. She certainly listened attentively to testimonies about Communism; her perception, however, was somewhat neutral, which means that it was tied in with her knowledge of the two sides of the scales, both weighted down more or less, but definitely weighted down. For me, Jane was part of my American initiation, like Henry Miller's books and Louis Adamic's reportage on the immigrant underclass. In other words, I profited from our conversations, maintaining a small measure of distrust in response to those traits of hers that were typical of American liberals, to whom it is exceedingly difficult to explain the demonic nature of certain regimes. Jane voted for the left wing of the Democratic Party. I don't know if she voted for Henry Wallace (the man who went to Kolyma and observed that the prisoners' living conditions there were first-rate), but I do recall that later on she was active in support of Adlai Stevenson's candidacy.

Jane was still in Paris when I found myself living there in 1951 as a fugitive from the Eastern Imperium, and her presence was important for me because it looked as if, despite all my reservations about her American "blind spots," she was mentally closer to me than the Polish émigrés, even the most sympathetic and well-meaning among them. Her convalescence was progressing slowly and she lived in constant fear that she would not regain her mental acuity. I was writing *The Captive Mind* at the time and I suggested to her that she translate the book into English. She agreed and thus her great adventure began; literally, her struggle to return to life. She saw the translation as a test: if she succeeded, it would mean that she had conquered the disease and could live and work normally. By the end of 1951, my text was almost ready; she began translating it at once and continued working on the translation after she returned to New York in early 1952, I think. Our collaboration went well; she didn't give me the slightest reason to doubt her perceptive understanding of the text, and I valued her critical comments. Nonetheless, she didn't have an easy life with me, so to speak. Friendship is one thing, but when it came to accuracy, I was implacable. I tormented her, and this was good for both of us. The translation is excellent; it reads as if the book had been written in English. Thus, the test that Jane set herself turned out as successfully as possible. It cost her a great deal of effort, however, and despite the many offers that she received after *The Captive Mind* appeared in 1953, she did not become a professional translator. I believe that her only other book was a translation of essays by Leszek Kołakowski which appeared in New York in 1968 under the title *Toward a Marxist Humanism* and included the famous essay "The Priest and the Jester."

Fate brought Jane to Geneva, where she lived for many years; she even became a Swiss citizen. She visited us in Berkeley during her business trips (she worked for the Swiss Tourism Bureau). In 1980 she came to Stockholm at my invitation and considered it the happiest day of her life. She died a couple of years later in Geneva.

Pruszyński was a valuable façade for the Warsaw government, but the period of façades didn't last very long, and he rapidly descended from his post in Washington or at the United Nations in New York to the position of ambassador in The Hague, which meant he had been sidetracked. In Poland, Stalinization was progressing rapidly; it had begun immediately after 1948, after the international Peace Congress in Wrocław, which was thought up and organized by Jerzy Borejsza, who thereby handed the Eastern bloc a valuable weapon. Who didn't attend that Congress! Western intellectuals and writers vied with each other in their enthusiasm. I elicited a message from Einstein, but since his message called for the creation of a world government to control atomic weapons, the Russians requested that it not be read. Either that event or something else (it's still a secret today) caused Borejsza's fall. That character deserves a thorough monograph, but real biographies of Communists will never be written.

$\mathcal{N}$OVEMBER 27, 1987

In The Hague, Pruszyński was thoroughly guarded; he couldn't sneeze without its being reported, since everything was supposed to have a political meaning. 1950 was an ominous year, its atmosphere determined by accusations of deviationism, trials, hangings of innocent people, and deaths in unexplained circumstances. This could not be felt yet in the posts in America, but I had been in the embassy in Paris that autumn and declared that it was a death trap. In those conditions, every month abroad was a godsend. Pruszyński, however, set out for Warsaw in the summer, apparently chiefly on account of Julia, whom he intended to marry; he had already divorced his first wife. I don't remember who told me that he had purchased a traditional golden sash, praising its usefulness, since one side was for a wedding and the other for mourning.

He was driving across Germany, alone, at night. Somewhere in the vicinity of Hanover he collided head-on with a truck and died instantly. Nothing happened to the driver of the truck. In another, politically less terrifying period, it might have been considered an ordinary accident, but at that time millions of unfortunates were being sent to forced labor in the gulags on the same continent and a pestilential wind was blowing from the East across all of Europe. Officially, Ksawery perished in an auto accident; however, various versions circulated both abroad and among officials in Warsaw. I shall set down what I heard.

First of all from Cecilia, a beautiful Englishwoman with a professional career, the only person whom he, under observation in The Hague, could confide in. Cecilia deliberately initiated this conversation with me in Paris; it was important to her that I should know. According to her, Ksawery left for Warsaw fully aware of the danger he was exposing himself to; it was an act of courage or defiance. Just as he had at the front, he believed in his lucky star. He had been warned. By whom? By none other than Jerzy Borejsza. "They want to put you on trial for Spain, for being there on behalf of the Polish Second Section," Borejsza supposedly said, and I doubt that Cecilia could have made that up. (The Second Section included the prewar Polish government's security and espionage organs, later transferred to London.) I believe that is exactly what was said, and that Borejsza advised him not to come back. Those who are aware that Spain kept coming up in the trials of Rajk, Slansky, etc., will admit that the idea of yet another accusation is quite probable. On the other hand, Borejsza's behavior is puzzling. It may be that, isolated by the Party and ill (he'd been in a mysterious car accident), he had undergone a serious philosophical crisis and had begun to live by ordinary human standards. Yet another hypothesis is also possible. Borejsza could have been acting in the interests of the Party or of those Polish Communists who wanted to avoid the kind of show trials that were taking place in Czechoslovakia and Hungary and were trying to oppose another Party group or the security organs which were at work building up false accusations. Pruszyński would have to be depicted as a deceitful class enemy who had worked for the London Second Section all this time, even in his ambassadorial and consular posts.

This leads to the conclusion that it was a matter of importance to someone that Pruszyński decide not to make the trip or not reach his destination. It may well be that we will never know what threads were entangled here, what forces were at work. We should note that it is easy to construct a logical system of clues, whereas reality is rarely logical. The fact that he was warned does not necessarily lead to the conclusion that something bad had to have happened to him.

Jane held some conversations in New York, in the late fifties, I believe, after the famous affair of the high-placed secret policeman, Światło. I don't remember whom she was quoting, because of course she didn't get access to Światło himself, who was carefully hidden away somewhere by the Americans. According to her, Światło was supposed to have testified: "That affair was entrusted to the German comrades"; in other words, the appropriate East German organs did what had to be done.

November 29, 1987

On board a plane to New York: after hours of confusion at Oakland Airport, the plane did not take off; a transfer to San Francisco Airport and a different airline. Overwhelming exhaustion, my asthma won't let up, and the stupidity of this trip, but I can't disappoint the Poetry Center on 92nd Street. Instead of arriving at eight in the evening, I land around one in the morning. My reading is the next day.

One more person emerges onto the stage. Comrade Stanisław Skrzeszewski. He was Minister of Foreign Affairs at the time, having succeeded Zygmunt Modzelewski, who had a heart condition. What I expected happened; Paris turned out to be a trap. In December 1950 I turned up in Warsaw for a brief holiday visit. Trusting in my lucky star, like Pruszyński. Countries can be divided into those which it is difficult to enter and those which it is difficult to leave. Considering the atmosphere of fear in Warsaw, my arrival was explained in hushed conversations either by my madness or by exceptionally powerful shoulders in the Polish security organs; in either case, the best thing was to avoid me. In the Ministry I learned that I wasn't going to be let out. I asked for an appointment with Skrzeszewski. He confirmed that they had decided to detain me for my own good, so that what happened to Pruszyński shouldn't happen to me.

"What happened?" I asked. "After all, it was an accident."

"No, according to our information, he was eliminated by the London Second Section."

"But I was in Poland during the war, not abroad, and I had no ties with London."

He considered this for a moment. "Yes, that's true. Nonetheless, we have decided to detain you."

Was he lying and had he made up this little intrigue with the Second Section to stall, or did the highest Party functionaries really believe this? How could this be reconciled with "entrusting it to the German comrades"? Had they decided that in the event of a successful attack the London Second Section would serve as camouflage? None of these questions can be answered.

In the opinion of Jan Meysztowicz (Pruszyński's ex-wife's brother and my schoolmate from Wilno), it was simply an accident, and that is what the family continued to believe.

In The Hague, Pruszyński was a new and not very skillful driver. He was driving at night, he was tired. It is very likely that it was an accident. It can also be conjectured that capricious reality played a joke on the plotters. That it preempted what would have happened anyway; for example, on the road in East Germany. And could it be that this accident, which was not caused by the German comrades, so astonished the indirect and direct plotters that they came up with the explanation of a rival act, the work of the Second Section?

This story about Pruszyński conveys to a certain extent the anxieties and practices of that time. No fastidiousness as to methods. Often, diplomats suspected of intending to defect were given an appropriate injection and loaded onto a plane.

DECEMBER 1, 1987

The preservation of states is a thing that probably surpasses our understanding. As Plato says, a civil government is a powerful thing and hard to dissolve. It often holds out against mortal internal disease, against the mischief of unjust laws, against tyranny, against the excesses and ignorance of the magistrates and the license and sedition of the people . . . Our government is in bad health; yet some have been sicker without dying. The gods play pelota with us and drive us about in every way . . .

—Montaigne, *Essays*

I copied this out of a Polish translation of the *Essays* on the plane from New York to San Francisco. Even though I was exhausted, I managed to have conversations with Matson, Richard and Jody, Brodsky and Inez (they all came over to the Algonquin Hotel), to meet with the marketing staff at the Ecco Press, and then to give my poetry reading at the Poetry Center. I read well, too. A book signing, a reception, then dinner in an Italian restaurant with Dan and Renata.

DECEMBER 2, 1987

In New York, discussion of an excerpt from *Conversations with Milosz*, reprinted in *The New York Times Book Review*, about Professor Blejwas's letter to the editor and my rejoinder. I still believe that what I said is true. After all, from my experience as a professor I know how much could have been accomplished in America, and I also know that even those Polish-Americans who have money contribute nothing in support of culture. The millions of Americans of Polish descent could have been an enormous political force; they could have changed Slavic studies at the universities so that they would cease to be what they are now: Russian studies.

I think I have already written about this somewhere. Ernest Simmons, a professor of Russian studies, approached me as cultural attaché in 1948, if I'm not mistaken, with the suggestion that Poland should endow a chair in Polish literature. Since he put forward the name of Manfred Kridl, curator of our Literature Students Circle (Creative Writing Section) in Wilno, he found an ally in me. Zygmunt Modzelewski, an old Communist who was Minister for Foreign Affairs at the time, understood the propaganda value of the chair and came up with the necessary sum (high for the time) of ten thousand dollars annually. It was not very nice to have a wealthy American university go begging from a Communist government. But there was no chair of Polish literature in America before that, and I am the one who created it. Then all hell broke loose: for a couple of years afterward, all the Polish-American papers raised a hue and cry about Communist infiltration (Kridl a Bolshevik!), although the thought that they themselves could have endowed the chair never once crossed their minds. Several years later, when the subsidy from Warsaw ran out, the chair ceased to exist. Of all my books, *The History of Polish Literature* probably has the lowest print run.

Why are they like that? I explain it now in New York: yes, Poland is a country of unheard-of caste differences, from heights such as are rarely met with elsewhere, to depressing lower depths, and perhaps the most powerful strata are the two extremes. The lowest, those who emigrated in search of bread, undoubtedly had no one to emulate, because the higher castes were too high for them. Naturally, the lowest over there, in the old country, were only coolies over here; they bore the mark of unskilled laborers, and one can understand their sensitivity to the middle-class contempt expressed in Polish jokes. Those were definitely class-based jokes, but also so ethnically poisonous that I could feel the poison when, for example, I picked up a pencil labeled "Polish pencil"—a pencil that one couldn't write with because it had erasers on both ends instead of on only one.

$\mathcal{D}$ECEMBER 5, 1987

On the significance of one's self: The history of each human life can be boiled down to a back-and-forth game between one's image of oneself and one's image in the eyes of others. Between pride and humiliation, with many intermediate stages. Every minute that we spend among people, in a store, in an office, at the post office, in a bus, offers us cause for melancholy observations about that fragility and sensitivity to gestures, words, that have the power either to bolster us or to drag us down. So pitiful in our petty pride, we require a little circle or clan in which we can be recognized, in which it can be reaffirmed that we are worth something.

Once upon a time, the tiny Żagary group was enough for me; things were more difficult in Warsaw, where, ultimately, I was reputed to be one of many talented young poets. In contrast to the *Wiadomości Literackie* [The Literary News] crowd, I did not relish the sweetness of displaying one's peacock tail in the Café Ziemiańska or of exchanging greetings on Mazowiecka Street, even though Mortkowicz's bookstore, located on that street, was apparently the only place in Warsaw where copies of my *Three Winters* could be found. (Under the marketing system employed by publishers at that time, it was the designated distributor of the book.) Today, my recalcitrance, my bristling whenever someone wanted to stroke me, and various other idiosyncrasies strike me as quite odd, although it is strange to think that the fame of that café and that street have vanished, while the shy, arrogant man survived.

Some people need to be recognized by many; others, extremely egotistical, are satisfied by their own and a few other voices. During the war, my friend Jerzy Andrzejewski was still basking in the glory of the Young Writers Award he had received in 1938 for his (weak) novel, *The Harmony of the Heart*, and enjoying the homage that accompanied it on pre-war Mazowiecka Street. There was a period during the war when we used to frequent a bar called "Under the Rooster," in the company of a certain Kudelski, a wealthy black marketeer, one of those characters who just turn up and later no one knows anything about them. Kudelski loved to torment Jerzy, addressing him as

"Mr. Adamczewski," because Jerzy used to introduce himself ceremonially, holding out his hand and declaring, "I am Andrzejewski," testimony to his regard for his own famous name. Corrected, Kudelski would beg his pardon, and a moment later say, "Mr. Adamczewski." I must confess that I was never accorded such disrespect; there was no reason why I should have been.

The bar "Under the Rooster" (I'm not certain that was its name) deserves to be mentioned here. The waiters were all actors. I had seen Milecki as El Cid in the Reduta Theater in Wilno. Kempa died during the Warsaw Uprising, in the explosion of a German remote-control tank in the Old City. Maria Leszczyńska ran the coffee bar; she was the companion of two poets, first of the consumptive Jerzy Liebert in the last stage of his life, and then of Stefan Flukowski, who was interned in a P.O.W. camp during the war. Her house on Narbutt Street, or a street that ran parallel to Narbutt, was a veritable Jewish orphanage under the aegis of her Catholic exaltation; one could truly say of that house, "The Holy Virgin hovers over their table." Whenever I came to visit, there were several Jewish tots seated around that table.

December 6, 1987

Yesterday in Zellerbach Hall to see the Japanese ballet, Kinkan Shonen. The program describes the theme ("A boy's dream about the beginning of life and about death"), but I doubt that anyone in the large audience that gave the company a standing ovation understood the metaphor. For me, it was almost a model of Pure Form—that is, of pure dance movement for its own sake. The music and the movement made such a deep impression on me that I had a dream at night, a visual-verbal dream. The hero was a Jewish sage in the style of Buber; the subject of his dance-sermon-recitation was a truth of the Old Testament.

During the night a storm, wild gusts of wind from the ocean, and rain beating against the windowpane above my head. But my asthma is almost gone.

The need to believe in the importance of one's own self is a good clue. That need was the decisive factor in my sticking with the Warsaw government after the war and in my first America. If I haven't figured this out until now, that's worth noting, although obvious things are the most difficult to analyze.

We should consider the fact that the 1939 emigration was the final extension of interwar Poland where virtually no one knew of my existence as a poet. The reading intelligentsia's taste did not venture beyond Skamander. Mazowiecka Street—Mieczysław Grydzewski, the editor of the London-based *Wiadomości* [The News], that is—still ruled over literature in London. In 1946 I visited Jan Lechoń in a New York hospital; I had known him in Paris and did not like him, but he deserved respect as one of the masters of my youth, and he was said to have cancer. This same Lechoń, however, treated me contemptuously in his writings. When the so-called Milosz affair exploded in 1951 and people began writing disgusting things about me (I regret that the "white book" of clippings I collected has disappeared), genuine irritation at an impostor shone through what was said: Who does he think he is? Who cares about his aesthetic problems? Time, however, condensed by the wringer of war, had changed many things over there, on the banks of the Vistula, including openness to certain thought forms. I existed over there, especially after the publication of my *Rescue* in 1945, and I also had created a function for myself in the ongoing struggle. This is the secret of that time: unknown to anyone in America, just a petty bureaucrat in one of the satellite embassies, I scribbled away, writing, translating poets, decked out in the cloak of my importance in that distant land. I can imagine someone commenting: "How petty such motives are! How he unmasks himself, confessing that he was a slave to his personal ambitions!" But fate was a factor here, and the understanding of certain rules of the game ought not to discredit someone unless he is a hypocrite.

$\mathcal{D}$ECEMBER 10, 1987

Leonard told me what happened when a Dutch poet gave a reading on campus. The area's Dutch people marched into the hall in closed formation to support one of their own. The poet was dismayed. "I don't want this type of audience!" he shouted. So, I am not the only one with such a problem.

A letter from Janek Ulatowski in response to my having sent him the new annotated edition of *Three Winters*. He writes:

That it's "under the influence of a daimonion" is obvious from the photograph—the photograph of a *man who is damned*—and what comes later confirms this. We seem to have a recording of your laughter, and it makes the flesh creep.

Kisiel's assessment is the most equitable, I think: ". . . But you'll disavow all this tomorrow!" It's plain to see that only in literature does Kisiel not make a fool of himself.

DECEMBER 12, 1987

Again, splendid weather. Hass and I are swamped with the proofs of my volume, *The Collected Poems*, 520 pages that have to be corrected immediately. I am also working on a foreword to a volume of Joseph Brodsky's writings in Polish translation.

During my last visit to New York I became acutely conscious of the gap between the social roles of a "name" and of a person as an individual human being (my snob value for agents of the booksellers' network or people standing in a long line for autographs at the Poetry Center). No. Correction: I have known this for a long time, raging at the mania people have (especially Poles) for being photographed with me as if I were a bear. But there are many degrees of grasping something, with distractions and memory lapses, that contribute to weakening understanding. This time I became aware that I have coped with applause almost instinctively as with something external to me. For instance, my entire stay in Poland in 1981. An unbelievable triumph, a moral allegory and a fable: the wise brothers lost and the foolish brother won. If writing was the center of my passions (and it was), if recognition is central for writing (and it is), my return to Poland in glory was the acme of my life. And yet it wasn't, because I was preoccupied with and protected by completely different problems, very private, very personal.

Now, in New York, fame appeared to me in a different light, in the light of the Manhattan literary-publishing circles; I started discerning a ritual, the tribute paid to success, in the warmth and goodwill of several famous members of those circles. Suspicious Lithuanian that I am, I was obliged to remind myself once again that in such circumstances sweet words are part of the ritual, and to repeat to myself, as I did in Poland, the words of Krasicki's fable:

That incense is for me, said the rat haughtily to his kin,
As he sat on the altar during Mass.
Suddenly, as he choked on the billows of smoke from the incense burners,
A cat leaped from the side, caught him, and strangled him.

DECEMBER 13, 1987

I have read Ksawery Pruszyński's marvelous contribution to the new edition
of the anthology *Land of Our Childhood*. How clearly he understood that
that older Poland whose roots were in the Kresy and in an enduring gentry
heritage had in 1941 already vanished forever. Was he right to break with
his comrades-in-arms and with the London emigration, voluntarily accepting
the brand of traitor? He was quick-witted and had an open mind on international matters; he didn't deceive himself as others did that a new war would
erupt at any moment. Another conservative, Stanisław Mackiewicz, did the
same thing later on. Thinking historically and soberly: the centuries-long
rivalry between Poland and Russia for control of Central Europe ended with
Poland's total defeat. It was necessary to draw conclusions from this and not
to abandon oneself to daydreams; that is, to the hope that the Imperium
would nobly spit out what it had swallowed. And yet he was mistaken, because
his decision assumed a choice between one or another world power. But
that's not what his choice boiled down to. Over there, one had to become
either a Communist or nothing, a marionette pretending that he is not being
moved by strings. Unfortunately, only faith in Communism could justify
the transformation of an independent country into a province controlled by
foreigners. Planetary thinking was opposed to independent thinking. The
Polish right, political descendants of Roman Dmowski, had once accepted
Polish subordination to tsarist Russia for geopolitical reasons; Pruszyński, an
opponent of Endecja, suddenly found himself thrust into the company of
ordinary collaborators.

What am I aiming at? At lifting a corner of the curtain, because Poland's
tragedy, which has few equals, remains concealed to this day. For the simple
reason that the division into homeland and emigration has forced people to
accept either one or another warped perspective. It was necessary to pass
over many things in silence "in order not to give the enemy ammunition."
To this day, some terrible truths are still not spoken aloud.

$\mathcal{D}$ ECEMBER 20, 1987

A sauna and a swim. At night, dreams with the familiar fauna of a wartime nightmare.

There is no room for Poland on this earth. The distant causes of this situation must be sought in the activities of Romantic friends of the people:

> *Disguised in sheepskin coats, walking from village to village,*
> *They blew their warm breath on folklore and similar primroses,*
> *Until at last they produced vast numbers of wondrous national signs.*
> *That was the hook—and they hang from that hook themselves.*
> *—"Toast"*

In essence, around 1820, Germany and Poland were hotbeds of political romanticism or, to use a term more rooted in earth, of nationalism. In order to raise folklore and "the soul of the people" to the second power and to maintain the idea of a nation, education is necessary (students, Philomaths), and also humiliation (which wasn't lacking in a Germany defeated by Napoleon or in partitioned Poland).

Throughout the nineteenth century, the French countryside south of the Loire still spoke the Oc language, but no one thought of appealing to an Occitan nation. It may be that the French Revolution, in introducing an entirely different idea of the nation than the one derived from Herder (see Alain Finkelkraut), successfully bolstered an all-French patriotism.

The Wilno Romantics, if we apply the criteria of a later nationalism to them, were still shaky on the national question. They loved the people, but the people spoke Lithuanian or Belorussian. The books of the students of Wilno University, written in Polish, nonetheless would crystallize two nationalisms—Polish and Lithuanian, and also, thanks to poetry, would contribute to the birth of Ukrainian and Belorussian nationalism.

In order for language to come to be considered the indicator of a person's membership in one group defined in opposition to other groups, a major revolution was necessary. Humanity had gotten along well enough without such important demarcations, and especially without the idea of a nation that aspires to its own state.

If after World War I the principle of self-determination of nations had been applied literally, Poland's eastern border would have followed the Curzon line. I shall forget for a moment about the real disposition of forces; one way or another, Poland, Lithuania, Belorussia, and Ukraine would be neighbors. Similarly, the principle of self-determination would have in any case dictated the present eastern border after World War II in the event that the Western Allies' absolute dominance had not led to the Yalta agreement. "Poland" would have denoted a narrow belt along the Vistula, too densely populated to stand a chance. No Western government would have come up with an idea like Stalin's of expelling millions of Germans from their centuries-old settlements and giving that land to Poles. Thus, one can say that Poland exists by the grace of Stalin.

During the interwar decades, there was a period when the American Communist Party had a peculiar cure for the "Negro question." It proposed that the Southern states, with their majority black population, should be recognized as Negro states, and that blacks from the other states should be resettled there. The plan was rejected as "un-American"; also, it was too reminiscent of the Indian reservations, of the Trail of Tears when tribes from Georgia and North Carolina, decimated by hunger, cold, and sickness, made their long trek to the territories set aside for them in Oklahoma.

But the plan must have pleased Stalin, who liked simple solutions, smooth and definitive. After all, he transported the entire Volga German Republic to Siberia. We have to admit that the crime of expulsion is contained *implicite* in the division of territories according to the language or race of their inhabitants. Thus, the Poles, expelled by Hitler from the territories incorporated into the Reich during the Second World War, forced by him to move to designated streets in their own cities, were coerced after the war (by fear of deportation) into an exodus from cities where they constituted the majority (such as Wilno and Lwów) and from numerous regions with mixed populations, and to accept complicity with Stalin's work in the "Western Territories."

In 1945 the Polish Communists were right: Poland could exist in the shape given it and guaranteed by the Soviet Union, or it could cease to exist. When Jakub Berman screams at Teresa Torańska in her book *"Them"* that, were it not for the Communists, Poland would have become a pancake, he's distorting the truth to a certain extent, because before 1939 the defense of Poland's territory was not one of their aims; one has to admit, however, that he was right in the sense that no government formed on the basis of free elections would have been given the Western Territories as a gift from Big Brother.

DECEMBER 21, 1987

Homeland, fatherland, the nation: *les choses vagues*, hazy things, as Paul Valéry called them, eluding definition, too loaded with emotional meaning. It's best, then, not to insist on anything in this area. Especially since it is not very good when a person's chief identifying characteristic is his membership in a given nation. Valéry did not have to be concerned with France or even to ponder what it means to be French; Frenchness was the air he breathed. But a Pole is first and foremost a Pole; a Lithuanian is a Lithuanian, a Ukrainian a Ukrainian. And it is curious that when he wants to serve his nation with his mind, his pen, his art, his achievements are flawed in direct proportion to his national fervor.

Ksawery Pruszyński, or, going home. He was not the only one facing an exceptionally difficult choice at that time. Speaking bluntly, it was difficult because to go home was natural, since that's where your nation was; to remain abroad meant that you were washing your hands of the nation as a whole and of your national feelings and devoting yourself to your profession, family, friends. You became a citizen of the world.

"How's that?!" people object. "What about the émigré's mission that has been tested for generations, the Paris streets that Mickiewicz, Słowacki, Norwid walked on!"

But in 1945 there were no facts that would justify emigration as a political act, unless one did not wish to understand the situation soberly. Today, events that took place later are being factored in retroactively; and silently accepting the additional assumption that the nation's struggle for independence has always been unchanging, people accept the idea that holding on to lost positions made sense.

Let us imagine that Pruszyński was a biologist, a painter, a physicist. He could have remained abroad without getting entangled in contradictions. But he was a politician, and there was nothing for him to do in the West. In addition, he was a journalist, and where writing enters into the game, everything takes on a different appearance.

DECEMBER 23, 1987

I don't see many similarities between myself and Pruszyński; I am not using
him to make my own reckoning easier. His case is clinically pure, since he
cannot be suspected of any leftist leanings. Nor of voluntary or involuntary
blindness. He knew everything about Russia; he had observed it in Kuibyshev
and had rescued people from the gulags. His knowledge encompassed the
mass deportations after the Hitler–Stalin pact, Katyń, the betrayal of the
Warsaw Uprising. Still, he went over to the side of Warsaw. For geopolitical
reasons.

DECEMBER 25, 1987

They were blind because it was easier that way, and then they saw the light:
this schematic explanation lingers on, as if it were all right to talk about us
the way people talk about the French or the English. In Warsaw during the
occupation I had perfectly good information about the gulag archipelago; I
didn't have to wait for Solzhenitsyn to enlighten me several decades later.
My past included my escape from Soviet Wilno—something not many people took a chance on, because the price of being caught at the border was
fairly well known (eight years). In addition, my knowledge of Russian allowed
me to do some serious reading in the Russian émigré newspaper published
in Berlin, which, despite the censorship, was much richer in news than the
rest of the officially permitted press. The French collaborationist *La Gerbe*
also reached Warsaw, but it was pitifully fatuous. The Russian paper offered
many eyewitness accounts, letters, documents, whose authenticity could not
be doubted; they came from the vast reaches of the Soviet Union. Anyway,
the editors' intentions clearly did not coincide with the aims of German
propaganda; they were attempting to steer a middle course. Kroński, who
did not know Russian, used to give me a hard time about this unhealthy
reading.

Recently I read and was pained by a slim volume of recollections and
opinion essays about the Paris journal *Kultura*. Must I always be punished
for my spiteful stupidity? At the beginning of my stay in Maisons-Laffitte
they assumed they had to educate me, so I would open my eyes wide,

pretending to be a child, "How can that be? Do they have forced-labor camps there?" And poor Zofia Romanowicz, in her recollection of 1951, took me literally.

All this happened a long time ago, and now it's the end of the century and the time to balance the accounts of our century is approaching. Screens, fogs, veils obscure the view and it is difficult to determine where things are, what is more important, what is less important. Anyone who has dabbled a little in the history of literature knows how elusive are divisions into schools and trends, and how mistaken the bestowing of laurels can seem after the passage of a decade or two. Perhaps the ultimate criterion will be the dose of reality present in a given work, demanding allegiance to the truth. Then those books that dispel the fog behind which the monster of Leninism–Stalinism used to hide will enjoy a great rehabilitation. I have observed over many decades how reluctantly they have been received and how quickly forgotten.

In Wilno in the early thirties, one Olekhnovich, a Belorussian former prisoner in the Solovki Island prison camp, received from his Polish readers the same reception that Poles who were released from the camps later received from the English public: sympathy, but disbelief, because the witness must have done something wrong; after all, no one is punished unless he's guilty. In those same 1930s, Panait Istrati and André Gide, with his *Return from the U.S.S.R.*, presented an opportunity for an organized campaign against the disillusioned, the "traitors." Victor Serge, Arthur Koestler, Ignazio Silone, and George Orwell were placed on this list immediately; Albert Camus was soon added. The progressive intellectuals conducted a whispering campaign—actually, not so much a whispering as a gesticulating campaign—which was much more effective than defamation in the press. They dealt with those inconvenient writers as they did with the servants of the bourgeoisie: without resorting to words, with an unspoken, mutually agreed-upon system of grimaces, snorts, dismissive gestures.

I could give the titles of books that either were not published or were effectively killed by silence. Also of books that were published in one language but could not find translators or publishers in any other language. For example, Józef Czapski's *On the Inhuman Earth* and *Starobielsk Notes* (which are not available in English translation), and Gustaw Herling-Grudziński's *A World Apart*.

I wrote *The Captive Mind* in what may have been the worst year, 1951, when the Stalin cult in France was at its height, shortly after a totally implausible (from today's perspective) and widely publicized trial. The

Communist *L'Humanité* had accused David Rousset, a former German concentration-camp prisoner, of referring to the existence of concentration camps in Russia in his book *L'Univers concentrationnaire*. At the same time, Jean-Paul Sartre and Francis Janson were preparing to hurl mud at Albert Camus in *Les Temps Modernes* because of *The Rebel*, in which he makes the same arguments. (I read that book after I finished writing *The Captive Mind*.) Thus, the only suitable word for all that is probably "psychosis." But also "power," fortunately without "police." Sartre's and Janson's articles were simply denunciations, a cry for Camus's punishment. When I was looking for a translator, a young man was recommended to me, a beginning writer of Polish–Jewish descent; he assured me that he would very much like to do the translation but could not, because no one would publish him afterward. André Prudhommeaux, an anarchist who fought in Spain, undertook the job for me. He worked as a copy editor at *Preuves* in Paris. But Prudhommeaux did not know Polish, so I dictated *The Captive Mind* to him in its entirety, sentence by sentence; all he did was correct the style.

DECEMBER 29, 1987

Writing *The Captive Mind* cost me too much for me to boast about it. That is, it required a series of preconditions: first, my departure from America, because Joe McCarthy was in the process of directing his witch-hunt for Communists, casting a pall of terror over intellectual circles. Obviously, no self-respecting person would join an anti-Communist campaign that was interpreted as the beginnings of Fascism in America. The intellectual level of the hunters justified such an assumption. I read somewhere a stenographic report of Bertolt Brecht's testimony before the House Un-American Activities Committee. He played with them like a cat with a mouse. Shortly afterward, he left for East Berlin. The unfortunate Whittaker Chambers can stand as an example of what awaited those hotheads who violated the code of this circle. The longtime editor of *The Daily Worker* broke with Communism because of a real inner crisis and stepped forward as a key witness for the prosecution in the espionage trial of Alger Hiss. From that day until his death, he was excluded from the circle of people worthy of having their hands shaken, he lost all his friends, and his posthumously published letters testify to the depths of his despair. He was firmly convinced that no one understood the essence of Communism and the danger it poses to humanity, and that he, by deciding after a lengthy inner struggle to make a public statement, had lost. Obviously, he had once been fascinated by the Historical Necessity of the triumph of the Soviet Union. The circles that condemned Chambers consisted by no means exclusively of Marxists and their sympathizers of various stripes; they also included broad circles of liberal opinion united in their enmity toward anti-Communism. "What would have happened if . . ." is always a risky business, but I think that had I stayed in America I could not have written *The Captive Mind* without exposing myself to ostracism by the only circles I could rely on in this country. It was even worse in France, but I had anticipated my foreignness ahead of time, as it were; I would be a leper, I assumed, forever.

In 1954 or 1955, in the lobby of a Paris theater where a Polish play was being performed, I bumped into Jarosław Iwaszkiewicz, who turned and snapped, "I cannot greet you, darling." I was told that Iwaszkiewicz had discussed *The Captive Mind* with Sartre at some meeting in Berlin. Sartre: "It's not enough to be smart, you also have to have *sagesse.*" *Sagesse* implies both wisdom and caution. Naturally, I was not cautious. That book trailed after me for a long time. It elicited denunciations by Poles to the American Embassy in Paris (for being crypto-Communist), which meant it wrecked my chances for a visa to America for nine years; it earned me the "mark of a traitor" among progressives; and also, something I didn't at all like, it meant I was considered a prose writer, a scholar in the field of *political science. Nota bene*: It did not help me obtain a position as professor of literature; on the contrary.

A second, inescapable condition was my pitiable frame of mind. I think a lot about ideology now, about the almost limitless capacity of people to get themselves pulled into a downward spiral from which there is no escape. The "Hegelian bite" can simply be explained by a traumatic experience of weakness—one's own weakness or that of one's country—in relation to a force that is advancing like an iron roller. "Europe is ours." After all, in the years 1945–50 no one believed in a self-sufficient capitalist Europe. I wrote to extricate myself from that downward spiral. Although only another act of self-therapy, my novel *The Issa Valley*, rescued me from abstractions and gave me back to poetry.

DECEMBER 30, 1987

All people are physically constituted the same way, and thus they can understand each other in their elemental feelings. The uniqueness of the way good and evil are blended in each individual is therefore all the more astonishing. Exploring my psychology will yield nothing; in any event, I am unable to do it. Especially since there is, of course, a link between *The Captive Mind* and my poem "To Myself in an Album for the Year 1950."

January 1, 1988

Sixty years ago, in Mrs. Klecka's boarding house. I can't remember all the people who were there. Ostrowski, a balding fraternity man and law student, a young bull and a triumphant bachelor; what happened to him is not known. Irena Osiecimska, beautiful, a student of Polish literature, but one of those who study only long enough to find a husband; our unexpected meeting on the street in Sopot when I returned to Poland from America for a vacation in 1949. "We are slaves here!" she shrieked. I said nothing in reply, but she could at least have been comforted by my knowing what she was talking about, because I came home sick from that vacation. Marysia, I've forgotten her surname, was still a high-school student, I think, in the last class of Gymnasium, just like me at that time; I will never know what drove her to New York, because a postcard I sent her in the sixties was an unfortunate mistake. It showed a small burro, a California ass. I was appalled by her response: She didn't want to know me, because I had insulted her husband. I had a hard time ferreting out what the problem was. Her husband, X, was known in Wilno as a bonehead, so the burro that I had selected in all innocence and quite by chance was supposed to have been an allusion to those Wilno matters.

One of the rooms in Mrs. Klecka's boarding house was a mystery to me and I saw its interior only once, when the door to the entrance hall was left ajar. An actress, Kossecka (?), rented it. The smell of perfume and powder, a woman's presence, a robe on the armchair, softness, the secret of the other sex. I believe I saw her, too, only once, in passing. She didn't interact with our boardinghouse at all; sometimes we could hear voices there, which means she had her own circle, inaccessible to me, well beyond my reach. I was probably somewhat in love with her, deep in my imagination, without even having a very good idea of what she looked like, but I would not have dared to approach her.

Mrs. Klecka's boardinghouse has come back to me because of that actress, as a matter of fact; she has been visiting me recently and I am trying to put together some data about her completely unknown life. I also suspect that it's New Year's of 1929, not 1928, that I'm thinking of, the 1928–29 school year. That year on a side street (what was it called? Stroma?), almost at the corner of Mickiewicz Street, was a happy year, better than the years before and after. My fights with my teachers were over, my grades were up again, I had experienced the delights of friendship in the P.E.T. club, and in that period before my graduation exam the future—indefinite, lacking any clear shape—enchanted me. I read a lot (including William James's *The Varieties of Religious Experience*) and also did poetry-writing exercises systematically, borrowing a model and my inspiration from Joachim du Bellay's sonnet ("Happy is the man who like Ulysses . . ."), which I had found in a French textbook. Did I want to become a poet? I knew I had been called, but probably to be something greater than "a poet." Did I want to "express my feelings"? No; those were exercises in style, very cold and objective. I remember one or two lines about the autumn threshing in the countryside.

Now, on the first day of the year, I think again about how all one has to do is cast a net blindly and one will pull in faces and names. And also, running ahead, that it is worth it to continue this memoir even though it is unclear how many pages will accumulate. Imagine transferring this into the last century: someone was already writing in 1828 and that same person was still writing in 1888. Incredible, unbelievable!

$\mathcal{J}$ANUARY 3, 1988

This January is exceptionally cold and rainy for California. My asthma acts up from time to time; there's music in my chest. My bad thoughts find no medicine in the things I see.

And what if I should start to say everything? Naturally, I'm afraid. I am afraid of people; why offer myself to them with all my weakness, sin, and bad conscience? What would be the use of that? One more contribution to the so-called psychology of creativity? But I am also afraid of my writing. Because my opinions about myself and my life are merciless, and perhaps that is all very well and good, but one opinion infects another; when I write they combine into a whole on the basis of form, bypassing other opinions that are not as dreadful. We are doomed always to partial self-revelation, at best with the good intention of avoiding falsehood. And it seems we always reveal ourselves more in code than directly. Last year in Paris, Stomma told me about my brilliance as a lecturer in our high school. I listened with disbelief, but that's probably how it was; in other words, one should constantly correct one's unflattering opinions about oneself.

I mentioned the name of Jarosław Iwaszkiewicz and the thought immediately entered my mind that there will be fewer and fewer people who knew him, that I am therefore obliged to talk about him. During his life, few people dared to attempt his portrait. There were various reasons why; at the very least, because for many years he was president of the Writers' Union.

I shall start with a time when I did not know him, when I was still a child. In Wilno in the spring of 1920 I caught a hint of the aura that surrounded him—a twenty-six-year-old man at the time. His poem "Valse triste," which was written somewhat later, was an attempt at conveying that aura:

> Ah, those dances, those dances, oh wartime!
> Guns in sunshine and strewn with spring flowers.
> A platoon that was ever so merry.
> Why is it now in mourning?
>
> Ah, wartime, ah, wartime, what Joy!
> Even posthumous joy is triumphant!
> Joy that was ever so merry.
> But why is death now in mourning?

In Henryk Wereszycki's reminiscences, published in the May–June 1984 issue of *Znak* [The Sign], I came across the following:

Merriment was characteristic of the Polish officer; as a matter of fact, of the entire Polish Army. Everything was done merrily, even with bravura. I had a friend—my age, naturally. We were twenty-one, twenty-two; we thought of the twenty-three- and twenty-four-year-olds as those old guys. Suddenly, for no reason at all, my friend would climb out of the trench to demonstrate that bullets couldn't hurt him. Utter nonsense, but that's how it was. Everything merrily. Before I became an officer, we were fighting the Ukrainians in Eastern Galicia. Whenever we entered a city or a small town, we would sing, and how we sang surpasses imagination. Girls would be standing on the balconies, we men were all merry, there was great, great joy. It was sensational. In 1916, when I was in Vienna as a Legionnaire, one of my mother's trusted friends looked after me (in other words, he gave me money and so forth). When we were leaving for the front, he came to the railroad station. Later, I saw the letter he wrote to my mother. "These Legionnaires," he wrote, "are unbelievable. How merry they were, how they sang as they boarded the train." After all, it was 1916, Austria was exhausted by the war, but these lads did everything merrily. This is very characteristic. It was the same in 1920.

How can we explain such joy? Could it be that people had an intuition that the war would end happily for them?
Wereszycki:

When the retreat began, I was convinced that in accordance with historical tradition we would stop only in Paris, that we were going into emigration once again because this war was, just as in 1831, a failed uprising. But this time the uprising succeeded.

JANUARY 5, 1988

I have to force myself, however, to sit down at my desk. Apparently the exhaustion that I experienced with my asthma, from lack of oxygen, has returned.

Wereszycki: A failed uprising as historical tradition! Hm.

No one now will be able to reconstruct that spring of 1920 in Wilno, although it's debatable whether it should be reconstructed. Because if it really should be, then it ought to be reconstructed as it appeared to various pairs of eyes, not just mine. Where do those images go, those perceptions? Do they perish along with specific individuals, or are they preserved somewhere in some realm that stores everything that has ever been experienced? For me, Wilno at that time was the colors of a uniform, the uniform of my father, a captain in the Engineering Corps, or perhaps already a major, and of his regimental colleagues. We were living on Embankment Street, right on the corner across from St. Jakub's, but the regiment was quartered on an estate where vegetables were grown (I remember the huge vegetable gardens), also on the Wilia River, but upstream, just beyond Antokol. Pines and sand. This happened after my revelation of the green in Szetejnie, after our return from Russia in 1918. "The Wilia, mother of our streams, / Has a golden bottom and azure cheeks." In other words, this landscape was new for me, because in Szetejnie the Niewiaża did not flow over a sandy bottom. Although I remembered our stopping at what I believe was the Rukła estate on the Wilia during our flight from Szetejnie before the advancing Germans in 1914, somewhere in the vicinity of Vievis (a Lithuanian name), and there was sand and pines there, too. That's the place where the Cossacks, whom I mention in *Native Realm*, were stationed.

"Guns in sunshine and strewn with spring flowers." Yes, merriment was all around me. Wilno was happy and rang its bells a year before, in 1919, when the Polish uhlans drove out the Bolsheviks. Polish Wilno rejoiced, although there were other Wilnos, too: Russian- and Yiddish-speaking. I was immersed in Polish Wilno, however, and that spring I went to school for the first time, stunned, not comprehending what was happening and what was wanted of me. I liked one girl and I remember her name: Bańkowska. But the fat letters on the front pages of the newspapers soon garnered everyone's attention: the front was approaching and my schooling did not last long, just a couple of weeks. Then came flight. Father retreated with his regiment. Mother returned to Lithuania through the Vievis forest with me, my brother, his nurse, Antosia, and a goat.

JANUARY 6, 1988

Yesterday evening, a sauna and a swim.

That generation, Iwaszkiewicz's, was lucky: their lovely war ended in independence. Although for the transplants from the east, even for young people like Iwaszkiewicz at that time, there must have been many blows and conflicts. Elisavetgrad, Kiev, Tymoszówka, the Black Sea steppe, a Greek Ukraine—all this can be reconstructed on the basis of his books, because he was different from his Skamander colleagues. The people of Poland's eastern borderlands, the Kresy, a region that had been retreating in several waves, had had a taste of Russian *prostor*—of wide-open spaces. Their situation was better than that of the Russian émigrés because they were in a country that spoke their language, but there was still poverty and the difficulty of adaptation. The young Iwaszkiewicz earned his living as a tutor.

To tell the truth, I have no intention of painting a portrait of Iwaszkiewicz. I shall limit myself to considering him as a poet, his influence on me and on literature, which, in turn, influenced him. I was growing up in Wilno, which was a safe place after the 1920 victory, and for a time was the capital of the state of Central Lithuania. Not long ago I read Siedlecka's book about Gombrowicz, *Little Lord Nobleman*, and I was stunned. Absolutely no similarity with my own childhood and youth, two different countries, two different social spheres, although supposedly the same landed-gentry background. I had none of that multi-branched family, none of the wealth, none of those social rituals, not to mention the good breeding, the social freedom, the mockery. What connection could I have had to those Gombrowicz estates, the town houses, the visits, the dinner parties, the steady income?

After demobilization, my father went into partnership with another man and founded a construction firm, Budmost, but we weren't exactly rolling in clover at home and I learned to be frugal at an early age. For a while I was friends with Ignacy Święcicki; I used to go over to their house on Makowa Street to shoot crows. Just recently, in Philadelphia, Ignacy reminded me that they had had to carry in buckets of water from the courtyard, which means that level of existence was normal for me. After the firm went bankrupt as a result of the bookkeeper's embezzling funds, my father, ever the romantic traveler, set off for Brazil; in the twenties, there was a lot of talk about colonial "possibilities." He planned to set down roots there and bring the family over, but it didn't work out. Afterward, for many years, he was a district engineer in Suwałki, and then in Głębokie. My family supported me when I lived in Wilno at the Biszewskis' boarding house and then at Mrs. Klecka's, but I suffered constant pangs of conscience that grew stronger after I entered the university, so I started working out deals: scholarships, occasional earnings. *Little Lord Nobleman* made me conscious of the poverty and provincialism of my Wilno. Yet Gombrowicz and I had one thing in common: Polish literature in school. Now I ask myself: Didn't he, despite his rejection of Polish literature as weak and devoid of universality because of its service to Polishness, take from it the romantic myth of the bard, annointing himself as a genius, a leader in the spiritual sphere? And didn't my early feeling that I was called also derive from that myth?

I wouldn't be able to reconstruct my readings between age sixteen or twenty. In poetry, it was Leopold Staff and *Skamander*, or, "And in the Spring let me see Spring and not Poland" (Lechoń). What was the source of my quarrel with the literary fraternity? No one doubted at the time that the greatest poet was Tuwim; Słonimski and Lechoń also had their admirers, but I, on the other hand, was in love with Iwaszkiewicz's poetry, and that was considered an eccentricity. Tuwim's poetry reading in Wilno drew a crowd; Iwaszkiewicz's reading was an embarrassment. I was still a high-school student at the time. Aside from me (I wouldn't have dared approach him), there were perhaps five or six people in the large hall of the Theater on Pohulanka Avenue. He read one of his stories, which confirmed the general opinion of him as a "swooning aesthete."

So what was the source of my enchantment, my obstinacy? I owned *Dionysiacs* (1921), *Qasidas* (1925), and his prose works, *Legends and Demeter* (published in 1921, but written in 1916) and *Escape to Baghdad* (published 1923, written 1917–18).

JANUARY 7, 1988

Iwaszkiewicz's slender volumes, their grayish, but good-quality, paper, their coarse covers, were not books but cult objects for me. That is, they had taken over the place occupied a couple of years before by my colored botanical and ornithological atlases. The simplest explanation is that this was my first encounter with modern poetry. More modern than what I could usually find in the issues of *Skamander*. I shan't probe into where he might have gotten it from; that's for the literary historians. It's possible that literary Russia was more modern than Poland; in any event, in terms of color, of the sensual weight of words, he, who had been brought up simultaneously in two cultures, set them against each other, experimented with the way Western ideas sound in Russian and in Polish. It's a fact that what repelled me in the poetry of Young Poland attracted me in him. In the final analysis, *Dyonisiacs* is thoroughly *art nouveau* in its cacophony of subject matter and, when subjected to sober analysis, is really quite stupid; the poems also leave something to be desired in terms of their versification. Nonetheless, I was indifferent to Jan Kasprowicz's *Hymns* and I liked Leopold Staff only briefly. So it must have been the sensuality of his poetry that captivated me; Iwaszkiewicz instead

of Rimbaud, whom I did not know. But why not Tuwim, also a man of two
cultures, if it's a matter of two languages in competition with each other? It
seems that Tuwim, in his Lodz, did not get even a taste of the refined sugar
that sustained the Russian intelligentsia on the eve of World War I and that
was so easily obtainable in Elisavetgrad or Kiev. Tuwim would periodically
come under the influence of individual Russian poets (Pasternak, for example); Iwaszkiewicz, in contrast, was not under Russian influence lin-
guistically, but his Polish genealogy is hard to discern. What, after all, is
the origin of those adventures on the steppe, Astrakhan, Jafis, the Oriental
exotica in *Escape to Baghdad*, which was written in 1916, and in *Legends
and Demeter* (1917–18)? Perhaps from Tadeusz Miciński.

To tell the truth, the logic of Iwaszkiewicz's poems and prose struck me
as more absurd, more dependent on free association than it really was, and
their mysteriousness only heightened their charm. I also found a great many
words that I didn't know; "ocarina," for example. Furthermore, his early
stories constructed a fantastic, spacious land; I journeyed through it and it
was ample in space and in time; in it, the twentieth century bordered on
the eighteenth, or the seventeenth, century. And the whole took on erotic
coloring under the control of a teenage Eros. I must not have applied any
labels then, because today, were I to pick up similar passages, I would
immediately notice the homosexual code in them.

Iwaszkiewicz's land was linked in my imagination with the Ukraine of
Malczewski, Słowacki, Goszczyński, Zaleski, even—why deny it?—of Sien-
kiewicz. I cannot completely rule out the possibility that he enchanted me
as a "writer from the Kresy," and I would not swear that when he lost his
Ukrainian aura later he did not also lose some of his power. In any event,
while I admired his novel *The Moon Is Rising* (although not as much as his
early poetic prose), *Hilary the Bookkeeper's Son*, which is set in Warsaw,
thoroughly disenchanted me.

JANUARY 8, 1988

In a sense, Iwaszkiewicz was the culmination, the final phase of the Kresy
manor, with the addition of Oscar Wilde and a cult of Dionysus. The young
masters, their horses, their carriages, the Orthodox priest Father Wasyli and

his daughter, Hania, who participates in the Dionysiac rituals performed in the nude on St. John's Eve, the French marquis, owner of the neighboring estate, who solemnly observes the autumn holiday in the Temple of Demeter, and even, to make it more fantastic, a letter from Florence, from Julek (Słowacki, d. 1849), whom the hero had recently met in Lebanon. Primarily, however, Dionysian religion is contrasted with Apollonian religion, the syncretic ideas as developed among the St. Petersburg Graecophiles, Professor Faddei (Tadeusz) Zielinski and Vyacheslav Ivanov. We are in the midst of the *Moderna* and not that far removed from the peacocks, topazes, and amethysts of Stanisław Przybyszewski.

As a writer of poetry I owe a great deal to *Dionysiacs* and even more to *Qasidahs*; they were an illumination, a revelation of a verse form liberated from meter and rhyme. When I attempt today to grasp my delight as a reader then, I find myself tripping over the obstacles to getting close to one's former self; I don't understand how apparently completely contradictory tastes could have coexisted in that young man. Quick-witted, intellectually developed, at the same time childish, he marked out a sphere in which, as it were, he renounced control and reveled in pure sensuality.

I probably knew Iwaszkiewicz's *Zenobia Palmura* at that time, although I'm not sure. I have reread it and realized what a rational reader I am, the I of today. A perfectly constructed novella in poetic prose, more avant-garde than many other so-called avant-garde ideas of the time (1920), akin to Witkacy. Kiev, 1912; a handsome young man, Prince Yura Mavricky; his valet, Józef; Zenobia, who is employed in Mrs. Banasińska's pastry shop, Palmira; the philosophy student Jarosław Iwaszkiewicz, identified by first name and last. Also, the tsar's family on holiday in Livadia, because Yura's sister is a maid of honor at the court. Józef is Zenobia's former lover; he both loves and hates Prince Yura; Zenobia gallops on Yura's phallus (see Podkowiński's *Madness*), hating herself for her lasciviousness. Jarosław is a friend of the prince, and also of the valet; when drunk, they screw the same wench. The author addresses the friend to whom this story is dedicated (Georgii Miklukho-Maklay), apologizing for Prince Yura's being a parody of him. Zenobia is transformed into the Queen of Palmura and, assisted by Józef, murders the naked king, or Yura, stabbing him with a stiletto. So, sadomasochism as an ingredient of the religion of Dionysus, and certainly of modern art, too (Witkacy's corpses, Artaud's "theater of cruelty," and so forth). In the early Iwaszkiewicz, particularly in *Dionysiacs*, this tension of eroticism and murder is always present. I assume that what fascinated me was precisely this sadomasochistic violence, probably more than the gold of autumn and ripe fruit, although no doubt I was barely conscious of it. What linguistic daring in *Zenobia*!

$\mathcal{J}$ANUARY 9, 1988

Two days ago I saw Bertolucci's film *The Last Emperor*. It is a film about the beneficent influence of prison pedagogy, which, after ten years of brain-washing, is capable of transforming even a former emperor and collaborator with the Japanese into an honorable citizen. A hymn in praise of *ispravi-tel'notrudovye lageri* [Russian for "corrective labor camps"] in their Chinese incarnation. I remember the film A *Path into Life* about the superb peda-gogues of the NKVD. But the American public, enchanted by the grandeur of the stage sets, does not even notice the thesis that is being served up to it and assimilates only the information that the Japanese were naughty and the collaborators were punished humanely (*gumanno*).

I notice that I have overlooked the most important thing: Jarosław's poems are words to music for which the score has not yet been written but which is, in a sense, already present. It differs from the "musicality of poetry" which is common to many poets, because his words do not create music; they only allude to it, often they are heard between one response from the orchestra and another. Most characteristic of Jarosław are his songs, lullabies, arias; isn't one of his supreme achievements *Summer 1932*, a cycle of songs? That is also why the simplicity of the words, disturbing in an age of avant-garde revolutions, does not grate: the verse continually replicates itself; it exists "against a background." Of the Skamander poets, only Jarosław had had a musical education, and although he did not become a composer, he was obedient to its summons. Not especially musical myself, I had heard a lot of music, nonetheless, and this music, which was for everyone to deduce or compose anew, captivated me with its richness.

I summoned up the courage to write to Iwaszkiewicz. A correspondence developed and he invited me to Warsaw. Probably my brief visit to Stawisko (a week?) strengthened my rebellious inclinations toward the Warsaw literary, progressive café. I must admit that I didn't understand the code in which Jarosław and his wife, Hania's, circle communicated. The names of French writers, composers, painters, etc., which constantly surfaced in their conversation meant nothing to me; I didn't know them. Allusions to friends of the household and anecdotes relating to them intensified my feeling of exclusion. I was certainly poorly educated and also closed to particular areas of conversation; for example, Mrs. Iwaszkiewicz's metaphysical interests, with frequent references to Proust, eluded me and also irritated me with their snobbishness; they weren't for my socially bottled up self of those days. Also, one of Stanisław Ignacy Witkiewicz's lectures in the Union of Writers on Foksal Street (what year? 1932?) about the lack of really serious metaphysical thinking among the Polish intelligentsia found in me a dull, scarcely comprehending listener.

I do not understand this. Because in the same period, more or less, when I met Oscar Milosz in Paris, he devoted a very flattering testimony to my intelligence in one of his letters. Why was I stupid with some people and clever with others? Why did I assimilate some codes, but not others? Who was I intellectually—wise and foolish by turns, studying furiously throughout my entire life, so that today I am enrolled in the highly trained tribe of mandarins? And what about those others, all the people for whom my present code is inaccessible?

JANUARY 12, 1988

I did not betray Jarosław's poetry. As succeeding volumes of his poetry appeared, I found confirmation of my choice and never came to appreciate the other Skamander poets. They might be significantly more accomplished and not shock or even amuse me as he sometimes did with various capers of dubious intelligence and taste. Nevertheless, the sources of Jarosław's poetry were significantly more mysterious, and that mysteriousness lay concealed behind its words, not in its words, which were usually too simple to convey it. Was he an intellectual poet who used a certain strategy of multilayered meanings? Probably not. In avant-garde circles he was considered the least intelligent of the Skamander poets, an aestheticizing snob. Such evaluations are usually relative and subject to change with the passage of time. Wikta Winnicka, Tuwim's close friend, often repeated what her half brother, Józef Wittlin, used to say: Tuwim is proof that God exists: if such a stupid man can be such a great poet . . . The Skamander poets were accused of vitalism and a deliberate absence of any program, which probably did not exactly convey the quite justifiable annoyance at their insouciance, and also their conviction that they were smart enough and that poetry does not demand intellectual work. Iwaszkiewicz would sit and write in an even, beautiful script; I don't think he struggled, crossed words out. Then he would shrug his shoulders: It's written down, and that's that. He was supported by his great vital energies, and I doubt that he gave much thought to his poetic strategy.

I think what may be important is Iwaszkiewicz's weak connection with so-called political and social reality. His colleagues responded to that reality— Lechoń in his "Crimson Poem," Tuwim in his political verse, the always publicistic Słonimski, and Wierzyński in his poems about Piłsudski. And that is precisely what assured their fame. Iwaszkiewicz's poetry resided in remote regions; it was preoccupied with sensual experience, with love and death; it was no more realistic than *Zenobia Palmura* as a portrait of Kiev. And it resided in the regions of what I would call pure fantasy.

JANUARY 13, 1988

I certainly wasn't bothered by that unreality; for me, there always existed a gap between words and reality, and that gap was no smaller in Iwaszkiewicz's supposedly more sober rivals. It's interesting that he never wrote about the Word, about his poetic workshop, as Tuwim did—but I don't wish to develop that argument here or to delve, for example, into the activity of the Russian formalists during the twenties and their frequent discussions with the poets.

Iwaszkiewicz as a famous writer. He would sit down at his desk every day and systematically fill up pages with his tiny script; that's the way his numerous stories, theatrical works, and novel after novel came into being. I think he shouldn't have done that. His *Red Shields*, supposedly a historical novel, is cut from the cloth of dream, not of waking reality. He was not good at "slice-of-life" prose, but, then, no one was good at it anymore, because its time had passed. I liked his *Young Ladies from Wilko* very much, but I was unmoved by his novels in which the action takes place in the present. One could infer from them the author's receptivity to various fashions—for example, the myth of the great writer, the Nobel Laureate, which was inspired by Thomas Mann, or the myth of the vigor of young nationalists. Iwaszkiewicz was not the only one to be obsessively haunted by an image of himself as a Nobel Laureate; in later years, Jerzy Andrzejewski was, too, and many other writers; Borges, for instance. Jarosław's industriousness and productivity were stimulated by this image and bolstered it in turn.

His life in the thirties. He joined the Ministry of Foreign Affairs and served as an attaché in the Polish Embassy in Belgium. Family tragedies coincided with others that had an odor of scandal about them, which gave rise to various rumors after the war. I note this, not because I want to confirm them, but only to give an idea of the unpleasant aura surrounding him and, more generally, of the opacity of that time. I can't stop thinking with distaste about my own opacity, and to this day I interrogate myself about the extent to which its causes lay inside me or were rooted in my surroundings and penetrated me by osmosis. The best expression of all these interdependent facts, I think, is in Stefan Kisielewski's novel *The Conspiracy*, where universal inertia—political and social—is manifested in the protagonist's sexual impotence. As a metaphor of meaninglessness, my memory has preserved from the late thirties a girl by the name of Anka, who, it is true, was beautiful. Since she had a fiancé from a wealthy family and was supposed to be married in a couple of months, why did she go out on dates with me? Since her views, her social set, were abhorrent to me, why did I get involved with her? She belonged to the ONR, the right-wing Radical Nationalist Party; she idolized its leader, Bolesław Piasecki, and even insisted that I had to meet him and took me along to their meeting. A "blond beast" with a great deal of energy, magnetic, soft-spoken, secretive, definitely a leader. Because of this meeting, I was able to understand later why the NKVD took note of him and decided not to shoot him, but rather make use of him.

The war swept all the Skamander poets into emigration; only one, Iwaszkiewicz, was left, as if to overturn all those neat distinctions. And so it was: the "aesthete" assumed the role of citizen. Indeed, this was the beginning of Jarosław's duties as a farmer and a generous host, in the style of the old landed gentry. Stawisko was immensely significant for underground literary-artistic Warsaw. It wasn't just that those two individuals, Jarosław and his wife, helped many people, including many Jews; Stawisko was also, and most important, an institution that signified a certain continuity even amid the ruins. Events in underground Warsaw were discussed there; judgments were formed about underground publications and their anonymous authors, whose names we knew; information was exchanged about the fates of writers, actors, musicians, museums, libraries. Small-scale readings for a selected few were held there. Jarosław read his own new works; others, including me,

gave readings. Stawisko also attempted to maintain the remnants of its pre-
war splendor, occasionally putting on magnificent dinners (white tablecloths,
wine, servants); an invitation to these affairs was no small honor. I do not
remember all the participants in these feasts. Wilam Horzyca and his wife,
the musician Roman Jasiński, Mauersberger (or Mauzio), possibly the Stro-
mengers (he was a musicologist), Władysław Zawistowski, a sort of underground Minister of Culture, probably some young people, too, maybe Staś
Dygat or Wanda Wertenstein. Wertenstein was a physicist; her family owned
a home next to Stawisko. Since they were Jews, they had to flee, but instead
of going into the ghetto, they rented a little house in Komorów, on that
same commuter rail line I mentioned before. Professor Wertenstein managed
to get to Hungary, where he perished toward the end of the war. Wanda
continued her life "on the Aryan side" and became friendly with Jerzy
Andrzejewski. Of the writers who frequented Stawisko, I can remember the
above-mentioned Staś Dygat and the poet Roman Kołoniecki, who served
for a time as Jarosław's secretary, but beyond that there's a gap in my memory.
Of course, I heard that Krzysztof Baczyński was among the younger writers
who came there. Jerzy Andrzejewski and I were more or less constant visitors.
Thus, Stawisko seemed to me entirely different from what it had been in
the old days; it was already quite dilapidated, but the change was to its
benefit.

One time Jarosław invited several people to a reading of his new work,
"The Battle of Sedgemoor Plain." That he would write such a story at that
time (1942) gave me a lot to think about. It also illuminated many later
events when he chose an open, programmatic collaboration with the Communists. Does anyone today remember what those religious-political factions
that we learn about only by studying the bloody history of seventeenth-century
England were actually fighting about? The author, not without reason, took
the time of "troubles" as his theme—actually, a time of frenzied murders
in the name of a faith that was equally strong on both sides and that excluded
compromise. The characters in this story about Monmouth's rebellion are
capable of every sacrifice; they refute the image of man as a being who is
concerned above all with his own interests. The true name of their heroism,
however, is futility. Nothing remains of their faith, their yearnings; time
carries everything away, ashes cover their traces. In old age, the heroine
views her own youthful steadfastness as pointless; she cannot even remember
why she acted one way and not another. Looked at from the perspective of
some future time, the author seems to be saying, won't our cruel era lose

the clear boundaries which now appear to delineate irreconcilable oppositions but which, for later generations, will be a matter of utter indifference?

In one of our conversations, Jarosław mocked the work of historians who rifle through the centuries in search of great syntheses; he quoted from a history of the Far East: "From the seventh to the thirteenth century there was continual turmoil in China." Then I remembered his "Battle of Sedgemoor Plain."

January 15, 1988

It's only a few years since his death and no one wants to judge him yet; his subservient odes ("A Letter to President Bierut") are only amusing, the details of his biography will fade, and his books, good and bad, will remain.

For refugees from Warsaw during the Warsaw Uprising and until the Soviets' January 1945 offensive,* the commuter rail line turned into the chief center for meetings, conferences, consultation on what to do next, trade in hard currency, mourning the dead. At the same time, the transit camp in Pruszków, from which transports to concentration camps in Germany departed, was still functioning, and daily roundups were still taking place. After we (Janka, her mother, and I) were rescued by a nun from behind the barbed wires of Okęcie, we traveled by cart, avoiding the railroad because of the roundups, to Władysław Ryńca's recently purchased house in Piastów. Providentially, he had transferred the manuscripts I bought for him to that house, including Kisielewski's *The Conspiracy.* However, some manuscripts of books that I had just purchased for Ryńca remained in our apartment on Independence Boulevard: a volume of new essays by Karol Irzykowski, and Herodotus in Witold Klinger's translation. They were lost; as we learned later, an artillery shell tore into the wall exactly at the level of the second floor, destroying our apartment and also our neighbors' apartments. If the authors had copies, they were probably destroyed, too, in other parts of the city.

* On August 1, 1944, in expectation of the Soviet Army approaching the Vistula, Warsaw rose against the Germans, but the Soviets halted their offensive and after two months of cruel battles the city was turned into ruins by the German aviation and artillery.

Piastów, Komorów, Podkowa Leśna (Stawisko). As I said, it was time to think about what to do next. Some people prepared to flee to the West; Stanisław Dygat writes about this in *Farewells*. A great many castaways were camping out at Ryńca's, as in almost every house, and an ordinary bandit raid of that house when the sky was lit up by the fires of Warsaw seemed to exceed the bounds of even the universal absurdity of those days. The bandits were young and were not interested in politics; they took our money and valuables. Stawisko was a campsite on the model of Ryńca's Piastów. I visited it once more in yet another phase. We wound up there with Zyg and Futa Poniatowski, and Dziak—the people with whom we had reached Okęcie after fleeing from their home on Kielecka Street. Now we had decided to move on together; it was impossible to find an apartment near the rail line and there were constant roundups. So, one after the other, Grodzisk, Żyrardów, Skierniewice, and finally the village of Janisławice. I am still interested in village life under the German occupation. At night, the passage of the forest partisans, who were never mentioned by day; lone Soviet soldiers, escapees from German camps, or possibly deserters from German support detachments, heading east across the fields; occasionally, at dusk, a Jewish neighbor with a sack of food for his family's bunker in the woods; conversations with the locals, sudden but meaningful pauses, acquiescing in the end of what had existed in the village until that time. Nearby, an estate. Our unpleasant visit there: the strangeness of a vanishing *mentalité*; a lot of nonchalant youths in high boots, patriotic ladies. Shortly afterward I learned that Maria Rodziewiczówna had sought shelter there in her flight from Polesie, and that that was where she died, her death coterminous with the death of the Polish manor. I would have attended her funeral, but I heard about it too late.

During those months Jarosław had time to consider what to do next. People from the Kresy probably had a broader historical perspective and a great deal of fatalism. Didn't Stanisław Stempowski, who was, like Jarosław, from Ukraine, tell me in 1945: "It seems to me that this dirt is going to spread throughout the world"? Whenever I read statements expressing astonishment at the treason of writers who went over to the side of the invaders, I think that at least Jarosław's case is clear, because his choice can be seen as consciously cynical and consciously opportunistic. He had decided beforehand that one must pay while collaborating and he was prepared to pay; that is, he was prepared to accept humiliation and not to appeal to his honor. His decision was a serious one; in comparison, the noble rhetoric of his steadfast émigré colleagues, Lechoń and Wierzyński, gives the impression of weightlessness. But even the none too clever Tuwim, praising the "new nation of one hundred nations" in the East, accepted the burden after his return to Poland from America, for—as Wikta Winnicka, who was probably the best-informed person, told me—he intervened with Bierut to stay the execution of condemned Home Army members.*

Of course, people said that Jarosław would do anything to save Stawisko. That's probably true, but it should be seen as part of his instincts as a good husbandman. For his *La Belle Epoque* sophistication was grafted onto an ordinary farmer from the Kresy and first the one would be dominant in him and then the other; the other had quite a sentimental attachment to white-and-red flags, to the architecture of Sandomierz, to the "simple people," so that in the end he dumbfounded everyone by leaving instructions that he should be buried in the ceremonial uniform of a miner.

January 16, 1988

Last night, a reading by local San Francisco poets to benefit the PEN Club. Carolyn Keizer read an excerpt from *Ulysses*, someone else read from *Huckleberry Finn*, others read their own works. I read a few poems in translation: Herbert, Anna Swir, Zagajewski, then a couple of my own poems.

Jarosław had those yearnings even before the war, although the Communists and the ONR [Radical Nationalist Party] were somewhat prophetically confused in his mind. The old rural Poland without a plutocracy; healthy, plebeian. But why am I dabbling in literary history? I keep trying to fathom the secret of his poetry's charm and its influence on me. I would sum it up as the "ecstasy of ephemerality"; his "Song for a Dead Woman" can be seen as a key:

> In the midst of great love
> Everything is conceived
> And everything is meaningless
> —but very holy.

---

* In Poland, overrun by the Soviet Army in 1945, the soldiers of the Polish underground units who had fought against the Nazis throughout the war were arrested, deported, or executed as potential obstacles to the Sovietization of the country.

I don't think that Jarosław was completely aware of his strong points and his weaknesses. He was probably the opposite of the clan of poets who know or gradually learn their own trajectory and eliminate whatever diverges from it. His productivity pins me to the wall, forcing me to ask questions about the aging of literary works. I have to admit with all due respect that his poems, starting at some point in the late thirties, do not move me at all, with perhaps one or two exceptions; they roll off me like water. Their subject matter is familiar; it's the same old thing. Family portraits, love, travels, Venice, Sicily, literary-artistic myths, ephemeralness, reminiscences about the dead, loneliness—everything that it was customary to put into so-called lyric poetry. But why is all this deprived of intensity, color, as if it lacked one unknown ingredient that would unify music and word? There is a theory, rather forgotten today because it is romantic, that says lyric poetry can be written only at a young age, or up to the point when our vitality begins to decline. In other words, lyric poetry is a product of our hormones; afterward comes the age of the mind. It cannot be ruled out that Jarosław was able to be Dionysian only as long as he was young; later, the time for crop rotation came, but he didn't take advantage of it.

There is another possibility. Namely, that I had equipped his poetry with something that was never present in it, transferring my own eroticism, my own voraciousness, my own music into it. And when I myself turned into a different reader, what happened was what sometimes happens when we meet a woman who was once the object of our love: it is difficult to understand how we could have attached our emotions to her. Although I do not really think that the value of Iwaszkiewicz's pre-war poetry can be attributed to my purely subjective judgments.

A reader such as I am today will pick up Iwaszkiewicz's poetry from that second phase and set it down, thinking, "He has nothing to say." And this will be followed immediately by anxiety. Because the cruelty of such an opinion reminds us of our dependence on time, which, hour by hour, month by month, imperceptibly eats away at our attachments and our loyalties. After we reach the age of seventy, we undergo a great reassessment of values and find ourselves doubting ever more frequently whether literature has anything to say at all. The power of time to strip things naked becomes increasingly palpable. More than one "immortal work of literature" disappoints us, and the stitches with which it was sewn together, the hidden seams, come into view. For example, I reread Stendhal's *The Charterhouse of Parma* last year and found none of the enchantment I had experienced long ago in Wilno on my first reading. That obvious marriage of pen and time, and also delight—what else should a reader be guided by?—occurs less and less frequently. At the very least, this discourages me from functioning as a literary critic, and it also reminds me of my own fate as a creator. One must always assume that the treasure of pure gold we are hording may someday turn out to be dry rot.

The war years definitely affected Iwaszkiewicz profoundly. It is one thing to know about human suffering; it is quite another to lose one's young friends, as he did, people he knew well, who were executed, tortured, killed in battle. After the war, Jarosław kept summoning their shades with his incantations, and their names return in his poems and stories.

The story "The Flight" was conceived as a response to Albert Camus's *The Fall*. To Camus's universally significant moral allegory, in which the refusal to help a drowning girl is shorthand, a metaphor, Iwaszkiewicz replies with a list of the sufferings imposed by history on the Poles—in other words, the elephant and the Polish question yet again. A very weak outcome to a duel with a Western writer.

January 17, 1988

Yesterday a visit from Tatiana Tolstaya, who is here for two weeks as a member of a delegation of Soviet writers. I know her stories (good, but very sad), so she might have considered herself honored, especially since, when I found out that she is Mikhail Lozinsky's granddaughter, I went over to my bookshelf and pulled out his translations of *The Divine Comedy* and *Hamlet* to show her. The conversation was completely unconstrained, without pretense or posturing. I referred to the empathy in her stories. Her response: "*Zhalost'* [Russian for "pity"]. What is left for us poor people if not *zhalost'*?" She was born in 1951.

Jarosław may well have experienced a lot of unpleasantness from his protean nature and his acceptance of various social roles. In the last decades of his life he was turning into an institution and performed his duties as an official with dignity. I wasn't in Poland during his lengthy tenure as president of the Writers' Union. A membership card was handed to me in 1981 with the embarrassed explanation that my file had "disappeared" and had not existed since 1951. Shortly after 1981, the Union was dissolved. I don't know what Jarosław was like in this office; he was probably the best among those who could have been president. I can only imagine the infinite number of stratagems and games, the compromises; he must have had tremendous expertise in this, since he held the position for so long. He swam in mud, but I never heard that he played dirty tricks on people; on the contrary, he helped and protected them. In other words, apparently—though it's not for me to judge—his strategy of saving what could be saved, not for nothing, but for an often painful price, did pay off.

One of his greatest services as a conservator was his work as editor of several periodicals after the war, especially *Nowiny Literackie* [Literary Novelties] and, after 1955, *Twórczość* [Creative Work]. Whatever else can be said about it, during his directorship it had the richest contents of any literary journal in the Polish language, and its failings should be evaluated while imagining what Iwaszkiewicz protected the journal from, what he would not let it become. The decline of *Creative Work* after his death was proof of this.

Distinctions, awards. As he ages, every writer—Jarosław even more than most—likes to anticipate that the volumes of books on his shelf will earn him a laurel wreath. It is doubtful, however, that he had a chance for international fame. The more his poetry was his own, sensual, the more untranslatable it was, because of the associations of the Polish words and the music that accompanied them. I became convinced of this when I tried to translate him into English. I included one poem, "Quentin Matsys," in my anthology *Postwar Polish Poetry*, and really only so that Iwaszkiewicz would be represented in the anthology, although I realized that he is not for export. But his prose, too, shares the features of his poetry to a large extent, and aside from a couple of stories, there is not much to offer foreigners. Not a single novel. His theater pieces are quite old-fashioned. He has been translated a little into the Continental European languages, but his complete nonexistence in English-speaking countries meant that such awards as the Neustadt Prize and the Nobel were out of the question. I never even heard him mentioned as a candidate for the international Formentor Award.

How would he have taken the awarding of the Nobel Prize to someone who, not so very long ago, had been his own young disciple? I admit that if it had happened during his lifetime, it would have been somewhat painful, and I would have felt embarrassed.

January 18, 1988

Pruszyński, Iwaszkiewicz. And now I am visited by a totally different man and writer: Józef Mackiewicz. Before the war, he worked for the Wilno *Word*, whose editor, his brother Stanisław Mackiewicz, made a lot of noise with his editorials, dabbled in politics, fought duels (with a sword), and wound up in the Bereza Kartuska internment camp because of his opposition activities. Józef, on the other hand, held a position somewhere in the editorial offices, and that is all that people knew about him. Later, everything was turned upside down. Stanisław will go down in the history of Polish writing as a journalist, and Józef as an outstanding novelist.

In 1938 Józef Mackiewicz published *The Revolt of the Marshes*. These were reports from the Wilno region which he had gathered on his travels by bus and horse-drawn wagon along the roads of Belorussia. Now, in California, when I think about that region it seems fascinating, with the uncommon richness of its interwoven ethnic, religious, and class threads, and also the richness of its history. I am even more capable of appreciating it now because I have read a thing or two about colonial history; for example, the Caribbean Islands. Exotica, palm trees, a tropical sea—and the horror of an absolute historical vacuum, greed, exploitation; at best, the criminal chronicle of white adventurers and pirates. Even though it was gray, situated between pine forest and marshland, the Wilno region during the interwar years ought to have inspired many writers with both its past and its present. And yet there weren't any writers. They would certainly have appeared; the two decades of the interwar period were simply too short. Besides which, there were obstacles. Those who wrote in Polish grew up in the traditions of the gentry manor and would have had to tear themselves from that orbit to see the larger reality. The Belorussians, marinated in their nationalistic resentment, had not yet achieved anything but patriotic poetry; the group of Wilno writers who wrote in Yiddish, Yung-Vilne, were from the same generation and had the same leanings as Żagary. Wilno produced an outstanding prose writer, Chaim Grade, a chronicler of the little Jewish towns in Lithuania and Belorussia, but he developed after the war, in America, as did Isaac Bashevis Singer.

In *The Revolt of the Marshes*, Józef Mackiewicz assembled his reportages with the independence and contrariness that were later to bring him much unhappiness. He had stepped outside the usual Polish orbit and had focused his attention not on the manor house but on the province of the "locals," whether they spoke Polish or Belorussian at home, and had shown particular interest in the phenomenon of the popular religious sects in that province, which were estranged equally from Catholicism and Orthodoxy. Also, a lot of information about the daily life of that region went into his book. A similar Wilno region is shown in Florian Czarnyszewicz's novel *The Lads from Nowoszyszki*, which was written in Argentina. Its main theme is the fighting between Catholics and Orthodox believers within a single village, which suggests not so much a national Polish or Belorussian choice as a choice of state: for Poland or for the Soviets. How the whole Wilno region would have fit into a different turn of history in 1939, we shall never know.

I hardly knew Józef Mackiewicz during my Wilno youth. A gruff fellow, one of those whose longish nose looks down into a glass of vodka; he wore a visored cap, usually dressed in homespun cloth and in high-top boots, and could have passed for a yeoman farmer straight out of the countryside. He loved to spend the night drinking in Wilno restaurants, like another of his colleagues from *The Word*, Jerzy Wyszomirski, but unlike him, he had no interest in writers. There was certainly no question of talking with him about poetry. Although it seems he was well read in one area that was not rare among us at the time: nineteenth-century Russian novels.

JANUARY 19, 1988

I couldn't possibly imagine him as a Warsaw or Cracow writer. He lived in the city that, for him, was still the capital of the Grand Duchy of Lithuania, and he was a patriot of that country. I think that today it is difficult for the younger generation to imagine the blend of loyalties I am talking about here and why people like him reacted to Polish patriots with as much disdain as they felt for Lithuanian or Belorussian patriots. I have been rereading Mackiewicz's essays and articles which were published in London, where he speaks of the "internal partition" of the Grand Duchy carried out by the Poles, Lithuanians, and Belorussians. "No heir to its entirety emerged. Quite simply, there was no such thing. Each group wanted to tear off a piece for itself." I consider him a writer who strictly speaks the truth and I think that he does not exaggerate at all when he writes, "This is the source of the argument, which is developing into an open struggle over languages, culture, tradition, the interpretation of history, religion. The battle was also carried out with fists and clubs in Catholic and Orthodox churches, with knives, wagon shafts, pistols, until in the end, during the last war, it was even fought with denunciations to the Gestapo and the NKVD. Hatred, in accordance with all the laws of nature, bred hatred."

According to Mackiewicz, the Polish side bears the greatest responsibility because "the heirs to the legacy of the entire land of the Grand Duchy" were Polonized culturally and politically, so that they were only able to oppose the growing nationalisms with Polish nationalism. "As a result, they found themselves in a drastic situation in their own land as spokesmen for another state, and from there it was only one step to their being treated as foreign agents by the absolutely overwhelming majority of the population."

The example of my own family? My cousin Oscar Milosz was the first representative of independent Lithuania in Paris, which for the Poles was the equivalent of treachery. My mother's parents, the Kunats, were loyal citizens of Lithuania, but they did not speak Lithuanian. My mother had dual citizenship, Lithuanian and Polish; she listed Polish as her nationality, and spoke Lithuanian, but poorly. Her sister, on the other hand, was fluent in Lithuanian. My father was declared a traitor in Lithuania because he belonged to the Polish Fighting Organization. He was blacklisted and was barred from the country of his birth. Nonetheless, on September 17, 1939, when he managed to reach the Lithuanian border from the little town of Głębokie, where he had been working as a district engineer, the Lithuanians showed themselves to be quite generous, as they were toward the many refugees from Poland, and although they knew who he was, they let him into the then neutral Lithuania. He was not persecuted there for his former sins.

According to Mackiewicz, the single conscious patriot of the Grand Duchy was Ludwik Abramowicz, editor and publisher of *The Wilno Review*. He proclaimed that all the inhabitants of the region had the right to inherit it in its entirety, acknowledging the absolute equality of all the peoples inhabiting those lands. His program differed from all federalist ideas, including Piłsudski's, because the others were all guided by Polish interests and the Polish *raîson d'état*. From this perspective, the Poles' violation of the Suwałki Treaty, their taking of Wilno, and the fiction of "Central Lithuania," placed a great burden on proponents of the "Jagiellonian idea." I don't know what Mackiewicz thought of Father Walerian Meysztowicz, who conceived of the Grand Duchy as the creation of his forebears, virtually the private property of the great noble families, and glorified the patriarchal relations between the manor and the peasant. Very likely, he counted him among those whose Polishness, "it goes without saying," was responsible for the Lithuanians' and Belorussians' distrust of the idea of a union, so that they even preferred dealing with avowed Polish nationalists.

JANUARY 20, 1988

Pre-war Wilno came back to me as I read the proofs (sent to me by the publisher) of Lucy S. Dawidowicz's memoir, *From That Place and Time.* Raised in New York, she spent the year 1938–39 in Wilno, doing research in the Jewish Scientific Institute—YIVO. This is very useful reading because it reminds me of an important other Wilno whose Jewish traditions earned it the name "Jerusalem of the North." Roughly one-third of its population had little in common with the state in which it was located; they spoke Yiddish and, to an extent, among the upper stratum, Russian. Dawidowicz's memoir (she did not know Polish) touches chiefly on the division into "we" and "you," and the persecutions related to that division. One of her Wilno friends, a journalist, lost his eye during the anti-Semitic student riots in 1931 (I remember them). The last year before the war brought the total triumph of the N.D. (National Democrats) program: picketing of Jewish shops, plans for the outlawing of ritual slaughter, a large number of regulations to enforce Polonization, and above all, a competition between the government press and the press run by the future saint, Father Maksymilian Kolbe, about who could produce more anti-Semitic propaganda. In Dawidowicz's narrative, Wilno is an unsafe city; there were repeated attacks by youths armed with sticks, and every encounter with young Poles carried the threat of a beating. Dawidowicz admits that women and children were not beaten, which didn't, however, reduce the sinister harvest of such events.

This Wilno is worth remembering when one speaks of the final end of the Grand Duchy. The energetic youth who beat their university colleagues with sticks and who organized hunts for people walking down the streets would soon look at Soviet tanks encircled by an enthusiastic crowd of Jewish youth, although I doubt that cause and effect were linked in their minds. Chaim Grade describes scenes of such joyous welcome on the streets of Wilno in his autobiographical book, *My Mother's Sabbath Days* (translated from the Yiddish), and since he was an honest writer and tried to be objective, he also describes how he went to the Cathedral that same day and how sorry he felt for the deathly sad crowd of the faithful assembled there.

My close acquaintance with Mackiewicz began in 1940 when Juozas Keliuotis, the editor of *Naujoji Romuva*, helped me reach Wilno, which by then belonged to Lithuania—a trip, by the way, that I considered to be part of my plan to reach Warsaw. Mackiewicz was editor of *The Daily Gazette*, one of the two Polish dailies that were being published in Wilno at the time. The assistant editor was my friend from Żagary, Teodor Bujnicki. I became a contributor to that paper, as did many writers, both locals and refugees, among them Światopełk Karpiński and Janusz Minkiewicz. Many years later, taking issue with my essay on Bujnicki, "On a Certain Recent Experiment and the Executed Bujnicki" (1954), Mackiewicz did not accept my description of his program as the defense of a "Polish canton" within the boundaries of Lithuania. It is indisputable that neither a "Polish canton" nor Poland nor Lithuania could have satisfied that heir of the Grand Duchy, since he wanted to follow in the footsteps of Ludwik Abramowicz. In practice, however, the program of *The Daily Gazette* led to such a solution and that is what differentiated it from *The Wilno Courier*, which became the voice of Polish orthodoxy as professed by the majority of Polish Wilno; for them, Wilno's incorporation into Lithuania was quite simply a Lithuanian occupation.

I never became close friends with Mackiewicz because we were of different generations and different mind-sets. I respected him as a writer and also as a man of goodwill who did what he could, and I never lost that respect. Which didn't prevent me from pondering the twists and turns of his destiny. Among the gentry of the Grand Duchy there were many sanguine troublemakers (I would count his brother Stanisław among them), but there was also a type of quiet but impassioned troublemaker, who would never give up. That's exactly how I picture Józef. The question arises: To what extent does a self-directed, high-handed individual, convinced that right is on his side, have the duty or the right to go against public opinion? It takes a great effort to forget what that opinion represents, and our sympathy or antipathy for it, but only then does the question of the social role of conformity acquire any power. Mackiewicz was stuck in his Wilno social circle of gentry like himself—former cavalry officers in the 1920 war, now ordinary bureaucrats, but also duelers and hunters, like his friend Michał Pawlikowski from the Minsk region, who edited a hunter's supplement to *The Word* under the title "Hear the Hunting Horns." Nonetheless, he struggled to break out of the mold. Powerfully influenced by the Russian Gymnasium and by his own fanatical interest as a schoolboy in books on zoology and ornithology (in this, we were similar), he was a naturalist by education and by his habits of observation. It may be that that positivistic training developed his skepticism toward "Polish Wilno." He incurred the displeasure of that Wilno from the very first issues of *The Daily Gazette*, publishing articles in which his despair and rage at the September defeat were poured out in furious attacks against interwar Poland as a whole, which did not leave one stone unturned. He did not like either Piłsudski or his presumed successors, but he went too far when he found a collaborator in the person of Piotr Kownacki, a "nationalist," and joined him in mocking the ranks of the "colonels," even though he had nothing else in common with Kownacki. This had the appearance of picking on defeated Poland to please his Lithuanian employers. *The Daily Gazette*, consistently butchered by the censorship and accused of subversive tendencies by the Lithuanians (why all that insidious talk about the Grand Duchy?), supplied the grounds for the defamatory arguments swirling around it in which the unspoken accusation was "collaboration with the occupier." In other words, Mackiewicz displayed a talent for presenting himself in such a way as to be attacked on both sides. This would be repeated later. Undoubtedly, feelings of rage and bitterness after the defeat were universal and he gave vent to them out of anxiety, not to please anyone. But the majority, even though they felt the same way, controlled themselves, because it wasn't nice to wash dirty linen in public at such a sad moment.

During that brief period when it was incorporated into neutral Lithuania, Wilno was jammed with refugees and was subjected to intensive Lithuanianization by force of statute and, if necessary, clubs. (The people who only recently had been beating Jews were now being beaten themselves for singing in Polish in church, though they were not the only ones who were beaten for using Polish.) With the industrious Lithuanians in charge, the city was a land of milk and honey; it had marvelous restaurants and cafés where hard currency was traded, passports and visas were purchased, trips to the West were planned. Most of all, it was a city of the most varied rumors and always bad news. Lithuania, surrounded by hostile powers, but appearing to be an island of salvation, attracted unfortunates who were ready to risk their lives by illegally crossing the "green border,"* but once they found themselves where they had dreamed of being, they realized they were in a trap. For a

* Crowds of people from areas occupied by the Soviets in 1939 attempted to reach neutral Lithuania by crossing the "green border" separating the states. The penalty for those caught without a permit by the Soviet guards was usually eight years in the gulag.

while, planes still flew from Kaunas to the West across neutral Sweden. I myself registered with the unofficial Polish representative in Kaunas, was deemed qualified, and already had my ticket when the flights were ended. (The delegates of the Polish government-in-exile, in Paris at that time, had facilitated air travel through neutral Sweden for young men who planned to join the Polish military units in France.)

I don't believe that I was particularly concerned about the Polish–Lithuanian tensions, although my friendship with Keliuotis, who organized Polish–Lithuanian meetings—that is, meetings of representative Poles and Lithuanians intended to reduce tensions—should have engaged me in that direction. *Nota bene*: Keliuotis, from Kaunas, did not know Polish and we communicated in French during my visit to Kaunas in 1938. (His studies in Paris turned out to be poor preparation for long years of imprisonment in the Soviet gulag.) The enormity and danger of events deprived the Polish–Lithuanian squabbling of significance, and I think I simply shrugged it off. In his above-mentioned essay, Mackiewicz accuses me of distorting the truth when I say that "a lot of the hatred between Lithuanians and Poles has been forgotten." He believes that in Wilno, owing to the nationalistic, unwise policy of the Lithuanian authorities, the enmity of the Polish-speaking population was intensifying. Locally, yes. Nevertheless, unrelated to the partisanship on both sides there is the basic fact of how the Lithuanian people behaved during the September defeat, and also, as I have said, the inappropriateness, even the ridiculousness, of nationalistic quarrels at such a historical juncture.

I can't re-create my thoughts from that time. It was one of my phases of intense, almost psychosomatic, pain, and externally, of activity in the service of a single obsession. I could not write poetry, which is, for me, sufficient proof that I was sick; instead, I expended all my energy on efforts to get Janka out of Warsaw and to take her to the West, but one after the other, the borders turned out to be too dangerous or impossible. Enough preoccupations to avoid clear thinking. Anyway, who could think clearly? The shock of September 1939 was so great that it took time for that experience to be assimilated.

So, Wilno was murky. But not so murky that I lost my political options. My collaboration with *The Daily Gazette* can be explained to a significant extent by the person of Bujnicki, because it was he who was in charge of the literary side of the paper. Aside from that, the "regionalists" were truly closer to me than the orthodox patriotic Poles, and as a blood relative of Oscar Milosz, who wanted Wilno for Lithuania, I could not generate any feelings of hostility toward the "Lithuanian occupation." The government of the Lithuanian state, however, didn't make matters easy for us in any way; on the contrary, it followed a stupid policy in Wilno, acting against its own interests. Their division of Wilno residents into various categories labeled the majority as "immigrating population" or "refugees"; even people whose great-grandfathers were from Wilno were included in these groups. The right to hold Lithuanian residency papers was granted only to people who could prove they had lived in the city in particular years, beginning with 1920, I think, while the "nationality" rubric included in these papers was aimed at limiting the number of people entitled to all the rights of citizenship. I preferred residency papers to refugee papers, but what nationality could I give if not Polish? Anyway, I would soon destroy my papers when I crossed over to the General Government, because they conflicted with my forged documents.

In Rudnicki's café across from the Cathedral, suddenly a loud clanking of iron, the invasion of Soviet tanks. To this day, that remains one of the saddest events in my life, because I had a clear awareness of the inevitable and a hideous feeling that I was witnessing the trampling of a defenseless people without any consideration for the law of nations. That is exactly what the awareness of calamity is like. France fell at exactly the same time. Two monsters divided up the spoils, initiating, as it seemed to me then, a thousand-year reign over Europe.

What would have happened had I not escaped from Wilno? I would have published in *Wilno Prawda* like Bujnicki, or been sent away to join the polar bears. I was too well known there. Although Janusz Minkiewicz and others ran a literary cabaret and survived. I know nothing about the contents of their texts, of course. What followed after the invasion has been faithfully described in Mackiewicz's novel *The Road to Nowhere*.

So, I didn't see Mackiewicz from 1940 until the summer of 1944, when he made his way to Warsaw. In other words, I was not witness to his activities in German-occupied Wilno. The accusations of collaboration came from the same circles that were furious with Mackiewicz in the 1939–40 period; in other words, the trail had already been blazed. When a kangaroo court judges one of the leading Polish novelists, without granting him the right of self-defense, it may be worthwhile to consider what views he expressed in his writings, and who his accusers were.

Mackiewicz is never devious in what he writes. We can believe him when he explains the misunderstanding around a surname (in his article " 'Editor' *Bohdan* Mackiewicz"). We can also believe him when he lays out his position in his novels and post-war essays. In my opinion, his position was so absolutely non-Polish, so opposed to what was considered a given in the minds of the vast majority of Poles, that even were he immaculate it would have been necessary to pin some guilt on him. The orthodox Polish view of the war assumed loyalty to the Western Allies and the return of the Polish state to its 1939 boundaries. That's what "Polish Wilno" thought, as did its armed forces, the Home Army. For Mackiewicz, those were the fantasies of a national minority who wanted to consider as permanent the temporary situation of the interwar years. In that part of Europe, victory would either be Germany's or Russia's, and the Lithuanians knew, as did the Belorussians and Ukrainians, that they could not rely on the West. The population in the territories of the former Grand Duchy (with the exception of Poles and Jews) greeted the Germans enthusiastically, and as we know, it was only the incomprehensible German lunacy that led to a reversal of those sentiments. What remained was Communism, which Mackiewicz considered a great evil. He placed the struggle against Communism in first place, above national interests, and accused the Home Army of acting on behalf of the Allies, thereby, in essence, aiding the victory of their ally, Moscow. Now, many decades later, it should be recognized that that realistic evaluation was a very good outline of the fate of Poland, which, opposing both, the one enemy and the other, placed its hope on the distant and indifferent Western Allies. Unfortunately, this realistic evaluation served only Mackiewicz the writer well, making possible his unrelenting depiction of history's blind alleys. As a political program, it was worthless. No one, not even Mackiewicz himself, would have supported participation in the German crusade, which was thoroughly compromised by the Germans themselves.

From his writings it emerges that if he could have resurrected tsarist Russia he would have done so, because he considered the liberalized Russia a state that respected law and tolerance, especially in comparison with what succeeded it everywhere in the wake of the First World War. Here, too, he took a completely opposite tack from Polish opinion, which is eager to place an equals sign between Russia and Communism. It's hard to find this surprising; for example, the Soviet policy of mass deportation of Poles from Belorussian and Ukrainian territory which was initiated immediately after the Revolution was only the continuation of nineteenth-century tsarist policy, except that the implementation was much crueler. Mackiewicz categorically rejected the identification of Communism as a specifically Russian creation and felt no enmity at all toward the Russian people, who were simply the victims of the calamity of Communist power.

It is hard to guess what he would have advised in Wilno under the German occupation. Were it a question of war between Russia and Germany, he would certainly not have hesitated to take a stand on the Russian side, but since a great game was being played for the liberation of nations from Communism, he appeared to be, theoretically, a proponent of some sort of waiting game or pact with the Germans, which, frankly speaking, is no different than collaboration. That much can be deduced from his post-war writings, because he was not an active collaborator in Wilno.

One of the main arguments offered by those who condemn Mackiewicz unconditionally is in Paweł Jasienica's article, "The Moral Remains of a Squire from Kresy," written by someone who was in Wilno at the time and who says, himself, "I served in the Home Army, I was assigned to propaganda, and one of my duties was an attentive reading of all the published rags." I have gone to the trouble of finding Jasienica's *Traces of Skirmishes*, the book in which this article appears. Jasienica, as we know, is a pseudonym. It is the name used by my friend from the Academic Vagabonds' Club in Wilno, Lech Beynar (whom we called "Bacchus"), a history student at the time. His name is by no means Jewish, as a whispering campaign asserted, but Tatar. Beynar was a descendant of the Tatar nobility, but he was not a Muslim. The name Lech, along with the surname Jasienica which he adopted later on, testifies to his own and his family's Catholic–Polish devotions.

If a serious historian and witness of events can write something so criminally thoughtless, then what can be said about other people? Beynar was a righteous and fearless man; unable to agree with what was clear to Mackiewicz, he fought to the bitter end in an anti-Soviet guerrilla detachment and was sentenced to death after the war. It seems he was saved by Bolesław Piasecki, the head of Pax. I don't recall that Beynar ever declared himself politically in our Academic Vagabonds' Club. We had only one nationalist, apparently—Kazimierz Hałaburda; he was deported and died of dysentery in the Soviet gulag. Of the other club members, our senior member, Gasiulis, was executed by the Soviet authorities for tearing down propaganda posters; Bujnicki was shot for collaborating with those same authorities; Jędrychowski was "elected" to the Lithuanian parliament and voted for the incorporation of Lithuania into the Soviet Union.

Beynar's moral indignation is sincere and by repeating after Joseph Conrad (*The Heart of Darkness*) "The horror! the horror!" he certainly expressed the sentiments of many of his generation. But if we examine the article more closely, there is little to it beyond an emotional state.

The first accusation touches on Mackiewicz's character. Beynar accuses him of cowardice: if he counseled resistance to Communism even at the price of the destruction of the entire Polish nation, why didn't he take to the forests (as Beynar himself did)? For those who knew Mackiewicz, this is only a demagogic device. The second accusation relates to the novel *The Road to Nowhere*, which Beynar calls worthless. Why? Because other nationalities are depicted favorably in it, while the Poles are defamed, and there is no mention in it of the ZWZ, or Union of Armed Struggle, from which the Home Army later developed. Also, there is no expression of love for one's native land in this book, as there is in *Pan Tadeusz* (?). But *The Road to Nowhere* exists and can defend itself. The attack on it demonstrates why it is hard to be a Polish novelist. If in the last century someone had depicted Poland the way Gogol depicted Russia in *Dead Souls*, he would definitely have earned the label "scoundrel." The third accusation is that Mackiewicz published in a groveling newspaper. He certainly did not have to do that. But what did he publish? Several chapters of *The Road to Nowhere*, which Beynar considered a lampoon.

A peculiar company collaborated in the attack on Mackiewicz; it included patriots and hidden agents of the perpetrators of the Katyń massacre. It was in the best interests of the latter that a witness should be denounced as a Fascist and collaborator. I have just looked into my file of Mackiewicz's letters to me from 1969–70. They are in reference to my efforts to interest American and German publishers in his books. Those efforts met with little success, because in every instance some Pole would get involved, anxious to kill any intention of publishing his book. Mackiewicz and his wife, Barbara Toporska, also a fine writer, lived in extreme poverty. I must agree with what Mackiewicz writes in one of his letters: that compared to them, Gombrowicz was extraordinarily well off.

JANUARY 24, 1988

Mackiewicz paid for his trip to Katyń in 1943 at the invitation of the German authorities. Ferdynand Goetel was the other Polish writer who made the trip. People in Warsaw remembered Goetel's open praise of Fascism before the war; in 1940 he had evinced cowardly leanings toward collaboration, because he registered as a free professional (writer) and urged his colleagues to do the same. A lot of people registered, thinking it was safer that way. Goetel, however, had a good understanding of the social pressures and demands of the patriotic code, and went no further in his conciliatory gestures toward the Germans. Even though he went to Katyń, no one in the emigration accused him later on of being a collaborator. But Mackiewicz, who was at odds with everyone, who did not take public opinion into consideration and was temperamentally litigious, only intensified people's unfavorable opinions of him by going to Katyń, and no one seemed to care that he made the trip with the permission of the Polish underground authorities.

Should the Poles, in the name of a higher diplomatic rationale, have refused to believe anything the Germans said and have added the Katyń graves to the other crimes of Hitler? That would have demanded the suppression of one's moral protest, an almost superhuman discipline. The Soviet state went to great pains to convince the world of its innocence, and its allies took it at its word, or pretended to, so that the Poles were left to stand alone—with the truth, but with a truth proclaimed by the German enemies. And who would have believed them, since they were known for their anti-Soviet "complexes"? What a paradoxical equation, worthy of philosophical analysis!

Not long ago, at the home of some acquaintances, I happened to see on their bookshelf a thick book by the American correspondent in Moscow, Harrison E. Salisbury, *Journey for Our Times: A Memoir*. I found the excerpt that reports on the trip by Western diplomats and journalists to Katyń; I read it and almost threw up.

Kathy Harriman was in Moscow with her father, now Ambassador to Moscow. She had a job with the Office of War Information and acted as her father's hostess, bringing life and gaiety to a banal scene. She turned the embassy ballroom into a badminton court and found a cache of old Hollywood films in the Spaso attic. They were so brittle they broke a dozen times during a showing, but we ran them just the same.

Kathy was present when the Katyn announcement was made and said she'd like to go along. The Russians promptly invited her and John Melby, a young embassy attaché. They laid on a special train—international wagon-lits, a mahogany-paneled dining car, quantities of caviar, champagne, butter, white bread, smoked salmon, cake, beef

Stroganov, cutlets Kiev—and we were off to look into one of the war's great tragedies.

The Russians had recaptured Smolensk in September 1943 and now they were about to explode their own propaganda bomb. The Western correspondents were invited as part of the stage setting. I don't think the participation of Kathy Harriman and John Melby was calculated U.S. policy. I think it was spur-of-the-moment impulse, but it is true that Averell Harriman was fed up with the "London" Poles and when we came back from Katyn he told me he had been convinced for a long time that the Poles had fallen for a German atrocity story and what we had seen strengthened his conviction.

I am deeply grateful to the Soviet press department for arranging this expedition. It was (and remains) a vivid lesson in Soviet methodology. There was the embarrassing extravagance of the train, outfitted with snowy linen, perfumed soaps, down quilts, white-jacketed waiters, luxury fit for the Czar. In fact, it may have been one of the Czar's special trains. To sit in the dining car, tables laden with bottles, crystal and silver, plates heaped with *zakuski*, and look through lace curtains at wooden freight trains where wounded Red Army men, heads in bloody bandages, arms in splints, legs amputated, gazed from the next track, shivering around potbellied stoves, was almost too much.

The author of this testimony, like the other journalists, was not convinced by the so-called proofs that were presented to them. Therefore, he refrained from expressing an opinion as to whose work Katyń was. But the American Ambassador in Moscow, Averell Harriman, let himself be persuaded. And having an American Ambassador as an enemy certainly intensified the catastrophic situation of the Polish government in London.

Józef Mackiewicz saw the Katyń graves and wrote what he saw. By chance, he was also a witness of the Germans' murdering of the Jews in Ponary, and he wrote an objective report of that, too. As long as Polish writing exists, those two documents on the horror of the twentieth century should always be remembered, to provide a model for literature when it retreats too far from reality.

Mackiewicz was a realist in his writing, and in comparison with his passionate reconstruction of "what it was really like," other varieties of realism reveal their pallor or their falsehood. All lofty sophistication of literary discussions was alien to him, and he never thought about the insuperable distance between reality and words. Nor about the universally proclaimed death of the novel. Stubbornly old-fashioned, he wielded his language as an instrument, not permitting his style to isolate itself and to take precedence over his writing hand. The novel was for him a "mirror held up to the highway," and he took care to maintain absolute faithfulness of detail.

The Road to Nowhere and *You'd Better Not Speak Up* together form an epic of the end. It is the end of the Grand Duchy of Lithuania and its remnants which lasted until 1939, the end, too, of Wilno as a city with a Polish and Jewish population. There is no chronicle other than this novel. It is also a portrait of life under the Soviet regime from June 1940 to July 1941 (Germany's attack on its former ally) and under the German regime. The last chapters of the second novel offer a portrait of Warsaw in 1944, where Mackiewicz landed as a refugee from Wilno.

Mackiewicz's writings about the war are a total exception to the abundant Polish literature on that topic. A patriotic pattern is obligatory in that literature: the battle between Poles and Germans. Mackiewicz remained more or less indifferent to that pattern; we can discern in this indifference his personal distaste for generally accepted ideas and also the influence of multi-ethnic Wilno. Two fundamental Polish propositions clashed with each other in this century: the independence of Poland as the goal of all struggles and undertakings, and the abandonment of this independence in the name of Communist internationalism. Neither of them is recognized by Mackiewicz; more to the point, his attitude toward them is hostile. Those who discarded independence in the name of Communism, like Dembiński or Jędrychowski in Wilno, are in his opinion not only traitors to Poland but also agents of a state that brings misfortune to the people of many nations. On the other hand, the proponents of independence (this is the source of his negative evaluation of the Home Army) are blinded by their concentration on a struggle with the German invader and do not realize that, by counting on the victory of the Western Allies, they are preparing the victory of these Allies' partner, Russia. Mackiewicz speaks out in his novels and his journalistic writings as a proponent of anti-Soviet internationalism, or of an anti-Communist international. Serious consequences, including literary consequences, derive from this position, because his characters are not divided according to nationalistic criteria. His sympathetic characters include Poles, Lithuanians, Belorussians, Germans, anti-Soviet Russians, all embroiled in various underground movements, potentially participants in a collective, international resistance to the system.

It is impossible to treat seriously everything that Mackiewicz the anti-Communist has written. Some of his articles are absolutely obsessive and border on paranoia, of the sort that sees agents everywhere. Thus, in putting together a selection of his journalistic writings, one would have to remember that he paid for the constancy of his views with fantasizing and even madness. All writers probably undergo a sifting out of obvious errors after their death, and the thought of this ought to caution us against appearing draped in the toga of a stern judge.

$\mathcal{J}$ANUARY 27, 1988

On board a plane to St. Louis.

I received two moving letters yesterday, one from W., the other from M. These women classmates, my own age, from the Faculty of Law at Stefan Batory University in Wilno, not only lead me back to the past along a thread of sentiment, they exist as individuals who are so precious that I consider myself fortunate to be able to think about them. For there were some unusual girls in our city, and how impoverished is everyone whose memory cannot call up such estimable human beings. I am saying this now when they are gray-haired women, raising their grandchildren, and I have some knowledge of their lives filled with mistakes and tragedies.

I was never close to M., but I used to watch her. I consider it a point in my favor that the thick eyeglasses she wore for her nearsightedness did not prevent me from recognizing her appeal. She was charming, with an alluring build, but of course there wasn't any foolishness in her head, since she was in furious pursuit of great goals. She and her sister belonged to the inner circle around Jędrychowski and Dembiński, the *In Plain Words* and *Karta* groups, and later, in post-war Poland, were among the recognized personalities in the "Wilno group." They came from a very Catholic family and discovered in Communism a new religion, just like Zosia Westfalewicz, Dembiński's wife, whose sister was a nun.

M.'s letter, written in her bold, decisive handwriting, includes a commentary on my poem ("Bypassing Rue Descartes") about breaking a taboo by throwing a stone at a water snake, which she discovered in the Polish edition of *The Witness of Poetry*. She adds, "Since we're on the subject of water snakes, let me tell you about fish. When I was a child I once entered the kitchen while the fish that our housekeeper had scaled while they were still alive were thrashing about. I always felt very close to animals. So I started killing them (out of compassion), smashing their heads against the wall. I was covered with blood. That was a situation for which there was no good solution. But I wonder if later, as a grown woman, I wasn't like those alumni of the Sorbonne."

She gives her own and her group's history in a few sentences. (Our Faculty of Law produced outstanding minds.) Compassion for people led her to commitments that were not a good solution. And the graduates of the Sorbonne, educated on Sartre's philosophy, were practicing a cannibalistic terror in Cambodia. M. continues:

> To make this more cheerful, I'll jot down how I remember you. The ramp in Śniadecki Auditorium; you're running at the head of a group of workers and students, chasing a nationalist fighting squad that wanted to break up an evening of poetry of various nationalities. You've got that werewolf face you knew how to put on, teeth bared, eyes bulging; you're holding the pieces of a chair. And howling.
>
> Another image: We are standing near the table in the Lawyers' Association, arguing about something, I don't remember what, probably politics, because you tell me maliciously, "You have always been and will always remain a zealot." Obviously, you must have struck home, since I remember it. I have lived through two devotions, but I no longer have the strength for a third. This is the result not only of old age but also, among other things, of the literature that has kept me company since childhood.

In another part of the letter, she speaks of Brodsky's speech in Stockholm in praise of literature: "Joseph Brodsky said at the Nobel ceremony exactly what I wanted to write to you, only much more beautifully."

My thoughts about them, those girls from Wilno, who today are old women, really cannot be conveyed in prose; it is all so loaded with abbreviations and so multi-layered that it would require a particular type of love poetry. Time would probably retreat in it to the years when we were in the lower classes at the Gymnasium, when M. was killing fish in the kitchen and W. wore the sailor-suit uniform of the Nazarene Sisters' school. Most likely, these stubbornly recurring images of community throughout childhood express my longing for a return, for *apokatastasis*, and also a longing for new beginnings, for the moment when nothing had to be what it would later become, when (imagining an entirely different epoch, different customs, etc.) we did not have to be parted. Who knows, perhaps such love poetry originates in dreams about Swedenborg's "angelic sexuality," in the desire for complete identification, for a virtual transformation into the other, not asexually, but by comprehending the other's sex as well.

It would be best not to write about W.'s letter, in which she worries about my health. Because I would have to draw out too many threads. I am always struck by her sad tendency toward self-deprecation; according to her, it is not true that she possesses exceptional virtues of mind and character. She always refers to herself, her illness, and her probably imminent death, with a shrug of the shoulders, carelessly.

The evening of poetry of various nationalities, which M. reminded me of. In opposition to "nationalist" Wilno, we had various contacts, and I think that some of their traces are remembered; for example, in 1972 in a train from Rotterdam to Paris, on the way back from a convention of poets, when we shared a flask of vodka with Abraham Sutzkever, who survived the Wilno ghetto and is the author of a book about the German crimes in Wilno. I also think that those contacts explain, at least in part, the secret of Władysław Ryńca. For how does one become a millionaire during a war by starting a transportation firm? Ryńca was from Silesia. He was in Wilno as a student—yet another of my law-faculty classmates. At the university, he became one of the chief activists in our anti-Endek bloc in the elections to the Students' Union; he also distinguished himself as a superb speaker. Later, he remained on the fringes of the group and did not draw close to Communism. I cannot say what he did from 1934 to 1939 (law practice?), and so I probably won't be able to figure out how he was transformed from a poor miner's son into a financial potentate, operating since 1941 where?— on the Wilno–Minsk–Warsaw line; that is, in ethnically mixed territories, precisely those described by Józef Mackiewicz in his novel *You'd Better Not Speak Up*. It seems to me that one of the factors worthy of our attention was the enormous quantity of ready cash in Wilno, in gold and dollars; it didn't pay to invest in anything. Ryńca's partner, Krywitzki, was a Jew from Riga; it's possible he's the one who mobilized their capital. Krywitzki worked in the firm's offices in Wilno and Minsk, which were liquidated as the front approached, and in 1944 he turned up in Warsaw, where I got to know him. He was protected by good Aryan papers; in general, Wilno had one of the most artistic printing plants for false documents. From Warsaw, not waiting for the Russians to arrive, he left for Prague, Czechoslovakia; he died there in circumstances that I know nothing about. Another factor in Ryńca's success was certainly his diplomatic genius and lack of ethnic prejudices. The firm was protected as a supplier to the army and had very highly placed Germans on its payroll. In actuality, it dealt in large-scale hard-currency operations on the black market. And its trucks kept rolling, loaded with everything but supplies for the army; with weapons, of course, but not destined for the Germans. Ryńca belonged to our socialist "Freedom," and through it to the "London underground," in which the ability to make use of such a transportation network was crucial. He transported money and arms for Home Army detachments, but I suspect that he had insured the road to Minsk, which led through forests under the control of Soviet partisans, by appropriate arrangements and services rendered. His trucks also transported Jews who were rescued from the Wilno ghetto, and not for money, if I can judge by the case of Seweryn Tross. Before the war, Tross, like my brother Andrzej, wrote for the journal *Plowing the Fallow Land*, and wound up in Wilno as a refugee from Warsaw. My brother hid his colleague for a while in our parents' apartment in Wilno, in Zarzecze, on Popowska Street. Then Tross and his wife were loaded on one of Ryńca's trucks and deposited in Warsaw, where I found a good hideout for them. Unfortunately, they died in the Warsaw Uprising, but not as Jews, simply as civilians exposed to German bombs. Everything the firm did was criminal from the German point of view, and it is hard to believe that there wasn't a single mishap. Ryńca's genius was evident here, too. He had put together a staff (I remember his drivers) on whom he could rely absolutely, cemented on healthier foundations than the relations between a boss and his underlings. The familial bonds of this group of "our boys" from Wilno ruled out denunciations, which were the most frequent cause of catastrophes.

I wrote about Ryńca in *Native Realm*, identifying him by the letter W., but I go back to him now because he truly impressed me, and to this day I am still trying to understand how he did all that. After the war, he founded a publishing firm as planned, and would undoubtedly have become the master of the publishing market; however, the enterprise was destroyed immediately by the regulations against private initiative. Then he became a lawyer and specialized in inheritance cases, including American ones, profiting from his connections with the "Wilno group" which enabled him to obtain passports for trips abroad.

JANUARY 30, 1988

At first, when we have to learn something new, it takes a lot of nervous energy; on the other hand, if we already have some experience, we only expend physical energy, which is a lot easier. This is true of plowing, of mowing, and also of the public recitation of poetry and of having to appear in the role of a film star. In St. Louis I read my poems, autographed books, allowed myself to be photographed, while in my thoughts I was somewhere far away. But where? In Ludwik Koniński's *Observations*, his diary from the years 1940–42, which is a profoundly tragic diary because throughout that entire period he was trying to convince himself that God exists, that evil does not have absolute power, but he was not very successful. I shall return to Koniński later; but now I must add something to my chapter on Mackiewicz, which was interrupted by digressions.

We won't get very far by judging Mackiewicz according to political criteria. Let us agree that he was a maniac, a Don Quixote, a utopian; nonetheless, his political passion enlivens his writing, which is strictly realistic but at the same time wants to serve, wants to be prose with a thesis. Those theses derived from his decency and his moral indignation. He kept on asking, "How is this possible?" He wanted to be a voice crying in the wilderness when everyone else was silent. Fortunately, he was not a politician.

The final chapters of *You'd Better Not Speak Up* reflect the differences in atmosphere between Wilno and Warsaw as Mackiewicz, newly arrived from Wilno in the summer of 1944, sensed them. His portrayal of Warsaw—crazy, carefree, indifferent to the shooting that was going on here and there, proud of its heroism, joyous because victory was near—is accurate. For Mackiewicz, this was the lightheartedness of children who don't want to know that in just another minute nothing will be left of their games, just as nothing was left in Wilno.

After his arrival in Warsaw, Mackiewicz expressed a desire to meet with me and Janusz Minkiewicz. We had a long conversation. On his side, it was the question, "How is this possible?" which he formulated in many different ways. So, now that it is clear to everyone that the Allies are far away, nothing's going to happen? No attempt, even at the last moment, to reach an understanding with the losing Germans, who by now are inclined to make concessions? After all, it would be possible to publish a journal now, to speak the truth about the Soviet occupation, the truth suppressed by the Polish underground as a service to London and, indirectly, to Moscow. We listened to him in disbelief, as one listens to a man who is not in complete possession of his senses. And we laughed at him. We told him that he had no understanding of the local mood, that no one would work with him on such a journal, that no one shakes hands with the collaborators Emil Skiwski and Feliks Rybicki, and that if he started publishing such a journal he would be labeled a traitor. Mackiewicz didn't mention the three issues of the newspaper *Alarm* which he and his wife apparently published in the spring of 1944.

I don't think I am making things worse for Mackiewicz by reporting that in that one instance he did propose collaboration, from which it might follow that he actually did collaborate earlier. Because it doesn't follow. He was in despair at the time, perhaps in even greater despair than Minkiewicz and I, because we still nourished some hopes.

It's a good thing that I mentioned Władysław Ryńca's activities in the Wilno–Minsk–Warsaw triangle, because they suggest the extraordinary density and complexity of human fates in that region under the German occupation. Their description ought to contradict Polish images of the period, which are immensely distorted by patriotic conventions. The reality of the war years in those territories has been thoroughly concealed and refashioned by official historians. It is a fact that people there greeted the Germans as liberators, and were it not for their insanity, the Germans would have had the local people totally on their side. The way things played out, the model of partisans and collaborators captures only a tiny fraction of the truth. It was a three-way game in which the vast majority of the population zigged and zagged, seeking insurance with both sides. In addition, there were also independent enclaves, separate statelets, as it were, cobbled together by little war lords. Mackiewicz's perspective was affected by his knowledge of all this; his objectivity was well served.

*J*ANUARY 31, 1988

Mackiewicz's novels inspire a certain skepticism vis-à-vis literature, which is forever being dressed up in some sauce or other, in the obligatory sauce of the moment, be it fashion, ideology, politics, or what have you. His books are filled with lively narrative; they hold your attention, so that "you can't tear yourself away," in other words, they fulfill all the conditions that used to be indispensable when the novel occupied the place that has since been taken over by film and television. Most likely, professional and non-professional literature have always existed. No one wanted to admit to reading Mackiewicz, both because he was so old-fashioned in a literary sense and because he was a dreadful reactionary, but people read him until their ears burned. And, in my opinion, he crushed his colleagues who wrote in much more elegant prose. He crushed them artistically. The Soviet soldier's saying applies to them: *Frantsuzy w shelkakh, no voinu proigrali* (The French wore silk, but they lost the war). His prose is tight, spare, functional; one sees what he describes, especially the landscape of his region. None of the Polish writers I know wrote like that. Yet, compared to him, both Bolesław Prus and Stefan Żeromski were professional writers. A yeoman squire, as I have called him, one of those stubborn, disdainful, passionate silent types, he wrote out of spite. Out of spite for the entire world that calls black white and in which there is no one who dares to exercise his veto. And it is precisely in that passion of his that the secret of his style resides.

$\mathscr{F}$EBRUARY 1, 1988

Karol Ludwik Koniński. I never met him and he wasn't within the orbit of my interests; I only knew his name. He wasn't one of my generation, and anyway, he published in the "national" journals—those journals, in other words, that were not considered serious in a literary sense. Now, I consider him a rarity in Catholic Poland—a man with a metaphysical temperament, like his friend Stanisław Ignacy Witkiewicz. Except that Witkiewicz thought Koniński's religious faith was an opiate, and it is possible that he used Koniński as the model for his neo-Catholic characters who pretend, without much success, that they are believers.

Koniński's diary, the manuscript of which has been deciphered by Bronisław Mamoń and published under the title *Observations*, moved me profoundly because it touches on fundamental questions, the most important questions for me and, in my opinion, for all twentieth-century civilization. I even experience pangs of conscience because I am wasting time occupying myself with something else. In short, it appears that we are probably witnesses and participants in an era of revolutionary change, which is the equivalent of the transition from paganism to Christianity under the Roman Empire. That was a slow process, lasting several centuries; it was by no means brought to an end by Constantine's proclaiming Christianity the state religion. We cannot permit ourselves much latitude in achieving a clear understanding of what is transpiring now. There are signs, but it is uncertain that they can be deciphered accurately. All my life I have tried to determine their meaning, and I continue to do this now in California. In academic circles, the number of people who profess a Christian faith is small; my students display ignorance of the simplest concepts deriving from biblical tradition, and indifference or even enmity toward religion. The scientific world is secular and it mainly professes a secular humanism, along with, for variety, the dreams of socialist terror that from time to time visit the freethinking graduates of libraries and laboratories. And yet the Christian churches, right next door to these temples of reason, are filled on Sunday, and no one knows to what laws this coexistence is subject. It seems to me that statistics are not important here, although the number of people who attend church is constantly declining in the West. What is more important are the reasons for their choice. This is something that has preoccupied me for years: people whom we call believers undoubtedly have a different way of thinking than believers of several centuries ago.

FEBRUARY 4, 1988

Koniński was a philosopher of pain, the pain of humans and of animals. A professed Catholic, he struggled with himself and tried to be a Catholic, but there was still a great deal of his father in him; his father was a Protestant and an agnostic who used to say that if someone did create this world it was probably Satan. The younger Koniński accepts the proposition that faith in God should not be purchased at the price of renouncing reason, nor should it do violence to our conscience. The eighteenth-century Deists also made these assumptions, but it was easier in that optimistic century to reconcile belief in God with reason and moral sentiment. Koniński wrote his diary in Rudawa, on the outskirts of Cracow; thus, he was in the vicinity of Auschwitz during the years of daily news about arrests and deaths, in the midst of general hopelessness, because the Germans were victorious on all fronts. The diary ends in 1942, probably during the illness that ended Koniński's life a year later. These conditions intensify his fundamental problem.

God created a world that "wallows in evil," and he remains indifferent to suffering. If, as people say, God is love, then there is a contradiction, both logical and moral, between his indifference and his love. What kind of love permits Auschwitz and *sees* what is happening there? True, in Dante, Hell, too, was created by Eternal Love, but for us it is absolutely unacceptable to condemn people to eternal torments; we think of a Christian Hell as a monstrosity. From the moment a man asks for salvation for himself and is spared suffering, temporal suffering, for instance, he has the right to inquire why he alone has this privilege while others beside him are dying in torment. As for eternal salvation, some receive grace and others don't, some are predestined for salvation and others go to eternal damnation.

As I followed Koniński's efforts at wriggling out of these contradictions, I understood—probably for the first time this clearly—that anyone who wants to think about religion in a really serious way must inevitably come up with heretical ideas. Koniński is prepared to forego placing maximal demands on our minds and not to demand that religious truths stand the test of reason; they may be beyond reason, provided they do not contradict it. And also beyond our moral judgments, provided they do not contradict them. But the balancing act is not very successful. His God is not the Old Testament Creator who summons the world *ex nihilo*, a capricious and unpredictable potentate whose orders must be accepted on blind faith, even if they are obviously absurd. He prays to a different, bright God, who is love, who fights against evil, suffers, and demands our human cooperation. In the religion of this bright God there is no room for eternal damnation; there is also no room for predestination.

To be sure, these thoughts are not new. The Epicureans discovered a powerful alternative: considering how badly the world is organized, either the gods are omnipotent but they are not good, or they are good but they are not omnipotent. If, however, they are not omnipotent, it means that some element which is older, so to speak, than they are opposes them. Thus, one can go all the way back to the Epicureans in search of the sources of the later gnosis and Manichaeanism. A bright God struggles with the evil which the world, created not by God but by a lesser demiurge, abounds in. Next, in the second century we find in Marcion the opposition between the God of love incarnated in Christ and the demiurge known as Jehovah. Many centuries later, William Blake will call this angry potentate Nobodaddy. Koniński prays for faith, wants to believe at any price that God exists and acts, although his is another sort of God, not an indifferent Creator. In other words, and getting into theology now, the Polish writer is drawing close to gnostic explanations, which may be inevitable in our century.

FEBRUARY 5, 1988

"If I must choose Catholicism or humanism, I choose humanism. If the Christianity that is able to harmonize with humanism is 'Protestantism,' I am a Protestant."

Koniński really makes things difficult for himself. For, as he says, "the meaning of my faith in God is that I should have hope that the noble and just yearning of the human heart will be fulfilled." And elsewhere: "God is the postulate of conscience! And only then am I seeking external possibilities for making that postulate plausible."

"I do not reject miracles if conscience affirms them. I do not reject miracles because the soul yearns for them, because I do not know by what law Grace subjugates Nature. God is deep and rich, because reality is fantastic."

". . . in Catholic Poland, where no one takes seriously either religion or atheism."

"A fine Good Father, who sees his child crawling into a well and does not grab him; a fine righteous Judge, who injected the accused with the rabies bacillus and then punishes him for his rabies with eternal imprisonment at hard labor."

" 'My kingdom is not of this world' is the truth. This world is not the kingdom of God, but would Jesus Christ have renounced that kingdom in the future? 'Thy kingdom come.' The Gospels are full of perplexing riddles that, for a critical mind, make reading them like treading on broken glass: jumping from one elevated safe harbor to another elevated safe harbor. The Gospels look like a landscape in a sea of fog; here and there loom clear, comprehensible peaks, but they loom up from a bank of fog in whose depths no ones knows what is hidden, what dark caverns there may be."

"Why religion and not atheism, even if it be a gentlemanly atheism, heroic, magnificent, Christian? Because religion appears to be truer than atheism. Because somehow it is the emotions, the imagination, convincing our intellect. Because it is a mystical and metaphysical conviction that the cosmos is not flat and mechanical but deep and vital, that Reality is rich, infinitely and profoundly rich, and that there is room in it for hell and heaven. And if there is a heaven, then there is a God; a heaven devoid of God is meaningless, it is just another hell, a hell of boredom. Reality, however, is fascinating, it is divinely interesting. Everything in us that believes in a richer and interesting world is truer than that which believes in a boring world that can be fully explained by a law of physics, as atheism postulates and presupposes."

In the final analysis, then, Plato's Eros, that mediator between the gods and humans, seems to speak for Koniński.

"*Filosofia ancilla theologiae*: philosophy always follows faith, whether that faith is theistic or atheistic, monistic or pluralistic. Philosophy systematically elaborates a *fundamental conviction*, provides the arguments in its favor, and then proves it. One can also arrive at a conviction by way of philosophizing, but not by philosophizing systematically; rather, by following the impulses of imagination, the emotions, custom. The heart points the way for philosophizing."

"How much less demonic was the pagan world than the Christian world! It is not true that Christianity brought light into the world of art; it brought dread and the demonic."

". . . but this is what shocks me, amazes me, attracts me: Why was it not reason and the logic of calm melancholy that emerged victorious, but heroic illogicality instead, which overwhelms the mind with a mass of unanswerable questions, and heroism, which commands us to live as if an evildoer, an evildoing thief, is forever stealing into our home?"

As the center of his Christianity, Koniński chose Christ's words: "My Father worketh hitherto, and I work" (John 5:17); that is, he chose the heroic philosophy of collaboration with God.

"It is not humility we feel in relation to God but pride, for there is in us that which is better than anything in all the cosmos; there is in us that which is in God."

"The dreadful torment of faith that clings to mystery with bare fingers, just as a person who is slipping down a precipice clings to a mountain slope.

"Catholicism, aware of this dreadful torment of blind faith, hammers in the iron pitons of objective proofs, *ex creatione*; oh, if only those pitons hold, if only that logic proves immovable! Catholicism is aware of the dreadful loneliness of man who has been left alone with God (until God bends down over him, and He bends down very rarely), and therefore it has enfolded the man of faith in the powerful cloth of communal prayer, communal ritual, communal sacraments, organizations, collective suggestions, authority, an official 'scientific' theology, all in order that man should not remain face-to-face with the Hidden God, with the night of mysteries."

· · ·

And the Church's diplomacy?

"Well, Samaritan gentlemen of Rome and German bishops, what do you have to say for yourselves? If you were unable to intercede for the Catholic Poles, how could you intercede for the murderers of Our Lord Jesus?"

"From Poland a new Catholicism, a Catholicism with prayers like those in Krasiński, and so forth? With the idea of a synod? With a Slavic Pope, at least just once, elected by that synod? With a Pope who would not be an accomplished and craftily frail diplomat, but a powerful, good-natured patriarch, a guardian of all people of goodwill, an honest representative of a kind God on this sad earth? Are these daydreams?"

I have copied out these sentences of Koniński's because they are close to my heart, and because they capture the inner strivings of "metaphysical not-quite-believers," as he calls them. It cannot be excluded that, just as he says, the religion of the majority has endured for centuries by force of convention, ritual, the fear of hell, politics, the splendor of sculpture and architecture, while the few seekers have always wound up in heresies, which did not harm the Church at all. Even though his hope for the Church's renewal was fulfilled, Koniński would have been a good candidate for the prisons of the Holy Inquisition and might very well have been burned at the stake. It is true, though, that Catholicism has abandoned the rigors of its dogma, moving closer to the Protestant faiths and the Eastern Church, and even to Judaism, which for centuries has allowed the independent speculation of cabalists to flourish without exposing them to persecution.

The mainstay of the Catholic Church appears to be the faithful who refrain from questioning, either because it's of no interest to them or because they have surrounded themselves beforehand with an impregnable barrier.

FEBRUARY 7, 1988

Committed to poetry throughout my entire life, I have had to situate my religious "yes" and "no" within the history of poetry from the eighteenth century to the present. Poetry's separation from religion has always strengthened my conviction that the erosion of the cosmic-religious imagination is not an illusion and that the vast expanses of the planet that are falling away from Christianity are the external correlative of this erosion. At the same time, the persistent strong presence of Old and New Testament images in the poetry of many countries raises a question about what phase we are in. What is poetry advancing toward—the disappearance of "relics" or their strengthening? The nihilistic foundation of poetry, as of all civilization, doesn't diminish its role as an organ of "metaphysical" knowledge. For Koniński, the profundity, the richness, the vitality of the cosmos is on God's side. And that, after all, is exactly what poetry proclaims in defiance of scientific formulas; that is what nourishes poetry, that is what poetry explores.

FEBRUARY 8, 1988

Kot Jeleński once wrote that he does not know anyone for whom poetry has become as much a part of his being as it has for me. At best, this can mean that one of the personalities who inhabits me is connected with poetry in just this way. And the other personalities not at all. Now, when I am drawing up the balance sheet of my life, I have to admit that my distaste for psychoanalysis was eloquent; that is, it testified to my having a lot to hide. In fact, I have never known *liberation*. The eight years I spent in the King Zygmunt August High School and the influence of Father Leopold Chomski made such a strong impression on me that the most I could manage was rebellion, but rebellion is not the same as freedom. The polite boy inside me was pious, diligent, superstitious, conservative, always on the side of authority and against anarchy. I was unable to reach the core of my repressions and to use them masterfully; Gombrowicz was able to. There is too much respect in my books for conventional virtues, and against my will, I could often pass as a moralist. Instead of saying, "Yes, that's me, that's the way I am, and that's that," I felt ashamed of my lack of virtue. That lack of virtue was rooted in the conflicts in my relations with the collective, first of all with my schoolmates, and could have been labeled extreme individualism, since collective values did not appeal to me. Although I could contradict this by mentioning my happiness at being a member of an exclusive "circle" at the end of school and later on of the Żagary group, as if I were in the bosom of the Philomaths of the 1820s.

I still distrust psychiatrists and have never sought their help. I don't know all the various personalities who inhabit me; at most, I can guess at the identity of one or another of them. Therefore, I cannot analyze the central fact of my life story: Janka's and my marriage. At most, I can distinguish an emotional dimension, which should be left undisturbed, and a dimension of moral engagement. When we were both working at Polish Radio on Dąbrowski Square during the period of our friendship with Józef Czechowicz, the Laski center and the Catholic journal *Verbum* were on my horizon. In other words, the Catholicism of Maritain as opposed to the hideous Catholicism of *The Knight of the Immaculate Virgin*, *The Little Daily*, and the other publications devoted to vilifying Jews and Freemasons. I was kicked out of Polish Radio in Wilno because of a denunciation in *The Little Daily*. Not long ago, someone in America asked me about Father Kolbe's responsibility. I answered honestly, I hope, and without concealing his views, but also without making him responsible for everything that appeared in his paper.

Laski (the intellectual anti-rightist Catholic center) and *Verbum*. I knew Father Korniłowicz, and Janka and I had a conversation with him about our problems, but it wasn't very successful. Janka, in fact, had made a concession, because she distrusted the clergy. That she was different from the Polish intelligentsia (this was partly a matter of her origins—her family were descended from the common people) had contributed to my infatuation with her. Laski preceded our meeting and continued, more or less, for some time afterward. I had even published something in *Verbum*, and Jerzy Andrzejewski and I used to go on retreats there, without any good results, but at least we honestly confessed to each other that the ascetic, prayerful atmosphere produced in us a wild craving for vodka and steak. I think this happened earlier, before Janka, not during the spring of my trip to Wisła with Marek (Stefan Napierski), my editor, who was publishing me in his *Atheneum*. Andrzejewski had been holed up for several weeks in a boardinghouse in Wisła, writing. The three of us set out on foot to Barania Góra and the source of the Vistula River. We arrived there in a not too sober condition, owing to the Silesian home brew that we drank in one tavern after another. It was charming. I remember that time, dear shades, as a moment when we were happy. That was in 1939, because it was at precisely that time that the radio broadcast the news of the death of Pius XI and I began to write a poem of farewell that was never finished; we understood perfectly well what that death meant in the gathering *nox atra*, the dark night of dictatorships. A few months later Marek was executed by the Germans. I don't believe I went to Laski at all during the Occupation; in the alternate ebb and flow of my Catholicism, that phase was more of a "no." However, I maintained contact.

I probably obtained Maritain's *On the Roads of Defeat*, which I translated, from someone in the Laski circle, probably from Marynia Czapska. The typescript had gotten to Poland via Holland.

Psychiatry would probably have revealed only the eccentricities of my scrupulous conscience, which I myself perceive as the cause of my depressions. A scrupulous conscience does not by any means have to be a sensitive conscience, and usually it is not a reliable conscience; that is, a conscience that does not allow itself to be shoved off the straight path. But a scrupulous conscience is incomparable when it's a matter of tormenting oneself, breaking records in masochistic guilt, even to the point of developing physical pain in the rib cage. This explains the fiery sword that guarded my fifty-year union with Janka, all the way to her grave in Berkeley's Sunset Cemetery.

Should I re-create the spring and summer of 1939? I won't be able to. In August, Bolek Bochwic invited Janka and me to Paulinów, his brother Bruno's estate in Polesie. Paulinów, located in the vicinity of Nieśwież and Baranowicze, was familiar to me from a spring visit (that year, or the year before) when Bruno and I hunted capercaillie. Paulinów was a forest estate—that is, without the usual contrast between manor house and farmhands' quarters—and this only enhanced its charm. The house was new and was not modeled on the traditional architecture of manor houses; it had a large terrace with a view of the pine forest, and we were drawn there every morning by the fragrance of Bruno's marvelous fresh-brewed coffee. There were usually five of us: the Bochwic brothers; the forester Mowczan, who was Ukrainian; Janka, the only woman there; and me. We were surrounded by forest, no neighbors except for one who supplied the topics of various amusing stories. He was a yeoman squire, pedantic and scrupulous, although not terribly literate. He had placed an inscription on his garden gate: "Whether you are entering or leaving, lock the gait [sic], and whoever does not do so will see what awaits him." Afterward, I often tried to imagine his fate somewhere in the Siberian gulag.

The aroma of coffee and pine woods, conversations, outings in Bruno's new Mercedes. We visited the palace in Nieśwież, which is to say, we were in the courtyard of that immense Renaissance castle. Out of nowhere, surrounded by wilderness and swamps: Italy. And right next door: Nieśwież, a little Jewish town. Years later, in Berkeley, when I was reading a doctoral dissertation on the economics of the Radziwiłł family fortunes, owing to that visit I was able to visualize the details in relation to the region.

The nights were mild, sparkling with stars; one fiery red star distressed us. Mars. War. It seemed that I would now have to experience the imminent fulfillment of my catastrophic expectations and also the prophecies of Oscar Milosz, according to which the next war would be the war of the Red Horse of the Apocalypse and would begin in Gdynia (in Polish, Gdynia is an anagram of *gniady*, or "bay"). I was in another phase, however, a much more stupid phase. In Warsaw I approved of the slogan "We shall not yield even a button" and, to the horror of Jerzy Stempowski (I remember our conversation), rejoiced (yes!) because the boil was about to burst. But an explanation for this should be sought in Stefan Kisielewski's novel *The Conspiracy*: the anguish of toiling away at the Radio; the internal disorientation and confusion, which also affected my feelings for Janka—a state of mind from which it seems war alone could rescue the novel's protagonist. My thinking at that time still strikes me as the strongest argument in support of the thesis that the same person can be either wise or stupid, depending on his circumstances and on his resistance to the surrounding temperature. However, it's possible that I'm exaggerating my stupidity, because it's as clear as day that some sort of blockage intervened, something took the place of something else. In any event, the focal point of my thoughts was now Janka, and also my timid efforts at discovering what it was that had caught me like that and was holding me.

I don't remember if we listened to the radio or if we in fact connected the news about the Ribbentrop–Molotov pact with the blood-red star Mars. We had one Warsaw newspaper which we would tear into to learn what happened next in "Niewieski's" (Gombrowicz's) novel, *The Spellbound*, which was being serialized in it. An incredible towel slithered like a snake, and suddenly the newspaper didn't come; instead, a general mobilization was announced.

February 9, 1988

Bičiulis means friend. From *bité*, honeybee, which is a mysterious word for me. Its connections with English *bee*, German *bini*, *bia*, Nordic *by* are clear; but it is not clear how it is related to Slavic *pczoła*, *bczeła*. *Bičiulis* is someone who shares bees with his neighbor. We are about to plunge into rural antiquity—Lithuanian, but not only Lithuanian. In rural America, "bee" also meant a gathering of neighbors, both male and female—for example, to shell peas ("husking bee"), and it appears that the old-fashioned plural form, "been," was used in the sense of "crowd." For me, a bee, or neighborly gathering (Polish *tłoka*, East Slavic *tołoka*, Lithuanian *talka*),* is as domestic as can be, it is familiar from my childhood; but is it familiar in contemporary Polish? And what about the bee as the heraldic device of dynasties in ancient Egypt, and also *biti*?

I have been proofreading Aleksander Wat's *My Century*, making a last pass in search of mistakes in the spelling of names, etc. So, after the passage of many years, this work, which was born in Berkeley, will appear here in English, published by the University of California Press. I remember that year, 1965, and the reluctance with which I undertook the taping sessions, only gradually being drawn into them and then carried away. I had made it possible for Wat to receive a fellowship, though Gleb Struve did more than I did. I was a bit peeved when Wat, euphoric, flew to Berkeley from Paris in November or December 1963, not waiting for Janka and me to return home from Paris, where I had been spending the autumn on sabbatical. It seemed as if he wanted to avoid having me as an intermediary, as if he wanted to believe that he had arranged it himself, everything himself; certainly he held an exaggerated idea of his own greatness, which America had finally come to appreciate. I was linked to him by a friendship that began, not in the years before the war, but at that terrifying New Year's Eve of 1951 at the Parandowskis' home in Warsaw: the Parandowskis and the Wats, outcasts, lepers, and I, pale, trembling. I had turned down an invitation to a New Year's Eve party at the Writers' Union because Mrs. Putrament was so confident: Milosz will certainly be there. To have gone would have meant to submit and to drown my dissent in vodka. Two days ago I saw the film based on Milan Kundera's novel *The Unbearable Lightness of Being*. One of the characters, Thomas, refuses to sign a declaration of loyalty because his fellow doctors are so confident: they have signed it, everybody will sign it. Just like me at that time.

My friendly feelings for Wat did not keep me from noticing his comical qualities, which I was even inclined to extend to myself and to the clan of poets in general. Egotistic, naïve, even somewhat childish. What didn't he imagine! That the students would sit at his feet and drink words of wisdom about Communism from his lips. That he would read everything that has been written on this topic and include it all in his seminal work. But it turns out there are thousands of volumes; he was swamped by them. No conver-

---

* These Slavic words are all related to the root meaning "crowd." In Polish, for example, the masculine noun *tłok* means "crowd," while the feminine *tłoka* means "bee" in the sense of "gathering."

sations in a European café, a fundamental lack of interest in his person, the glibness of superficial personal relations, accompanied, to be sure, by a good deal of matter-of-fact kindness. Quite simply, no one had time for him here. And I must admit that when we arrived a few weeks later I did not behave as I should have, given his excessive sensitivity. Or was that how my own feelings, wounded by his haste in flying to Berkeley, deviously expressed themselves? It's quite possible. You wanted to do it all by yourself? Good; now deal with it. Anyway, when he wanted to give a lecture on Futurism (in Russian, because he didn't speak English), I said, "Nothing could be simpler. Choose a date and a title and present a brief outline of the theme." This gruff, friendly advice, even though it was quite normal, was immensely painful for him. What's that? He should propose and announce ahead of time what he plans to speak about? But, after all, Professor Gregory Grossman, the director of the Slavic Center that had brought Wat to Berkeley, had gone to great lengths to calm him down and to convince him that no one wanted to extract anything from him in exchange for his fellowship. How then could he have suggested lectures to him? So Wat understood it as pressure? The initiative must have been Wat's. All that was needed was for someone, either he or I, to go to Grossman or to Kathryn Feuer, who couldn't have been more favorably inclined toward Wat, and say, "Here's the title and topic; let's set a date."

> They who support my arm, will they be stopped by the aroma of vineyards? . . .
> They who lead me by the arm and have a stony gaze.

This poem by Wat is dedicated to me.

Critics have sought an answer to the question: What is the source of all those contradictions in my poetry? In my prose, too, for that matter. I could enlighten them by referring to the several personalities who reside in me simultaneously, whom I have tried to suppress, generally without success. I didn't want to be so volatile, but what could I do? I hope that this diary goes further than the confessions I have made in my other books and that it will be valued as one more attempt at demonstrating that I was conscious of the incompatibility of my various personalities.

FEBRUARY 10, 1988

I never served in the army. First I had a student deferment; then I was declared ineligible and was transferred to the reserve category with the rank of qualified marksman. This is the category the politically suspect were usually assigned to if (and this also happened) they were not inducted into the army with the special aim of indoctrinating them with healthy morals. Every year I performed a few days' substitute service in Warsaw with a shovel. My companions were, for the most part, Jewish workers. The military powers were probably right, because I could have been a subversive element, a miasma.

On the way back to Warsaw from Paulinów or, more precisely, from Baranowicze station, we passed a number of trains filled with laughing, singing recruits. I am incapable of re-creating those days or the first of September, when we didn't realize immediately that the explosions were a bombardment. Tours of duty as a fire spotter, the desire to submit to someone's orders. Apparently, the penetration of my consciousness by the awareness of defeat was quite traumatic, because my memory revisits it unwillingly. Janka and I became separated. She had gone to visit her parents in Wołomin and was supposed to return to our apartment in Dynasy, but the radio broadcast the order that all men capable of bearing arms were to leave Warsaw, so I reported to my workplace, Radio Poland. It was evacuated that very night, and I wound up in the broadcasting truck. A night of slow, bumper-to-bumper movement in a great exodus; finally, in the morning, Lublin. A gap in my memory. I heard that Czechowicz had arrived in one of the radio cars. I tried to find him, but our radio truck (with a receiver, a megaphone, etc.) was leaving for the front, I don't really know why, and I volunteered, and we set out toward the Vistula line. Kurów in flames? To have to turn back immediately and not even be able to stop in Lublin, because the Germans were already there. Lublin had been bombed a couple of hours earlier, and Czechowicz had died in the bombing. Now what? Numbness. Lwów. Something was happening, after all: so many people, an awareness that one is part of an avalanche of trucks, army and police detachments, cars, all forced south. The beauty of a sunny day somewhere in the vicinity of Podwołoczyska, with the family of one of the radio workers in a rural Subcarpathian landscape—corn, pumpkins. Awareness that all of this was converging automatically on the bridge at the Romanian border, and telling myself: I don't want to. The evacuated institutes had gasoline, but family clans had also acquired gas; for instance, the aristocrats who organized themselves into the so-called Potocki caravan (*la caravane Potocki*). Jaś Tarnowski, who was something of a degenerate scion of the clan because he was too much a part of the artistic milieu, was also traveling with them. I told him that I had no intention of emigrating and that I preferred to return to Warsaw, come what may. It turned out that he had the same idea, and he suggested that we travel together. He had a small car and gasoline. We made a plan. The only possible route was north along Poland's eastern border and then over toward Polesie. So we set out against the current, traveling on narrow roads. It was not a long trip, but it is worthy of mournful recollection, because the day was September 17. The many low-flying planes, like bats, convinced us that something was going on. Soon we were told that Soviet tanks were on their way. We didn't talk. Jaś turned back; the faces of people crowded together in the villages we passed; we got there in time to cross the bridge into Romania. After which the two of us, stopping once in Chernovtsy, avoiding checkpoints, made it to Bucharest by driving along country roads.

ℱEBRUARY 12, 1988

There's a snowstorm on the East Coast, but here it's spring, hot, the trees are in bloom. Yesterday a sauna and then a swim in the outdoor pool.

My stay in Bucharest would demand such an extended description that I prefer not to attempt it. Suffice it to say that I hatched an insane plan to go home—a continuation of my journey with Jaś Tarnowski, which had been interrupted by a petty circumstance, the invasion from the east. And against all odds, I managed to carry out my plan, which is almost incomprehensible. Since the territories occupied by the Soviets had to be ruled out, only a roundabout route remained. I wrote to a friend, Keliuotis, the editor of *Naujoji Romuva* (I was a contributor to the journal), saying I wanted to come to Lithuania. He replied, sending me a *sauf conduit*, which was a sort of Nansen passport.

My return to Wilno, and then, in the summer of 1940, to Warsaw, is for me an example of the distinction between intentions and a true goal, which remains unknown or scarcely perceived during the moments when we are making decisions. For I obviously did not know that I was returning in order to experience, to observe, and to be able to fulfill my destiny as a writer.

FEBRUARY 13, 1988

The optimistic occupation of studying languages. An etymological dictionary of the Russian language, four volumes of Greek, Karłowicz's and Linde's dictionaries of Polish, *Modern Lithuanian*, Brückner's etymological dictionary of Polish, a dictionary of Indo-European roots in English. An optimistic occupation because it implies a goal, a utility that runs counter to common sense. Because what good is knowledge after the death that old age must be prepared for every day? It follows from this that dictionaries will continue to exist in heaven. There will be no complete knowledge there, because then it would no longer be necessary to study, and that would mean a state of passivity and boredom, but rather there is striving, activity, to the second power. In other words, philologists will receive laurels in the other world. Although it may well be that there they will also study languages that never achieved the level of writing and grammar.

FEBRUARY 14, 1988

I can hardly keep up with my numerous interests. The proofs for the Wat book, and recently the proofs for a five-hundred-page volume of my collected poems in English. Philosophy. Reading: the diary of Father Pedro Font from his 1776 expedition to California. What it looked like before the white man arrived. I trust this monk more than I do romantic fantasies about noble savages. The life of the Indians: filth, stench, constant fear of death because of the unending war of all against all, and most important, the virtually constant malnutrition that will draw them to the Spanish missions, because they were given breakfast, dinner, and supper in exchange for agreeing to baptism. Of all the various human characteristics, Father Font sees in them only the physical shape of man; otherwise, they are animals. This drives him to contemplate theological problems. Such poverty for millennia, and what about after death?

*F*EBRUARY 19, 1988

A couple of days in the mountains. Whiteness, brightness, so as not to forget what snow looks like. A ski lift. Alpine Meadows.

Driving along Lake Tahoe, just beyond Tahoe City, I recognized or tried to recognize the cabin that Janka, the boys, and I rented in 1961. A little patio right beside the water; I loved sitting there and looking at the high shores on the Nevada side. A trace of this remains in my poem about a moment at dawn, two fishermen in a motorboat, a resolution, and forgetfulness. How am I different from myself at that time?

> *Leaning on my Waterman*
> *I depart into the abyss*
> *Of eternal doubting.*

That's Gałczyński, from the time when he still allowed himself to doubt.

What is one allowed to confess in public? Doesn't there exist a sphere that should be left untouched by words because it would be deleterious to the health of the human species? Shestov would have said, yes, there is such a sphere.

*F*EBRUARY 23, 1988

It may well be that if we're talking about the future of religions, the intuition I had in Japan was right on the mark, and I am surprised that I have not yet expanded it. It came back to me in connection with the British anthology,

Tongues of Fire, which contains three of my poems and one by Wat ("Japanese Archery"). The volume's editor, Karen Armstrong (a former nun), writes of the distinction between a mystical experience and the religious practice of the majority of people who fulfill whatever their particular religion requires of them. Buddhism and Shinto in Japan survive through the power of tradition and are not subject to confirmation or contradiction. This is different, somehow, from the violent erosion of Christianity during the last centuries; it appears to be an enduring condition that ensues after a leap downward from that stage when religion ruled everything. Perhaps other religions are following the same path and Christianity in the West is settling comfortably on just as humble but powerful a rung, or else, to use another comparison, it will be a straight line which various other lines will cross— lines of personal expectations, charismatic movements, or mystic contemplation, and fundamentally not overly preoccupied with any particular faith, because in this view, for example, a Christian theist has a great deal in common with an a-theistic Buddhist. Obviously, the existence of religion as prescribed practices is important, because with its disappearance there would be no defense for believers' own thoughts or any stimulus for them.

FEBRUARY 24, 1988

It cannot be ruled out that our entire way of thinking about the history of religion demands a fundamental change. Centuries of burning faith uniting the peasant, the artisan, and the theologian, of religious enthusiasm and dedication, may be, to a great extent, the creation of later retrospective imaginings. In many countries the Christianity of the masses was dubious and the custom of attending church did not mean that the faithful could answer the simplest catechism questions. In the sixteenth, and even in the seventeenth, century the Lithuanian countryside was Christian in name only. But even France, which was converted to Christianity so much earlier, had a large urban population in the eighteenth century consisting of poor people who knew nothing about any kind of religion and whose existence explains the fervor with which during the Revolution the heads of the saints on cathedral portals were smashed. Mikhailovsky, criticizing Dostoevsky for his belief in the profound piety of the Russian peasant, argued that the Russian peasant was an atheist by nature. These examples, the first that come to mind, lead to certain suspicions: the history of religion, like history in general, bears the mark of the "learned caste." The splendor of architecture, painting, and music constructed an image of Christian civilization that was to a certain degree above the heads of average people, who are usually preoccupied with their earthly affairs, and it is impossible to draw any clear divisions here, just as one cannot isolate the magnificent temples of Nara and Kyoto from the amazing mixture of traditions that is called Japan. It is possible, then, that the various restraints that have hindered religion in the past (pagan customs, poverty, illiteracy) find their counterpart today in other restraints, so that a general reckoning would end up in a tie.

The "death of God," however, struck at the learned caste, and then philosophy, science, and art went their own way, no longer concerned with the opinions of theologians; and that is a fundamental difference. It is here, in this parting of the ways, that I see the chief problematic of modern poetry.

Poetry in place of religion; summoned, that is, by the same needs that turn man to religion. Such a formula would be accurate, but it is too general and can embrace divergent tendencies. Mallarmé is not the same as Rilke, and neither of them is the same as Whitman. It would be no exaggeration to seek analogies in the first centuries of Christianity, when, as a consequence of massive layers of intellectual refinement (Greek philosophy, the contemporary scientific world view, etc.), the new religion proved insufficient for the educated, and therefore various types of gnosis became widespread among them. Gnosticism would have been for that time what poetry (which can by no means be reduced to "aesthetic experiences") is today for educated people. In its most important creations, poetry is an exploration of man's place in the cosmos. That kind of poetry used to find its rival in the many varieties of historiosophical gnosis.

February 25, 1988

Outsiders, people who have not been initiated into the knowledge about literature which has been growing to stratospheric heights in recent decades, must find it quite difficult to understand why everything that used to be part of philosophy has now moved over into literary studies. Or into scholarship that uses literary studies as a pretext. A certain Alexandrianism in writing about writing, the three-storied edifices of formalism, structuralism, deconstruction, etc. This entire realm of writing, along with its contiguous spheres of activity, begins to look like a deadly-serious enterprise, quite possibly, in terms of importance, on the same plane as Hegelian historiosophical gnosis. Warm, getting warm. And what if one were to study the antagonisms, the collaborations, the rivalries of the two chief callings of the modern era—the social prophet-revolutionary and the artist?

*F*EBRUARY 26, 1988

I have an overwhelming aversion to discoursing on poetry, an aversion that sets me apart from the thousands of theoreticians, scholastics, martyrs of one or another "ism" who construct their university careers on that "ism." I prefer a poem that was written a thousand years ago by the Japanese woman poet Izumi Shikibu (974–1034):

> *If he whom I wait for*
> *Should come now, what will I do?*
> *This morning the snow-covered garden*
> *Is so beautiful without a trace of footprints.*

Is such a poem an instrument of knowledge? Yes, of knowledge, and on a more profound level than philosophy.

$\mathcal{M}$ARCH 1, 1988

In this poem our thoughts about a young woman who lived a thousand years ago, about one morning in her life, become part of our so-called aesthetic experience, which obviously cannot be reduced to aesthetics. A connection arises, a unity, her body, her breath, her admiration for the whiteness of the snow that fell during the night, something that is equally well known to us, but hidden. For haven't we, too, experienced moments when we would have wished for that purity to persist, immaculate, and then immediately felt ashamed because it's a foolish idea? The childishness of that woman. A mature woman, she is waiting for a man, and at the same time her eyes are wide open like a child's; she discovers the details of the visible world. And that world persists so objectively that the presence or absence of her guest does not emerge into the foreground. It is as if she were indicating the proper place for our passions, which ought to be subordinated to disinterested contemplation. But it is precisely through the complexity of her emotions that this Japanese woman is so tangible, so close to us, that she takes on the shape of women we hold dear.

$\mathcal{M}$ARCH 7, 1988

I cannot grasp in verse my basic theme. Experience teaches that in such cases one has to wait. Let's say for several months. But my hope that I will succeed in catching it is contradicted by my resignation, because, after all, the time will come when one does not write poems anymore.

MARCH 9, 1988

Stunning discoveries about the complexity of the human psychophysical organism. Would I be capable of describing it by offering even a few examples? This is a field that I have never enjoyed exploring, completely denying my own fragility and my body's dependence on its spiritual states, while at the same time knowing nothing about it. In other words, my self-awareness in this regard was minimal, and that is why it is true that I have been guided by powers wiser than I.

The film *Hope and Glory*, about World War II in London. An artistically flawed film, but faithful to the mentality of the West and the practice of self-deprecation. A teacher lectures to her class, explaining what England is fighting for: "To preserve the empire." But the audience knows that the empire fell apart. What of it? Will no one protest, will no one proclaim that that wasn't really what England was fighting for?

MARCH 13, 1988

A constant stream of publishing chores this year. I had scarcely finished the proofs of my thick volume of *Collected Poems* when I had to start working on the proofs of Wat's *My Century* and my own *The Garden of Knowledge* in French translation (*L'Immoralité de l'art*), and now it's my *Unattainable Earth* translated into French. Aha, also a revision of our slender volume of Wat's poetry in English translation.

I discovered, while reading the proofs of the French volume, the degree to which a mature language, refined through literature, is unreceptive to poetry. In French, there are prepared formulas for all the word combinations that we put together with such effort, seeking our own means of expression, and that obviously is the source of the translator's tendency to use these formulas. I say, "At the beginning of the world"; the translator says, "À *l'aube du monde.*" But *à l'aube* means at daybreak, at dawn, which is trite. I: "He reads a curse"; the translator: "*Une formule magique*"—and what has happened to reading? And so forth. I don't feel like giving multiple examples. And all this has somehow or other to be caught. I can do it in French. But what happens in other languages? Horror. Today a journalist of Hungarian descent phoned me from Brazil; he is preparing a translation of my poems into Portuguese. He said that the translation of my book that was published in Budapest is marvelous. How does he know? Did he compare it with the original? It may be true that it is marvelous, but I can't check it out. Just as, in the final analysis, I cannot evade certain translation monopolies.

March 16, 1988

The day before yesterday, I held the second of my three seminars at the university. It was successful, but more and more often I find myself thinking that, aside from the poems that I will leave behind, I don't have too much to say, because my theoretical observations could be pursued equally well by someone else. I spoke about objective art, about Schopenhauer, for whom Dutch still lifes were the highest achievements of objective art; I read aloud fragments of his lectures and then my poems from the cycles *Lauda* and *La Belle Epoque.* And that's fine. But at my age one thinks about one's own mistakes; I think, too, about those people who were wiser than I. Many were wiser, and it is not much consolation that there were also many who were more stupid. For a long time my driving force was the certainty that I was right; today, that's a bit of a joke. During this seminar I realized that I continue to speak like someone who is passionately formulating plans, who confronts one genre of poetry with alternate forms; I am still the poet who knows and struggles against the subjectivism of contemporary poetry. But, as a matter of fact, I ought to shrug my shoulders and limit myself to what I have written. "Czeslaw, don't talk, you'll say something stupid. Write!" Despite this wise council from Zygmunt Hertz, I pursued a university career, but now I've probably had enough; my skepticism toward sage posturing, including my own, keeps growing.

MARCH 19, 1988

I found a letter from Kot Jeleński written in 1982 which for some reason was not with his other letters; it moved me like a message from beyond the grave. It confirms yet again the *perfection* of Kot's response to the written word, his absolute decency and wisdom. He writes about the exchange of letters between me and Melchior Wańkowicz which was published in the journal *Creative Work*. A less loyal friend would have hesitated; he would have been reluctant to express a bitter truth. Kot responded to that document with sadness and insisted that the exchange lowers my image in the eyes of admirers of my poetry and is even more incomprehensible since, at that very same time, I was saying the exact opposite in my poetry. In his opinion, Wańkowicz was in the right and my arguments were dishonest and marked by an impermissible self-assurance and self-pity. He advises me to take the bull by the horns and finally write about my work in the foreign service after the war—not contritely, but without attempting to defend indefensible positions.

Kot was right. My arguments were false and concealed my true motives, either because those motives could not be admitted or because they would have demanded too complicated a self-analysis. The unfortunate magnanimity that led me to give Ms. Ziółkowska permission to print it (she knew what she was doing, because the correspondence presents Wańkowicz in a positive light) has taken, and will continue to take, its revenge. Adam Michnik, with the best of intentions, advertised this correspondence in his essay and in the book *Polish Questions*, but as a result of his lavish quotations, his defense of Milosz appears weak and is unexpectedly strengthened only when he quotes from the poems, actually demonstrating, on a different plane, the logic of my position.

From the beginning, my departure from Poland occurred under the sign of deception, because I was guided by a single desire: to leave. And then we'll see. Before her death, my mother simply ordered me to leave. Later, finding myself in America, I noticed that I had absolutely nothing to do there, in any sense at all. Aside from earning my living, along with "eating, defecating, and sleeping." My conflict with *Kultura* when I wound up there in 1951—a conflict that may seem funny today but wasn't funny then—gives some idea of the extent to which any integration at all into émigré circles was internally impossible for me.

ℳARCH 30, 1988

Do you really like Gombrowicz's novels and plays? Now, be honest! No. I don't envy him his having written them; I would not wish to be their author. Do they disturb me? Yes. Because if people really exist only for other people, if the cocoon we have spun vanishes in a cosmos about which we can say nothing, not even whether it exists (at most, that it exists in our minds), if this is so, then perhaps we really do live in hell. My anxiety derives from my thinking of Gombrowicz as a modern writer, so that I have to consider myself old-fashioned. A polite little boy who believes in a dear little God, who tries to avoid sin, encounters an uncivilized rapscallion who sticks out his tongue and thumbs his nose at the authorities of two millennia. In the final analysis, what I can oppose to Gombrowicz comes straight from the storehouse of ancient concepts:

"The world exists, not just in my mind."

"And how do you know that?"

"Because it is observed by God."

This reminds me of Descartes's reasoning. Descartes cured himself of doubt by basing his argument on the idea that God cannot deceive us. But, says Gombrowicz, that was cowardice on Descartes's part.

So be it. Yet I have a tremendous need to go outside of myself, beyond my persona; the more I am aware of my aging organism, the stronger is this need, this desire to be somehow a part of God's thoughts when he observes the world, a need for perfect objectivity, for a sphere that *endures* independently of people's fleeting interconnections. I have tested this; my poetry is like that, it moves outward, it travels beyond me. The ideal: to be able to say that, although things are not good with me, the world endures and moves along its path, and in this world, despite all its ghastliness, there is another side, a true side, a lining visible to the eyes of the Divinity. In other words, my quarrel with Gombrowicz really revolves around his "argument about the existence of the world"; that is, his stubborn denial of assertions that something other than our perceptions exists. That is one of his attacks on objective truth. The other is the way people entangle themselves in a single interconnected body; hence, the truth is always *their* truth, God is *their* God.

I am not a very passionate admirer of Nature, because Nature is pain, but I still feel the presence—inborn, inherent—of a tree, an animal, a flower, while for Gombrowicz these exist only as a threat. For me, too, but there is also something beyond them. Would Gombrowicz have been able to write a Zen poem? Was contemplation, other than contemplation in the act of creating a work of art, within his reach? Whatever I might say in my own defense, in defense of a superstitious child, he could easily turn it against me. You pray to God? You are praying to yourself. Feuerbach *da capo.*

My fate propelled me in the direction of accepting Gombrowicz's opinions, not leaving any room for transcendence. Illness in one's immediate environment has to have such an effect. The soul's absolute enslavement to the cells of the organism is laid bare at such a time. How many years I was forced to witness this!

Last Sunday was Palm Sunday. In the Church of St. Mary Magdalen I experienced once again that immersion in the ages of humankind, identification with the millions of men and women who have participated in the Mass throughout the centuries; this is hard to put into words, however. There was also an intuitive understanding that Christ exists because every individual is alone with his threshold of pain, of dereliction, and I in my egoism am unable to enter into my fellow man. No matter how often I think about total empathy, I am overwhelmed by panic: Why am I, as egoistic as a cat, thinking about this? To tell the truth, I treasure my cat-like nature.

My childish thinking incorporates centuries-old habits. Namely, I think that people live as long as they fulfill what they were destined to fulfill, and that if I have nothing left to do, I will soon die. What does such an idea mean? Is there room for it in an a-theistic religion—in Buddhism, for example?

My asthma is making me weak and once again I am convinced that poetry, for me at least, demands all one's physical powers, an enormous concentration of nervous energy.

By chance, yesterday I heard a tape recording, made in Poland, of my poems being sung or chanted to music (whose?). If I wanted to live longer, it would be only in order to correct the evil that I have done. Including all my poems that promote that moaning-noble-patriotic Polish blockheadedness. Or can be recited that way. Alas. Leśmian didn't write a single poem in that cause; what tempted me? A polite little Boy Scout who was incapable of liberating himself from his short pants. Only my bouts of national orthodoxy, not my flirtations with Communism, are stains that cannot be washed clean.

$\mathcal{A}$PRIL 1, 1988

Keiji Nishitani's criticism of Western thought in *Religion and Nothingness*, especially the "subjectivization of atheism" in Nietzsche and Sartre, can be applied in its entirety to Gombrowicz, who is entangled in the old dilemma of Western philosophers: subject–object. What remains is to reflect on the virtually inescapable conclusions of extraordinary intellects like Gombrowicz (because, after all, Sartre and Gombrowicz arrive at the same conclusion independently of each other), and to consider also the probability that the post-Christian West opens to the philosophy of the East where the subject–object problem is crossed out.

$\mathcal{A}$PRIL 4, 1988

Literary Life has printed Gombrowicz's letters to the Świeczewskis. He was convinced that his letters would be worth a great deal and advised them not to lose them. Why didn't I worry about my own letters? And why didn't I ever consider the possibility that I should say something or not say something out of concern for posterity? Does that mean humility, or lack of faith in my own greatness? I can't be my own judge. Or perhaps it is total arrogance: I feel I am superior to any game of literary greatness, that the game is quite stupid. After all, I did have to situate myself somehow or other in pre-1939 Poland where Tuwim was the greatest poet; I would not have disputed

Iwaszkiewicz's greatness, and would have placed Czechowicz above myself. So how did it appear then? How did my consciousness compare with a different level of unavowed convictions? (Or, at least, what was not expressed in my opinions?) I am inclined to picture it this way: a hierarchy exists and on its pinnacle are those poets who are initiated; not a single poet of that rank exists in Poland, but Oscar Milosz belongs here. I have no hope of ascending to the pinnacle, but by virtue of my awareness of its existence I stand higher than the Polish poets around me. I think that's about it. And did I have aspirations later on? Was I jealous of Przyboś's fame, of Gałczyński's? Probably a little bit jealous, but somehow or other, that passed me by. Now, Iwaszkiewicz—*he* was convinced of his greatness and he stylized his letters, although his entire myth of the "great writer" (see the Nobel Prize winner Zamoyłło, a character in one of his novels) only amused me even before 1939.

The day before yesterday, Holy Saturday, I went to the cemetery. A beautiful place; my ashes beside her ashes. This is how it should be, I thought, not Sopot and the Kunat family tomb.* If only as recompense for the way I wronged her by being incapable of loving her as she deserved to be loved.

Sex. In the final analysis, lust is chiefly a matter of legends. A man and a woman are primarily a game of self-love. And that is why this whole realm is so suspect, so impure. My guilty conscience. And at the same time I know that Swedenborg was right: a true marriage is heaven on earth. That is what I sought and that is what, but only briefly, I experienced with Janka.

APRIL 8, 1988

On board a plane from Oakland to Seattle.

Yes, obviously, we are defenseless against time that will come after our death, against all changes in taste, customs, scales of value, fashions. They will take what they want from us, discard what they don't need, and who can foretell to what extent that image will be similar to our own self-image? Sometimes I think that the fabric of speech—language, music, painting—

---

* Sopot, near Gdansk, on the Baltic coast, was settled after World War II by refugees from the East. Members of the author's family on his mother's side (Kunat) are buried there.

is composed chiefly of traces from which it is impossible even to guess who a particular person was; that what will remain as an example is one poem, one still-life canvas.

I am being pressured to authorize the publication in Poland of my underground anthology, *The Invincible Song*, from 1942. I say, "I don't want to, that was a long time ago and I have nothing in common with it." But my book *Three Winters*, from 1936, has appeared with commentaries and it gave me a great deal of pleasure. Which means that I endorse *Three Winters* and I don't wish to endorse *The Invincible Song*.

April 9, 1988

In the Mayflower Hotel in Seattle.

I fulfilled my obligations (a seminar and a poetry reading) without revealing how much every effort cost me because of my asthma. Obviously, reflections about aging and the not-too-distant end are always in the background, especially after that card from W., who writes that she is growing weak with old age and illness, that she has no strength for anything, even to thank me for the packages I sent her.

Inter arma silent Musae. (The Muses are silent in wartime.) There is a good deal of truth in this; the Muses, that is, have their own precincts: gardens, the order of the seasons, loving couples, musical instruments. And, no doubt, the strangeness of existence. But contemporary poetry, as I said yesterday at the seminar, is a search for how man should behave in an untenable position, confronting a cosmos that he does not understand in the least, or which, the more he understands it, the less he understands. This is comparable to the need that people feel when a friend or someone close to them dies: *something* should be done, but what? No one knows. It is good if religion, with its liturgy, enters in. But if it doesn't? How should one behave in the face of ultimate things? Couldn't poetry be the creation of a substitute liturgy?

Inter arma silent Musae. What enduring works of poetry really arose in the clatter of arms during World War II? Melchior Wańkowicz's wife and daughters gave me fragments of Tuwim's *Polish Flowers* for my anthology *The Invincible Song*, but I censored them, on my own recognizance, because his posturing was unbearable. Despite my finickiness, which was greater than that of the editors of competing anthologies, there is a lot of patriotic rhetoric in *The Invincible Song*. Indeed, the rhetoric is almost exclusively patriotic, and even though I could see that, what could I do about it? No doubt, other anthologies were better; they did a better job of rousing people to action, because their editors didn't have scruples like mine; they weren't, in other words, aesthetes.

If a person takes his vocation seriously, he ought to realize that he is bound by a strict hierarchy based on the principle of rejecting everything that does not meet the highest demands; rejecting, that is, anything that intuition tells us is marked by the characteristic features of false, cheap values. Who knows, perhaps the entire realm of the so-called noble feelings, social rebellion, patriotism, etc., should be included here; one should admit, that is, that hierarchy imposes a certain inhumanity. My first volume of poetry sinned against that hierarchy with its social themes, but the second, *Three Winters*, strictly preserved a contemptuous, arrogant hierarchy.

*A*PRIL 10, 1988

A couple of weeks ago, Carol planted an apple tree. The planting of an apple tree is optimistic, as in the legend of Johnny Appleseed; we will pass on, the apple trees will remain. But the deer went after it and ate half its leaves, just as in the last few days they have eaten all sorts of flowers, pansies, even the spirea and whatever else Carol buys to add to the garden. As I write these notes, a search is under way for means of outsmarting the deer.

A strict hierarchy means that one is able to catch the thread of one's own (no one else's) fate and that no temptations will distract us from behavior focused on a single goal. Which is very difficult, because we live among people and are in their power, we share their emotions, desires, and fears. The intensely emotional pressures of the collective. You have one life, do something with it. From the perspective of future generations, who cares if you yielded to the demands and expectations of your contemporaries? Does this mean that I am an advocate of art for art's sake, that I want to preserve its purity, that like Mallarmé I still advise people to turn their backs on the crowd? Of course, but only in a hygienic sense. Not in the sense of a chalk circle inside which only word-weaving is permitted.

I am amazed at this and do not understand it. Where has this taken me!

How can I draw a line between my purer poetry and my poetry that yielded to the supplications of my age? More precisely, between the poetry in which that age was appropriately transformed and the poetry in which it appears in its raw state? Sometimes I think that my life ought to have ended after *Three Winters* and that all the rest was an unnecessary addendum. Because then my madman's face, as Janek Ulatowski says, my face of a *possédé*, would have appeared clearly, without any pretenses. I have undoubtedly always been this way. Gombrowicz about Janka and me: "I don't understand how such a wise woman could hang in there with such a madman (*avec un fou pareil*)." And once again he was right.

*A*PRIL 12, 1988

A letter from London, from a reader I don't know, Sebastian Barker. But what a letter! How many letters like this can one receive in a lifetime? Probably only toward the end of one's life. But what can one do with such a letter if one considers oneself *un fou pareil*?

I watched an hour-long television program about Robert Lowell, one of a series on American poets. A weak series; they pretty much bungled it. Assorted comments about Lowell by various poets, many by my Robert Hass.

During my first stay in America, *Lord Weary's Castle*, Lowell's first volume of poetry, was a sensation. I was bowled over by it and I was the first to write about him in Polish; that was before Stalinization. I don't recall how it came about that Lowell visited us in Washington, in our cheap first-floor apartment on Sheridan Street, which we rented from a Mr. and Mrs. Miller. Maybe since he was a rebel (he had gone to prison rather than participate in a war that in his then Catholic opinion was unjust), he considered it necessary to demonstrate his independence from "red"-hating public opinion? Look, you aren't going to be contaminated by "reds," you can see at a glance that they are people like everyone else. He hadn't the faintest idea, of course, about our Polish complexities.

Later on, I saw Lowell during his visits to Berkeley. My aversion may have been provoked by his fame during the sixties when the whole pacifist youth movement considered him our great progressive; he confirmed their faith that all people, especially poets, think identically, because only swine think differently. Which is, after all, a constant in America: to be a poet is to be a so-called liberal. Add to this Lowell's divorces, his stays in psychiatric clinics, his interest in European (museum) culture, and we have a typical chronology of a life—too typical for my taste—in the service of a common-place milieu.

APRIL 14, 1988

I should return to the years of the Free Speech Movement in Berkeley, because it has already become history. That's when those Lowell readings took place. Just think how many people remember and are beginning to write memoirs about that period; for them, it was the most intense experience of their lives. And for me? A pitiable spectacle. Could it be that the grownups felt the same about our Dembiński "movement" in Wilno? Here, there was Mario Savio working the mass of students into a fanatical, hysterical trance, and Bettina Aptheker, from the American Communist Party (and how!), directing them. I was neither afraid, like so many professors who prostrated themselves before those youngsters, nor was I overly distressed. I gave the agitator who came into my classroom permission to address my students, but when I'd had enough of him, I grabbed him by the scruff of the neck, to his utter astonishment, and ordered him to leave.

The "revolution" lasted a couple of years and went through various waves of intensity. After the American bombardment of Cambodia, cells were organized in the departments, so students and professors could discuss the issues together or, more precisely, be appropriately indoctrinated. I extricated myself diplomatically by translating from the French an article by Prince Sihanouk that I found in *Preuves*. It coincided with my convictions, because the unfortunate Sihanouk, who was maneuvering and making small conces-sions to the Vietnamese, was the only man who could preserve his country's neutrality. The Americans had blundered in and ruined his entire cautious game plan, without any benefit for themselves. I read that text. One of the professors babbled some shameful "progressive" nonsense.

After the meeting I gave a ride home to a woman student who had come to Berkeley from Warsaw University.

"How is this possible, where have I landed?" she asked. "Did I escape from Communism only to fall into the same thing here? And that Professor X., what does it mean, who is he?"

Keeping my eyes on the road, I replied, "A prick."

I don't know how I would have reacted to the revolution of the sixties at the Sorbonne. I definitely would not have supported cutting down the plane trees on Boulevard Saint-Michel in order to erect barricades. It seems that here my views diverge from Kot Jeleński's. A couple of years after those events I had a conversation with Abrasha Zemsz, who is no longer among the living; he was a quaint character from the Left Bank, an always starving, eternal student (a Polish Jew who had had painful experiences in the Polish armed forces in England because of anti-Semitism). Abrasha played an active part in the revolution and even exerted some influence. I asked him why, but he didn't mention any ideology. Because it was a movement, because it was action, because it was a revolution in and of itself.

*A*PRIL 15, 1988

At the Oakland airport.

Driving to the airport, I was thinking about the hideous music of the second half of the nineteenth century. What were they thinking? That they were inventive, that they were progressive in comparison with the seventeenth and eighteenth centuries? Why did that miraculous equilibrium between the resistance of form and inventiveness occur just once, that heavenly sculpting of sound as in Bach, Haydn, Mozart, and not only in them; lesser composers, too, partook of that beautiful style.

En route from Oakland to South Bend (the University of Notre Dame), via Chicago.

My convulsive laughter whenever I heard Tchaikovsky, for example. Why did they do it? A composer, the dignity of the artist, the myth of the artist, the orchestra (so many months, so many years of labor by violinists, trumpeters, cellists); the public—ladies in corsets, bemedaled officers, frock coats. And all this so that posterity might laugh at their ritual, perhaps even at them personally, who took that ritual so seriously.

America has afforded me many joys, including negative ones—for instance, that no one has forcibly poured into my ears assorted varieties of Tchaikovskyism. This is one more reason why I could not live in Russia.

A volume of selected poetry by Oscar Milosz, in Lithuanian, a bilingual edition, Vilnius, 1980. Quite a large print run: 14,000. My thoughts are similar to those above about music. Entire lengthy periods of so-called worthless art, but also periods in the life of a given artist, a poet. The Lithuanians, instead of selecting according to modern taste, respectfully translated him "as is," from his early volumes, which are marked by fin de siècle verbosity. A lot of poems that I never read before because they were unreadable. Nonetheless, among them there are suddenly poems that will remain forever in French: "Karomama" and "Lofoten." Later, a surge: the splendid "Symfonies" from World War I and the post-war poems.

Kunas ir dvasia—body and soul. That sounds fine. I am sensitive to that sound because of my mother's family name: Kunat. Poor Gombrowicz boasted about the Kotkowskis in his family line; for me, names ending in "-ski" were always faintly ludicrous. Kunatas—obviously the name of a leader, evoking the virtues of a sturdy body. Kunat was granted the Axe coat of arms in the fourteenth century; according to legend, he was one of the few surviving members of the Jotvingai, a now extinct Prussian–Lithuanian tribe, who were slaughtered by the combined forces of Poles and Teutonic Knights. I think that when I showed up in Warsaw from Wilno in the thirties, a few people (like Marek Napierski) were excited by a genealogy like mine, which was almost American Indian. And Iwaszkiewicz included a certain minor Jotvingaian prince named Kunat in his novel *Red Shields*.

I like traveling by plane. Writing, reading, drinking. The number of miles I have covered by plane, in America and across both oceans, is astonishing. My high energy and a level of activity that even I find amazing coincided with the approach and completion of my seventieth year. To tell the truth, my energy in alcohol consumption, my sexual energy, and my creative energy were all linked. My opinion of my friend Jerzy Andrzejewski was tempered by compassion of a sort, not because he wanted so very much to receive a Nobel Prize and I'm the one who received it, but because he sank into alcoholism, which I escaped because I was able to either drink or not drink.

To have an active mind until the end; let the body refuse to obey.

.   .   .

Victory and defeat. Thinking about Andrzejewski, it's hard not to consider that opposition. I have seen so many illusory greatnesses, so many failures. In Poland, in France, in America. Sometimes it seems I won. Earlier, however, while still in school, I believed in victory only at a price. When people praise and applaud me (often with standing ovations), I would like to say to them: "If you knew my life, would you change places with me?"

APRIL 17, 1988

Aboard a plane from Chicago to San Francisco.

A conference on nationality problems in East-Central Europe and Russia, part of the ceremonial inauguration of Andrzej Walicki's tenure as a chaired professor at Notre Dame. No asthma, which points to its source as Berkeley allergies.

On the return flight from South Bend to Chicago, I told Professor Ivo Banac the contents of my poem about Szetejnie, Kalnaberze, and Stolypin. Also, what I learned recently after Piotr Kłoczkowski catalogued Kot Jeleński's archive. Kot had translated that poem into French and given it to Stolypin's grandson. The grandson read the poem to his aged father, who was moved by it, and said that he remembers it all: Szetejnie, the young Miss Kunat.

Banac and I agreed that Solzhenitsyn is correct on this point: the only person who could have saved Russia after the February Revolution was Stolypin. Because power lay in the streets and there was no one who wanted to go after it.

Banac and I discussed a plan for a conference at Yale on the cities of Central Europe as cultural centers. I am glad that he included the north at my suggestion—Tallin, Riga, Vilnius. I asked him why he didn't include Dubrovnik, his native city.

I am not writing down my memories in general, because access to memories is often blocked, images won't appear, they are censored by us. So, only fragments.

Autumn 1950. Rue Dumont-d'Urville, not far from the Etoile. They put me there after I arrived in Paris from Washington, and it didn't enter my head to say, "Thank you very much, but I prefer to choose my own place."

I wasn't *that* naïve. The house belonged to the embassy; embassy employees were housed there. The concierge saw who came in and when. She was a hefty middle-aged woman, actually rather elderly, a Pole from the north of France. She worked for the UB, the security police, of course, but also undoubtedly for the French police. A mystery that I have never been able to unravel is the Paris concierges' connections with the police: are they paid, or do the police have other means to control them? My room had a thin door that opened into the next room; you could hear everything, so I couldn't invite anyone. A fervent young Communist couple lived behind that door —the journalist Kozicki and his wife, Anka, Władysław Broniewski's daughter, who later committed suicide. I thought I remembered her from Warsaw, when I was at the Broniewskis' once in the Żoliborz district: a flaxen-haired little girl in a playpen, behind bars of light wood. Now she was a grown woman, very nasty, one of those fanatics with tight, narrow lips. Both of them treated me like a representative of an alien class. Just as the horrifying snake-eyed Egeria in the embassy did, a woman from Paris's Communist Polonia. There was no ambassador. The chargé d'affaires, Ogrodziński, didn't count, because he behaved like an animal caught in a trap. He had come into the Party from the Polish Socialist Party. There was an old Polish–Parisian Communist—Menzel, I think, I forget his name—whom I considered a decent man. The embassy was run by an agent of the security police, Wójtowicz. No one will ever find out what he thought. He soon outwitted all of them and emigrated to Israel, and either returned to his real surname or took another.

When I walk along rue Saint-Dominique now in the vicinity of the embassy, the locale of my former suffering, it doesn't seem to be guarded the way it was then. In those days, a civilian with a machine gun used to stand in a guard house; they used miners from the north for that.

I often think about people like the concierge on rue Dumont-d'Urville. Hundreds of thousands of people like her, millions, a truly infinite number of little terrified people who know that one has to connive in order to survive somehow, and there is no doubt that they would sell their fellow man for the price of a meal. There are always a great many of them, but totalitarian regimes multiply their number to an astonishing degree. (Didn't the concierge in our Wilno dormitory—I have no recollection of what his Polish title was—collaborate with the police?) And if by some magical means it became possible to ascertain the true, not the imagined, genealogy of the inhabitants of Poland, it would turn out that the forefathers, grandfathers, parents of a large percent of them (perhaps the majority?) were not very honorable individuals: informers, servile yes-sayers, lackeys of the police and the UB, double agents, and so forth. How does natural selection work here if it's the subservient and the unscrupulous who have the best chance of surviving and producing offspring, while those who are pure and devoted to simple moral principles perish? And what of Russia? It's horrifying to think who makes up their population after years of terror when those who denounced their neighbors survived and those who had no desire to make denunciations did not.

This thought, alas, leads to another: about the immense social class of lackeys, of subalterns of all stripes, the groveling, the obedient, those who know that their fate depends on their master's smile. Yes, a significant percentage of Europeans are descendants of domestic servants. But be wise, distinguish between honorable and dishonorable service, especially since you have no idea how genes combine and are transmitted.

I must have done something in that embassy for the couple of months from October to December. Even though only bits and pieces remained of the relative splendor of Putrament's ambassadorial tenure, when he hired brilliant people, when there were numerous receptions for the literary élite. I had a taste of that during my visit to Paris in the summer of 1949. I even gave a talk on Oscar Milosz in the Maison de la Pensée, a project of the French Communist Party, which was trying to monopolize all venues for lectures, concerts, exhibitions, etc., and was succeeding. And also those luminaries of French *lettres* on the embassy terrace. It didn't surprise me that Aragon was there, but since Supervielle was there, too, it meant that it was obligatory for the politically neutral to frequent the reds.

Not much came of that recent past, because the terror was contagious, after all, and the faces were sad, not party-going. Nevertheless, despite the revulsion that the "London Poles" felt for this outpost of renegades, the economic interests of a large number of people forced them to frequent this "court." These people were, first of all, painters and sculptors, usually starving, who were trying to get their hands on something—either meals or some paltry payment for sketches printed in the propaganda sheet published for the French Polonia. I tried to support the artists, although I had only modest funds. It's sad; once I organized a tea and they came, because they had to, but they hated it and I could feel it. I felt bad because of their humiliation; for instance, poor Zofia Stryjeńska. Some of them returned to Poland and were given studios there—Alina Szapocznikow, for one.

In 1949 the Krońskis were still in Paris, but I found them back in Warsaw, in their own apartment, when I turned up there for Christmas 1950. Their behavior at that time reminded me of Władek Borysowicz's behavior in Wilno after the city was occupied by Soviet troops in 1940. He was stroking his belly. He, who was always unemployed and dying of hunger, now had a job and a full belly; in other words, the superiority of the system. The Krońskis said nothing; they just kept talking about Mother. Mother is attentive, Mother gives everything, good Mother, the People's Democracy.

During my tenure, Pankiewicz's remains were brought from the South of France and buried in one of the Paris cemeteries, I don't remember which one. This had been initiated before my time. In 1934–35 I was part of a small group that would gather in the Louvre on Sundays to hear Pankiewicz's lectures as he led us from painting to painting. Other members of the group were Józef Czapski, who later wrote a monograph on Pankiewicz; Kazio and Fela Krance; occasionally the composer Roman Maciejewski, I think. And now Pankiewicz's funeral, with almost no one there, because the Warsaw embassy was burying him. A few other people and I. In a cold Paris rain.

I had a few friends in Paris, particularly those cynics from the newspaper, and also Nela, which is important. During the war she lived mainly within the small island of Polish intellectuals in Grenoble; nearby, in Laffrey, the death of her philosopher brother; her arrest and imprisonment by the Gestapo in Lyons (the head of the prison was the infamous Klaus Barbie). After the war the Miciński family tried to do a balancing act between Poland and France. The daughter returned to Poland with her mother and remained there, but Nela's other niece, her sister's daughter, was in Paris, and so on. In Paris, to tell the truth, Nela was always hungry; the room that she rented cost very little, but it was located in the Cité Falguière, an almost Asiatic slum.

My nerves were in very bad shape throughout those months. I understood that my position (first secretary) was a fiction, and I felt a gnawing anxiety about Janka, who was scheduled to undergo a Caesarian section. The principal reason for my condition was the necessity of constantly wearing a mask, just like Hamlet surrounded by spies.

April 18, 1988

Yesterday was the second anniversary of Janka's death. We went to the cemetery—Tony, Peter, the whole family.

I return to Paris in the autumn of 1950. The feeling that you are being followed can easily drive you into a kind of paranoia. The obliteration of the boundary between lucidity and hallucinations testifies to the miserable state I was in. Nela, awaiting appointment to a lectureship in Lyons, belonged partly to the embassy circle—the Krońskis, Julia Hartwig, a few painters. I would meet her in cafés, though, in order to speak frankly, tête-à-tête, and to seek her advice: Should I or shouldn't I go to Poland?

Nela categorically advised me not to go, while I insisted that they wouldn't do anything to me, because I had been accredited by the French government. Despite her advice, I went, only to escape from there barely alive. I met with her immediately afterward in an obscure café not far from Cité Falguière; we were certain that we were being followed. We changed cafés and the same characters turned up, one of them a woman in a green fez. We drove to the post office so I could phone Maisons-Laffitte, and the same thing happened. Like an oppressive, repetitive dream. Today it's more or less certain that they weren't from the Polish Security at all, but from the French Sureté.

$\mathscr{A}$PRIL 21, 1988

At the San Francisco airport, waiting for a plane to Dallas and Nashville.

About misanthropy. Others can say of us, "He was a misanthrope"; we ourselves don't say, "I am a misanthrope." But since there are many degrees of misanthropy, we can confess to a certain amount of it which requires keeping people at a discrete distance from us and which does not tolerate rubbing up against people en masse. From that perspective, America is better for me than the Slavic countries, and my Grizzly Peak has allowed me to survive various idiocies in the city below. A true misanthrope ought to live in a castle. Which is how the hero of Jules Verne's novel *Castle in the Carpathians* lives. His castle, in Transylvania, sits on an almost inaccessible, wild mountain, is surrounded by a moat, but that's not all; the current from high-tension electric wires will shock any daredevil who attempts to break in. There aren't any daredevils, however, because with the help of electricity the owner produces various incredible phenomena, so that people in the valley believe that the castle is inhabited by ghosts. The misanthrope lives alone with his faithful old servant and spends his time listening (on a phonograph) to the voice of a great Italian cantatrice whom he once loved, and watching her image on a screen (a prophecy of the invention of television!).

On board the plane.

The poverty of the human species. Physiological poverty, because what an absurd arrangement it is: genito-urinary love and a sojourn inside the female's belly; but also the poverty of mutually created unending myths that prevent us from attaining reality and seeing how things really were. Those myths that combine to form "culture"! Barely a half dozen or a dozen years pass, and people are already spinning threads and entangling a man, events, in a cocoon for their own benefit.

I have read many poems in several languages about Osip Mandelstam as a martyr for freedom. I have also heard the tapes of a Polish theatrical montage in his honor. All this has very little in common with the real Mandelstam.

A question: Is distortion, banalization, inescapable? Is it true that the wider the range—of fame, for example—the smaller the number of complications that are permitted to survive? And what is our role, we who already belong to the past, in inciting the myth? Which of our features, in other words, promotes it?

I once heard a recording of Konrad Swinarski's production of Mickiewicz's *Forefathers' Eve*. The not very modest thought comes to mind that Polish literature occasionally receives writers who are distinguished from the general mold by a certain sensitivity, and that therein lies the source of misunderstandings about aesthetic values, and other values, too—a mistaken conviction about a community of likes and dislikes.

Another thought, a modest one, but bitter. Perhaps my poems (many? several? a few?) contain a dash of kitsch which stimulates people's appetites for such recitations? After all, the more time passes, the more the law of simplification comes into play. Once upon a time, when he was writing them, Tuwim's poems also appeared innovative, but how many of them are banal today! All the more reason why I—living, striving, discriminating—do not praise such evidences of my own stumbling.

*A*PRIL 22, 1988

Nashville, Tennessee, the Vanderbilt Plaza Hotel.

Professor Donald Davie, Vanderbilt University, is retiring and returning to his native England. The Department of English is marking the occasion with a farewell ceremony at which Wendell Berry, Helen Vendler, and I are to appear. Wendell Berry was last night. The heir of the agrarian poets of the American South whose citadel was Vanderbilt University (Ransom, Tate). Defenders of traditional values, of an America of farmers, of Nature, now industrially poisoned. A local sarcasm: "Yes, his agrarian program is workable, provided one comes from a wealthy family, has inherited a large farm, and holds a professorship at the University of Kentucky."

Yesterday on the plane I reread Donald Davie's book on my poetry and discovered many apt observations, both pleasant and painful for me. An important distinction between the "I" of lyric poems and the "I" of dithyrambs (which is my case). The theme of this session is "The Poet's Responsibility." My reflex whenever I hear something like this: I would like to say that whenever I have tried very hard to be responsible I have been my least responsible. But that became apparent only much later.

*A*PRIL 23, 1988

It's over and I even extricated myself somehow from the usual compliments to the guest of honor, which absolutely must be spiced with humor. Helen Vendler delivered a lecture at four o'clock about Keats's views on the role of the poet, also quoting from two poets who were present in the auditorium—Donald Davie and me (my poem "The Poor Poet"). At eight in the evening Davie was officially presented with his Festschrift and then I gave my poetry reading.

I read Donald Davie's essay in *Durham Poetry* on the poetry of Zbigniew Herbert. Kot Jeleński is right: Polish literature today has become a world literature. Davie explains English receptivity to Herbert's ironic poetry in terms of England's post-war decline to an inferior position vis-à-vis America, like Poland in relation to Russia, and from this arises a demand for irony. An odd idea, to say the least.

At yesterday's reading, an enthusiastic group of young Poles. These new-comers of the eighties are everywhere.

My misanthropy cannot help but be tempered in America by an incredible, unexpected, astonishing discovery: that I can communicate with an audience through poems read in translation. I hold this against Western Europe: there's a lack of institutions there for the public reading of poetry. Here, as in Nashville yesterday, not only professors and students come, but also poetry readers from beyond the campus.

Not long ago, a high-school English teacher sent me the essays her students had written about my poetry reading at the University of Southern Illinois. She had taken her class to the reading. Their comments were clever, fresh; they amused me and moved me. They had never seen a Nobel Poet Laureate. They expected someone like Edgar Allan Poe (!) and were amazed to see such an ordinary man, talkative, and with a sense of humor. And also that they could understand the poems, even though poetry in general is incomprehensible.

APRIL 25, 1988

Aboard a plane from New York to San Francisco.

Exhausted more from drinking than from work. Though my reading in Polish and English at the Cornell Club at a benefit for the Polish Institute of Arts and Sciences did take a lot out of me; afterward, I could hardly stand on my feet. This time I sat around longer and chatted with various people, so I managed to repair the bad impression I made a few years ago when I left immediately after my reading, which looked like the demonstrative ar-rogance of a prima donna, although there really were reasons why I had to go.

Not only the Institute, but also a session about Gombrowicz at New York University under the auspices of the American PEN Club. The hall was full. Susan Sontag and John Simon read fragments from *Ferdydurke* and the *Diary*. Next, about Gombrowicz: John Simon, Susan, Janusz Głowacki, and I. Then dinner with other writers. Leon Wieseltier, literary editor of *The New Republic*, joins us. I learn from him that he is an admirer of Oscar Milosz's *The Noble Traveller* and has read it a couple of times.

To be at the bottom—to be on top. Our ambition ought to be satisfied;

this is healthy and normal, as long as one doesn't lose perspective on oneself. I blame myself for a certain lack of courage, a long-standing modesty that makes me incapable of reaching out and taking, of convincing myself that I deserve it.

From time to time I attempt to explore my former states of insecurity and timidity. What is disturbing is our gift for forgetting ("The ox doesn't remember when he was a calf").

April 27, 1988

Aboard a plane from San Francisco to Boise, Idaho.

I have blundered into various unanticipated realms, although I prepared myself for only one vocation. To me, having a strong "Metaphysical Sense of the Strangeness of Existence" meant "the strangeness of the existence of human society," or civilization, as we call it. My entire body of creative work should be divided into those works in which I attempted to express that feeling and all the remaining works, and only the former should be preserved: that would be in accord with my thinking. Although a lot could be saved from the latter group, too, in which the same thing is found under a different exterior.

It's just that I've managed to express so little, no more than flashes here and there.

A perspective that changes over time, no doubt. But also enduring elements. Above all, the piecing together of this whole human structure from the most animal-like individual beings amazed me already in my early youth. The institutions in which this is most clearly revealed: public toilets, brothels, cemeteries. I would say that the falseness of women results from the greater contrast in them than in men between their animal element and the mask they wear for their surroundings. A stunning young woman dresses and puts on makeup in front of a mirror in order to go forth like a conqueror, attracting the voracious eyes of men, yet a moment ago she was sitting on the toilet and she remembers that her bowel movement wasn't good and she is also aware that her period has just started and she is using a tampon. Taken together, this gives her a permanently guilty conscience, as it were, because she pretends so much, so often plays a role. Which probably encourages her to play other games, to practice purely utilitarian hypocrisy.

APRIL 28, 1988

At the Pendleton, Oregon, airport.

I have never been so far away—far away, that is, from everything. La Grande, Oregon, has a population of 11,000 people and a college, and prides itself on having an elevator operator, the only one within a radius of five hundred miles. The single tall building is seven stories high. A region about the size of Poland, with a density of six people per square mile. Mountains, forests (state-owned), wilderness. The name La Grande was given it by French trappers from Quebec. A living Nobel Laureate has never been seen in this college. People came to my reading from the surrounding area, too, which is to say from places two hundred miles away, but in the main they were professors and young people. The hospitality of George Venn, a poet who was attracted to this region with its environment unspoiled by pollution, and who teaches at the college and writes; he owns a home in the country, from which it's an easy drive to the "city." Along the road to Pendleton there are forests, more forests, an Indian reservation; in Pendleton I take a look at a woollens plant and the arena for the annual fall rodeo. A land of sheep, cowboys, Indians. And mushrooms. I envy them their boletuses and orange-latex milky mushrooms. Now, in the spring, they are gathering morels.

In a small propeller-driven plane, flying to Pasco and Portland. Over green rectangles that are intermingled with the golden yellow of unplowed land. The agriculture of dry regions: the land lies fallow for a year to soak up moisture, then wheat is sown, and then it lies fallow again for a year. We fly across the Columbia River.

My great joy at reading Barańczak's new poems in *Literary Notebooks* 22. Marvelous. His transitional phase has finally come to an end, his moulting; the snake has left his old skin (of Polish anguish) behind.

APRIL 29, 1988

At the Portland airport, waiting for my return flight.

Relief that this exhausting day and a half is over with. Yesterday, I thought I would collapse. The drive to Corvallis, in the rain, about two hours. Chitchat with the professors at an English Department get-together. A nap at my motel, fortunately, but not long enough. The reading was difficult, the auditorium was not entirely appropriate—a lack of direct contact. Then drinks with the faculty. The next day, this morning, that is, again the drive from Corvallis to Portland. Sitting on the campus, I prepare a new program for my performance from twelve to one; very successful, direct contact. Lunch in a restaurant with a few people, and then they drive me to the airport.

All the time, however, I'm divided into the person who already knows how to play the game the way they want him to, and another person who is immersed in his own thoughts. About human society as a marvel. And about Polish themes, thanks to that issue of *Literary Notebooks*.

When, in what circumstances, did that wise man, Jerzy Stempowski, make mistakes? When the perspective he favored, of looking back as if from eternity, encouraged him to treat current events as something that was old hat. True, for someone who is steeped in the Greek and Roman writers, there can be no entirely new products of the intellect, because everything is assignable to a known category. Nonetheless, the maxim "There is nothing new under the sun" is false. If there is no progress in perfection, there is at least progress in the complexity of cultural phases as they absorb what has come before them. Stempowski understood Gombrowicz in the same way the pre-war intelligentsia did—of which he was an exceptionally well-educated representative. That is, he saw in him immaturity, the arrogance of a young whippersnapper, mannerism.

$\mathcal{M}$AY 1, 1988

Only a one-day break in my travels. Yesterday, the christening of little Natalia, my goddaughter.

Aboard a plane from San Francisco to New York.

The question, I admit, is open: Can one have a good, classical, gentleman's education, like Stempowski, that would suffice for a correct evaluation of the present? Their evaluation is usually contemptuous. They are the ones, after all, who shrugged off Impressionism and, later, Cubism. From some distant perspective they may have been right, but their motives were wrong. I don't know, of course, what was Stempowski's attitude toward painting, because his early essay, "The Chimera as a Beast of Burden," is concerned exclusively with the sociology of painting.

I was on good terms with Stempowski. You could have counted the true liberals in Poland on the fingers of one hand, and he was a valuable ally for someone like me who could not tolerate "national" Poland. He was also a valuable ally for Giedroyc. His attitude toward the traditional Polish–Catholic mentality was expressed in his blasphemous witticism about Poland's geopolitical situation: "Fortunately, the Blessed Virgin created the Chinese."

How far did he err in his contemptuous judgment of Gombrowicz's *Diary*? *Nota bene*: I, too, said to myself when I read Kot Jeleński and Gombrowicz's correspondence about launching *Ferdydurke* in Europe that if I had to orchestrate my fame like that I would die of shame. I would have thought it beneath my dignity. So perhaps it was I and not "Master" Gombrowicz who was an arrogant squire? Or one of those Lithuanian grumblers? I did virtually nothing to launch myself; on the contrary, I acted against my own interests if I felt like it, although I didn't go as far as Jan Lebenstein, who threw the most influential critic in Paris down a flight of stairs.

I return to my main theme: the strangeness of human society. You don't need conspiracies, rebellions, or martyrdom to contemplate this. Even without such diversions, daily life will suffice for this. And there were certainly plenty of people among the Poles who were more philosophically gifted than inclined to throw bombs and blow up bridges. But their talent wasn't of much use, because they were in the grip of situations that had trapped them against their will. In France during the Second World War, Matisse, Picasso, and others peacefully went on with their painting on the Côte d'Azur. "Neither a sword nor a shield are the nation's weapon, / But a masterpiece is" (Cyprian Norwid). Is it any wonder that there are so few masterpieces in Poland?

Piłsudski, defending his choice of a revolutionary path, once said, "I could not live in an outhouse." And if someone was a writer, then he wrote protest works, like Żeromski. Obviously, I was always cognizant of this, but at a given moment I understood it differently, without fear of breaking a patriotic taboo. I have tried breaking the taboo, but always with a bad conscience. Now I see a conflict between the "chivalric ethos" and art, which always demands disinterested contemplation.

Society. The number of variations of customs, religions, and ways of indoctrinating the young seems truly without limit. Our imagination is capable of suggesting only a few of these. The testimony of the Spanish missionaries from the territories that are now Arizona and California, where they came upon "wild" people (an epithet which, despite the legend of the noble savage, reflects quite accurately the white man's revulsion): complete nakedness, stench, relieving themselves in front of everyone, almost instinctive thievery. And so on.

The famous "discovery"—organized by crafty anthropologists—of a tribe of cavemen in the Philippines who supposedly had never had any contact with civilization was meant to confirm man's dream of himself as gentle, sensitive, child-loving, serene, without violence or wars. Undoubtedly, anthropology has taught us to look for an unlikely complexity in every "primitive" society. To what extent, however, did the myth of innate goodness that has been spoiled by civilization motivate and cast its aura over those anthropologists' reports? I have had similar suspicions while reading an anthropological study of African Pygmies.

The remote accessibility of former societies. Soon the society I was a part of will also become unfathomable. Even Mr. Jerzy Stempowski, whose biography I often think about. Not only was he a so-called confirmed bachelor, but no woman was ever in his immediate vicinity. His life was the model of the gentleman scholar's complete withdrawal from those spheres where the affairs of mortals take place, as if sex were beneath the demands of good taste—just like religion, which he absolutely ignored, or the modern concept of a fatherland, which was alien to that sworn émigré. To be sure, even for me he seemed to have come from someplace else, from the era before World War I.

MAY 6, 1988

A day and a half in New York, in the Hotel Algonquin. Monday evening (May 2) we arrived with our baggage at the Manhattan Theatre Club for an evening of Polish poetry read mainly in English translation by Piotr Sommer, Stanisław Barańczak, and me. Other poets whose works we read: Miron Białoszewski, Ryszard Krynicki, Zbigniew Herbert, Wisława Szymborska, Anna Swir. At 11 p.m. we took off for Lisbon on Mrs. Ann Getty's private jet. We were acquainted with some of the guests. It was the first time this Wilno provincial had flown on such a plane, whose interior appointments (wood paneling, brass) reflected the good taste of millionaires. A writers' conference under the auspices of Getty's Wheatland Foundation.

MAY 9, 1988

The Central European group: Adam Zagajewski, Jan Błoński, Jan Józef Szczepański, Krzysztof Michalski, Czeslaw Milosz, Georgy Konrad, Danilo Kiš, Peter Esterhazy (a novelist), Mihajlo Lalić (a poet), Veno Taufer (a poet), Josef Škvorecký. Bohumil Hrabal and Ivan Klima were denied passports. The Russian, Soviet, and émigré group: Annensky (a critic), Joseph Brodsky, Anatoly Kim, Tatiana Tolstaya, Sergei Dovlatov (from New York), Grant Matevosian (from Armenia), Zinovy Zinik (from London).

An astounding get-together of Soviet and émigré writers for only the second time. (The first time was one year ago in Washington, also at a conference sponsored by the Wheatland Foundation.) When did our Paris meeting of Polish poets from Poland and the emigration take place? Probably in 1967. Iwaszkiewicz, Przyboś, and Artur Międzyrzecki from Poland, and from the emigration, Kazimierz Wierzyński, myself, Jan Brzękowski. That encounter, too, was a harbinger of slow change. The even more astonishing collision between the Russians and "Central Europe"—a term they were hearing for the first time. Their unconcealed horror at the hostility of the Central Europeans, which they had trouble accepting, because Russians, of course, are raised from childhood to believe that they are admired and loved by everyone. One particular exchange with the Hungarians illustrates their utter lack of understanding and our mutually incomprehensible assumptions. (Gyorgy Konrad: "Yes, you liberated us, but that was forty-three years ago. Take back your tanks already! It's been going on too long!") They don't comprehend the degree to which their thinking is imperialistic or, as Salman Rushdie remarks from the audience, colonialist. Joseph Brodsky attempts to defend them, attacking the concept of Central Europe. A colleague from Poland tells me later, "I felt terrible. They turned pale, they squirmed. And what about the non-Russians among them? They're in the same position as we are." It was worth coming to Lisbon just to witness such a confrontation, which would have been impossible even a couple of years ago.

$\mathcal{M}$AY 12, 1988

Hôtel L'Aiglon, Menton.

Nela asks me a lot of questions about events and acquaintances we both once knew in Bucharest, Paris, Brie, Montgeron. I keep replying, "I don't remember." My memory is totally selective, which leads to the question: Does forgetting last forever, or are there brain cells that preserve people and names, so that it is only necessary to stimulate those strata? For instance, for the longest time I was unable to recall the name of a street from the autumn of 1950, and then it suddenly leaped out at me: rue Dumont-d'Urville. This is unquestionably both a biological, or psychological, problem and a theological one (the Last Judgment).

We're having no luck with Menton. It's overcast. Rainy. But the weather's just the same in Lisbon and, according to the weather reports, in Paris. Exactly like last year; May in Europe.

The clash between the two panels in Lisbon, the Central European and the Russian, duly reported in *The New York Times*, deserves notice as the first confrontation of this kind since the end of the Second World War. The guests from Moscow were encountering the idea of Central Europe for the first time, which explains their anger and confusion. "We know Poland, Hungary, Czechoslovakia, and the literature of these countries," they said, "but what's this about Central Europe?" The émigré Joseph Brodsky took exactly the same position, which isn't news, of course; it has been public knowledge ever since his polemic against Milan Kundera. His friend and fellow Nobel Laureate, Milosz, in complete solidarity with his Hungarian, Yugoslav, Czech, and Polish colleagues, retorted that it is high time to break with Russian literature's taboo against any mention of the borders of the Imperium, and noted that it was Joseph Brodsky himself who first used the word "Imperium" in his poetry to refer to the Soviet Union.

The Russians' pained astonishment points to the touchy issues that lurk within any conception of the countries under their domination as a collectivity or union. It would be a good idea to reconstruct the process by which the term Central Europe came into use some ten years ago and met with relative success in the press of various languages. If it hadn't been accepted as an appropriate term, at least in certain literary circles, the organizers of the writers' congress in Lisbon would not have arranged a special panel under that heading.

MAY 15, 1988

Menton, Hôtel L'Aiglon.

In 1945, in Cracow, I experienced the end of Europe. It even amazes me that that acute consciousness of the end was registered so inadequately by me and by others. If someone had told me then that everything would begin *da capo*, at least in the western part of the European continent, I would not have believed him. In fact, the inhabitants of the western part also did not believe this; it seemed only a matter of months before the Communists would take power.

Those who expected that war would break out (the London emigration, for example) could easily find the fuel to maintain their fever. Despite this, America stubbornly began to bring the Marshall Plan to life—to save Western Europe, that is. When Stalin acquired the atom bomb in 1949 and immediately made war in Korea, currents of fear, if not outright panic, spread across the world once again. Janka's reluctance to accompany me when I left America in October 1950 was understandable.

It seems that Antoni Słonimski, embarrassed at the least honorable act of his literary career (his attack on me after my escape), justified himself by saying I had demonstrated my baseness by taking off after collecting my salary in Paris on February 1, 1951. That is what he was told. The enemy has to be a scoundrel, too. This did not accord with the truth. Instead of reporting at the embassy, I feigned illness and surfaced in Maisons-Laffitte at *Kultura*.

Kultura had only recently moved to France from Rome and was camping out in almost wartime fashion in a half-ruined house on Avenue Corneille, in a neighborhood of large parks that struck me as exceptionally gloomy, as did everything, by the way, that fall and winter. Announcing my impending arrival by telephone, I did not know what I would find, although I had deduced a few things about their Paris arrangements from Kroński's letters.

Both Krońskis wound up in Paris after their liberation from German camps (their excellent German had saved them), and initially they were on the side of "London." His article on Existentialism appeared in the first Paris number of *Kultura*, which later drove him to attacks of fear. Shortly afterward, however, they went over to the side of the embassy of the People's Republic of Poland. ("The Fascists pay too little," he wrote to me.)

That term, "Fascists," wasn't just an example of Kroński's humor; in Paris all opponents of Communism were branded with it—the entire Polish Army in the West and the new émigrés from the East. The complexity of my feelings, my dread at what was happening in Poland combined with my antipathy for the losers, made it very difficult for me to talk in that kitchen on Avenue Corneille, where the oilcloth-covered table was used for the phalanstery's meals and for opening the morning mail. For me it meant hitting bottom, simply because I had nowhere to go. To a certain extent, my wounded pride made my rudeness toward my hosts and my rabid sarcastic attacks on them a foregone conclusion.

My quarrels with them were largely triggered by my provocative behavior, by my pretending to be stupid in order to irritate those "reactionaries." Our mentalities were mutually alien because of the conservatism of Jerzy Giedroyc and also of Zosia and Zygmunt Hertz, which they still held to from their pre-war Polish phase and would only gradually let go of. I think that the confrontation with an exceptionally nasty but intelligent individual somehow influenced the direction taken by *Kultura*. Especially in regard to literature. Giedroyc had reached his decision to publish a volume of Gombrowicz containing *The Marriage* and *Trans-Atlantic* before I showed up, but Zygmunt's angry though quiet resistance and his screaming (when Giedroyc didn't listen) give some idea of their habits. What a distance between what Zygmunt was then and what he became later!

If *Kultura* had not demonstrated an extraordinary ability to evolve, it would have remained just like the London circles and would not have exerted any influence on intellectual change in Poland. In addition to his incredible perseverance, Giedroyc was characterized by absolute independence and sheer cussedness, which protected him from any conformist tendencies. Viewed in this light, his launching of the publishing activity in France by two reprobate writers—Gombrowicz (a jester, a megalomaniac) and Milosz (a red)—had an almost symbolic meaning.

𝓜AY 16, 1988

Paris, rue de Rennes (Mary McCarthy's apartment).

I sat in the library, miserable, suffering from a nervous itch that made me scratch myself until I bled. The library was dark with the smoke from my cigarettes and from the stove, which had to be fed lumps of coal. For the first few months, where I was staying was a mystery; I had simply disappeared. Even so, whenever I went down to the town center, Zygmunt never left my side, because a kidnapping attempt could not be ruled out.

Paris, the city of light, the city of poetry, painting, theaters, of architecture that acquires ever new colors "under the blows of the sun." Alas, to know a great deal about it means to know too much about the laws of human society. I compile a list of Paris's famous names and compare them today with what they were, what they published, in 1951. Do they blush? I doubt it. The current has kept them afloat.

May 20, 1988, Rue de Rennes

What number Paris is this by now? No other city could, unchanging, meet my transformed self as this one has, in my youth, my prime, and now in my old age. After all, Wilno and Warsaw have ceased to be what they once were; they are different cities now. But here: the same streets, the same metro stations, the same cafés; it's only I who see everything differently each time. Where I am staying is not far from the Catholic Institute on rue d'Assas and the Alliance Française on Raspail—in other words, my year 1934–35. Would I be able to reconstruct my distant self, the man I was then, and the way I processed the data of my five senses at that time? "The Gates of the Arsenal," which I wrote that year, is accessible to me from the outside, like a finished creation, separate from me. And Paris, because of its unchanging nature, is always a subject of contemplation for me, with the contrast between its firmly entrenched form and the torrent of human lives—fragile, fleeting, subordinate to time, they rush onward, slip past, perish, while the torrent flows on. The coeds in the cafés on Boulevard Saint-Michel! Where are those seventy-year-old women now? This is what is most worth pondering: the reality that appears before our eyes is always different and undergoes changes depending on our phases; at the same time it is different for the eyes of everyone in this human stream, and is also subject to the changes of the experienced moment. Taken together, an infinite number of Parises. I would speak of film frames were it not that each taste, color, smell, state of ecstasy or depression, is unique; in other words, photography is not an accurate enough metaphor. So the question: Where is the objective truth of this reality if this reality exhibits a myriad subjective hues? What does the eye of God see? This warehouse of subjective states, or some substratum, some "as it really is"?

One has to discriminate between microchanges and macrochanges. I used to be hampered in my contemplation of Paris as a human city in a "pure" state by the exoticism it held for me, a newcomer from a distant European province. One had to be French to accept its customs as natural, to not even notice them; that is, to perceive the flavor of certain speech intonations but not others, or of particular ways of reacting, as each generation of young Frenchmen learns in school. Not being French, I found that my access to certain mysteries—culinary ones, for example—was blocked. There were many other reasons why I, a savage, was intimidated. Gradually, however, a melancholy feeling of community prevailed, and one particular species, the French, no longer obscured the universal pitiful characteristics of the human race—at least for a thoughtful observer, since a foreigner will never manage to penetrate to the very center of French society.

The most fundamental change, however, occurred when I moved to America and began to visit Paris as a tourist. Earlier, Paris was something of a cloud-shrouded mountain peak that I *had* to ascend, like Balzac's heroes who come from the provinces to take the capital by storm. In theory, that is, because in practice this was rendered impossible by political hostility toward an émigré. Nonetheless, the Prix Littéraire Européen in 1953 opened doors of certain publishing houses, but then, almost deliberately, I ruined my chances by choosing to write a "conservative" book, *The Issa Valley.* One way or another, the tensions and anxieties of my poverty interfered with disinterested thinking. As a tourist, I could observe the city's currents without worrying whether I would eat tomorrow.

$\mathcal{M}$AY 21, 1988, RUE DE $\mathcal{R}$ENNES

For example, Paris in 1951. No matter how often I ride into the city from Orly Airport, I always wait for the taxi to pass the Porte d'Orléans and turn into Avenue du Général-Leclerc, and then I catch a glimpse as we pass of the building (that one, right?) in which Mac and Sheba Goodman rented their lovely apartment. Mac worked in the economic section of the American Embassy; he specialized in oil. Given the dollar's exchange rate at that time, his salary translated into a lot of money. Sheba managed the Paris branch of the International Rescue Committee, an institution which was founded in New York to deliver aid to Spanish refugees after the Civil War and which afterward assisted refugees from many countries. Both of them were New Yorkers. In their youth they had experimented with Communism and they told me, laughing, about their stay at a Marxist summer camp where a dynamic, positive, progressive spirit reigned and where the day began with a joyous summons on the megaphone to join in morning gymnastics: "Good morning ev-ery-body / It's time for ex-er-cise." They soon lost interest, but they carried away from their experiences an interest in the consequences of the Russian Revolution (attentive readers of Koestler and Orwell) and a fondness for refugees from the East. *Nota bene*: Janka, too, attended a similar Marxist camp in Poland around 1930, which is not insignificant, because there was something about her when we first met that distinguished her from the Polish young intelligentsia, who were generally right wing.

Mac studied physics in college, and it paid off. Coming from Jewish immigrant families that were not particularly well off, the Goodmans were poor in their youth; they were experiencing wealth for the first time in Paris, thanks to his position, and they knew how to enjoy it. Their apartment was furnished luxuriously, and Mac loved doing the honors at the bar. Their home was open, warm, hospitable to guests; they had frequent receptions and dinner parties. In a sense, that home was my Parisian refuge. I have never forgotten the Goodmans' warmth nor their faith in me—after all, they bet on me despite all the slander, and there was plenty of slander, not only on the part of the reds, but even in the political section of the American Embassy, with which Mac, to be sure, had nothing in common. A certain woman of Russian descent was employed there, and her adviser on Communist affairs was Ryszard Wraga. Before the war, Wraga (not his real name) was head of Polish intelligence in Russia. Stanisław Vincenz remembered him as a young lieutenant, blindly devoted to Piłsudski. This may not be sufficient qualification to become an intelligent espionage chief, and if one may judge by his activities in Paris, Polish intelligence had understood very little of what was happening behind the Eastern border. Wraga suffered from acute espionitis; he connected everything to the activities of spies and agents. In other words, he became a victim of his own profession, which drove him to become a sort of kook. This only goes to show how dangerous the profession of spycatcher can be. As for me, he was absolutely convinced that I was an exceptionally dangerous agent who appeared to have "chosen freedom," but was actually working for my Eastern handlers. And since *Kultura* had welcomed me, Giedroyc, in his opinion, was "objectively" guilty of acting as an agent. In this spirit, Wraga published a number of articles in Polish that were really denunciations, and then fed these and other denunciations to his Russian girlfriend (whom he later married). When *The Captive Mind* appeared, no further proof was needed: such a book could only have been written by a Communist agent.

Even though they didn't know Polish (which means I didn't exist for them as a poet), as friends Mac and Sheba understood my sufferings and Janka's efforts in America to get me a visa, which, as can be seen from my file in the American Embassy, was impossible. I met a lot of Americans at the Goodmans', many of them with the picturesque life stories of international ex-Communists—like Bertram Wolfe, author of monumental historical works on Lenin, Trotsky, and Stalin. There were also foreigners—for instance, the Hindu writer and philosopher Raja Rao, whom I met again many years later at the University of Texas. Did they have French guests, too? Rarely.

My friendship with the Goodmans continued after Janka and the children came to France. When we were living in Brie-Comte-Robert, the arrival of the Goodmans' long limousine would be greeted by Tony and Peter as a joyous, even if fairly frequent, family holiday, because, after all, we had no other family. Once we spent a vacation together, in 1955, I think, in the Aosta Valley at the foot of the Gran Paradiso massif, where the ancient royal hunting grounds had been turned into a national park. We had to observe certain diplomatic conventions in our relations with them, however, because of Hannah, who was terribly jealous and hated Sheba, which meant we had to avoid any encounters between the enemy camps. Hannah had been brought up in the Czech lands when they still belonged to the Habsburg monarchy, so she was culturally German; she had settled in France, and she and her husband had lived out the war on a farm in the Dordogne, but she spoke English fluently. I was never able to figure out the causes of her hatred of Sheba, but I believe she was responsible for pushing Sheba out of the International Rescue Committee in Paris. Sheba's kindness and some-what bovine gentleness, however, couldn't possibly have given any cause for those outbursts of rabid passion. In contrast to my friendship with the Good-mans, who had accepted me at once, my acquaintance with Hannah—at the Committee, where I had appeared as a petitioner—began badly. As she told me later, I didn't make a good impression; I was gloomy, ill at ease, secretive, and seemingly ready to provide plenty of material for suspicion. Only gradually, after the arrival of my family, did Hannah's distrust change into love for us, especially for the children, but it was a fanatical love in its exclusivity.

MAY 22, 1988, RUE DE RENNES

Mac and Sheba kept track of new publications and knew who was who among the literary names, but our conversations were not particularly in-tellectual. Mac considered himself a poet who was hampered by the necessity of earning a living; in other words, he was one of those minor writers whose number has been increasing steadily in this century. A couple of his poems

A YEAR OF THE HUNTER   245

were successful and I even translated one into Polish. He worked for years in his spare time on (yet another) translation of Paul Valéry's *Le Cimetière marin*.

Hannah, on the other hand, had a rare, gluttonous appetite for every sort of topicality—in literature, politics, art, film, theater, for books in three languages, for gossip and life stories. During her almost weekly Sunday visits to Brie, she would unload her week's collection of information in non-stop conversation with me, until Janka's head began to ache from our raucous exchanges. I shall describe Hannah and her circle of friends later on.

So, 1951 passed and suddenly it was 1952. I have to give a very abbreviated sketch of Jeanne Hersch. When Karl Jaspers taught in Heidelberg, he had two very talented women students. One was Hannah Arendt and the other was Jeanne. Arendt emigrated to America and became famous there. Her colleague did not have to emigrate from Europe because she was Swiss, but her language, French, placed certain limitations on her activities. Jeanne's father, Liebman Hersch, was from Wilno; he was an activist in the Bund there and had had to escape from the tsarist government in 1908, I think. As a political émigré in Geneva, industrious and robust, he became a professor of statistics at the University of Geneva. Jeanne's mother was a physician. They spoke Polish at home, which explains why Jeanne had some knowledge of the language, although she didn't speak it very well.

She was a friend of Józef Czapski's and that's how I got to know her. Now I have a problem: how can you describe a quite extraordinary person in just a few lines? A mind that was philosophical to the core (since childhood), perhaps even excessively inclined to discriminations, to precise *distinguo*. A love of truth and an ability to instantly seize on falsehood, but also a recognition of those hazy screens behind which philosophers often hide. (She couldn't stand Heidegger.) She was direct, sharp, obstinate, incapable of diplomatic tactics and compromises; participants (mostly men) in meetings and scholarly conferences were afraid of her, and I have had the experience of seeing her destroy their arguments with one thrust.

Apparently, she was a superb pedagogue, first in the Ecole Internationale de Genève and later as a professor of philosophy at the University of Geneva. For a while she was also head of the philosophical section of UNESCO. In addition to her own books, she worked for years translating Jaspers's works into French, faithful to the master of her youth. Thanks to her, I paid Jaspers a visit in Basel shortly before his death; he wrote the introduction to the

German edition of *The Captive Mind*. She also introduced me to Hannah Arendt in Paris.

Her singular nature: for it would not be easy today to find another person as consumed by moral passion as she was. From the tribe of prophets. "A daughter of the wilderness," as our mutual friend Stanisław Vincenz described her. Her socialism, derived from her family and confirmed by her membership in the Geneva Socialist Party, was a matter of moral obligation above all. On the same grounds, it ruled out any totalitarian temptations, not only Soviet, but also those contained in the work of Hegel and Marx. Jeanne was a staunch anti-Communist and she contemptuously dismissed the entire Parisian leftist fashion of the fifties as *baratin*. I needed her as a wall against which I could bounce the balls of my provocations, and those provocations demonstrated that I was suffering from the "Hegelian sting" and needed arguments capable of overcoming my arguments.

Our friendship lasted for decades, through periods of varying closeness and distance, with appalling quarrels, but also with humor. I have to steel myself to make a very difficult confession: I was afraid of her. Just as all the male participants in those meetings and conferences were afraid of her, although maybe somewhat differently. Unfortunately, Jeanne was doomed to isolation, because everyone was afraid of her. That air was so morally pure it couldn't be breathed. How could I, twisted, irresolute, and, in my opinion, something of a pig, endure it? And, to top it off, a man who loves to drink? For Jeanne, alcohol was Evil, a symbol of the eclipse of consciousness, of that which is most precious, since for her, after all, clarity of thought and behavioral correctness were inseparable.

Brave. Absolutely just. Demanding a great deal of herself and of others. Aggressive; you wouldn't want to contradict her. Her threatening finger. The rigor of her intellect, infallible, would turn against her as a result of what I would call a lack of flexibility. In the final analysis, one has to know when to let go and when to insist—in thinking, in value judgments. Kot Jeleński thought highly of her, but he didn't praise her ascetic moralizing. He, who was so supple, so curious about all sorts of points of view, had to accuse her of growing more and more rigid by holding firm to her unbreakable principles. Another of our mutual friends, Stanisław Vincenz, treated her like a good, kind daughter who also happened to be a bit loony, and he would laugh uproariously whenever he talked with her about her adventures. For there was much in her that diverged from the accepted norm, eccentricities that people considered unseemly (especially in pharisaic Geneva) and that derived from her habit of always staking everything she had, one hundred percent, without considering whether people would think about it or what they would think, and of being prepared to take on the tanks of accepted custom with her bare hands. She was not well liked. But she had loyal close friends and did not keep them jealously to herself. I became very fond of her co-translator of Jaspers, Hélène Naef, and the whole Naef family. In Geneva I also met the writer Denis de Rougemont, Robert Hainard, the painter of animals, and the excellent (I think so today) poet Jean Paul de Dadelsen.

May 23, 1988, Rue de Rennes

Jeanne's type of fastidiousness—about people, styles, books—appealed to me and I could trust her in this. When she said that something I wrote was good, I knew that she wasn't trying to boost my ego or give me an empty compliment. I was an even stranger creature for her than she was for me. She thought I was the most "instrumental" person she knew. That is, I was totally different in my life and in those hours that I spent at my desk writing, as if I lived only to serve as an instrument for that other self. (I could have cited Krasiński's lines, "A stream of beauty flows through you, / But you are not beauty"—but Jeanne did not know Polish poetry.) She had absolute faith in my talent, and no matter what anyone else may have thought, my literary prizes were no surprise to her.

She urged me to write *The Seizure of Power* for a contest. I shrugged my shoulders. I did agree to do it, but unwillingly, arguing that in the twentieth century the novel can no longer be an excellent work of art and that it wasn't worth it to practice that genre. As an experiment, and also to please her, I began working on the novel, producing a certain amount of text per day. The novel was finished in two months, more or less. She translated it into French and met the submission date. According to the rules of the Prix Littéraire Européen, financed in Geneva by Les Guildes du Livre, which was a book club of sorts, national juries in the European countries made the first selections and nominated their candidates. I was nominated by the French jury (even though the manuscript was marked *"traduit du polonais"*). The prize (five thousand Swiss francs) was divided between me and a German prose writer named Warsinsky. The sum of 2,500 Swiss francs (a large amount of money at the time) was less important than the book's publication by book clubs in Switzerland and France. This is how I was able to support myself by my pen and bring my family to France.

When I complained that I did not want to write a novel, I did not know that I would soon violate that principle again by writing The Issa Valley. For entirely different reasons, to be sure. As an attempt at self-therapy, in order to extricate myself from a dialectical bottleneck that was making poetry impossible, and also out of pure spite. It was not what was demanded by the Paris market, which was left-leaning and chased after the latest fashion. Jeanne appreciated that. The translation into French cost her a good deal of effort; after all, the French Academy had gradually removed from its dictionaries many old local words relating to farming, hunting, fishing, weather conditions, etc. Jeanne slaved away, surrounded by dictionaries, and she did this during a period of rancor between us, which made her achievement even more heroic. I don't think the book had good reviews. I remember my photograph, probably in L'Express, with the caption, "La metaphysique est facile." As if what is difficult and worthy of a writer are social and political affairs, and someone who is interested in metaphysics is guilty of escapism. Albert Camus liked the novel. But the book acquired faithful readers and had favorable reviewers mainly in West Germany, where Dr. Kaspar Witsch, at that time director of the firm of Kiepenheuer und Witsch, was its supporter and publisher. True, the quality of that translation was an unknown for me; I suspected a certain old-fashioned tone in the style of the translator, Maryla Reifenberg, a very nice lady who had come to Munich in 1912 as a girl from a Polish manor and had remained in Germany for the rest of her life, marrying a gentle giant, the half-Dutch art critic Benno Reifenberg.

Jeanne was a pretty good school for me in intellectual mountaineering, and I felt truly fortified whenever she said, "De nouveau tu as oublié d'être bête," which means something like "You've forgotten again how to be stupid." Philosophically, she represented Jaspersonian Existentialism and its "philosophical faith." Nota bene: I had a conversation with Jaspers on the religious upbringing of children. He attached a great deal of weight to biblical tradition, and although he disliked Catholicism, he advised Catholics to give their children a Catholic education as a path to the Bible. Somewhat like Albert Camus, who asked me if I wasn't surprised that he, an atheist, had his children prepared for their First Communion.

I was influenced not by our discussions alone but also by Jeanne's philosophical books—only somewhat by L'Illusion philosophique, but very powerfully by L'Etre et la forme. Much later, she produced a book that categorized political doctrines, *Les Idéologies et la réalité*; it appeared as a Paris *Kultura* publication in my Polish translation under the title *Polityka i rzeczywistość* [Politics and Reality]. I believe that her true arena, however, was always the towering regions of philosophy, not its social applications, the analysis of which brought such fame to Hannah Arendt. Jeanne stayed on the boundary between philosophy and theology. I regret that I could not listen in on her discussions with the superb Jesuit theologian Gaston Fessard; her friendship with him dates from my American years. Father Fessard was probably the only one among his contemporaries who elaborated a system of Christian historiosophy (I don't count Teilhard de Chardin, because I don't acknowledge him as a thinker) based on the Hegelian dialectic of the master and the slave and also on the Paulist dialectic of the Jew and the pagan.

These interests did not mean that Jeanne ever betrayed any inclination to convert to Christianity. She participated in the Castel Gandolfo seminar, but not as a Christian. Because I have always sought the company of pious people (to make up for my own deficiencies), I valued her piety above all; she was truly a priestess of transcendence as well as a voice obedient to a summons from on high. And in the name of that quality I was and am prepared to forgive her faults.

May 24, 1988, Rue de Rennes

A visit to the Broca Hospital to see Hannah, who is ninety-two and has been hospitalized because she broke her leg.

Métro Glacière. The stop for the former Palais du Peuple and, less famous, the Salvation Army shelter for the homeless. Lacking money for a hotel, the three of us slept there in the summer of 1931—Elephant, Robespierre (Stefan Jędrychowski), and I. It is hard not to be haunted by images of everything that was waiting in the wings for those three boys.

And now, Hannah. The Broca Hospital is *de long séjour*, which means it is primarily a home for the aged. I know these repositories for broken dolls. The senile dementia, the feeble steps with a cane, or gliding about in wheelchairs, the muttering, gibberish, and birdlike screams of the mad. Hannah is almost blind; it was hard for her to recognize me. But her mind is working well and her memory is good, although she complains that she can't remember names.

Hannah wrote her doctoral dissertation in Vienna on the work of Thomas Mann; it was published in 1925 on the occasion of Mann's fiftieth birthday. She emigrated to France in 1930. There, in the hospital, we talk about her friends and relatives—those whom I did not know and those whom I knew. I did not know her husband, a translator from the German, and I probably met Baladine Kłossowski only once; she was Rilke's confidante and the mother of two painters, Balthus and Pierre Kłossowski. I used to see Pierre at Hannah's. I did not know the art historian Elie Faure, who found them their place in Dordogne during the war. And Leon Trotsky, who used to be their guest whenever he came to Paris, is another era and would demand an entire essay on the Trotskyist sympathies of the American and German émigré left before the Second World War. Thanks to Hannah, I knew Alfred and Marguerite Rosmer, old activists in the French labor movement, whom we used to visit in their country home outside Paris.

Madame Weil, Simone Weil's mother. It was Hannah who led me to her, to that apartment in the Quartier Latin, high above the Luxemburg Garden. That was when I was working on Simone Weil's *Selected Writings* in Polish translation. Her room, the table at which she wrote. From Hannah one could learn that Simone had had lengthy conversations with Leon Trotsky, who could appreciate her dueling abilities.

First and foremost: Muriel. Here, various strands converge, and also our household. Muriel Gardner, an American, from a very wealthy family (Armour hams); she studied medicine in Vienna before World War II and after the annexation of Austria she became deeply involved in the anti-Hitler underground. The film *Julia*, about a courier in this underground, borrows from her life, which Lillian Hellman attributed to a certain Julia, in defiance of the truth. In Vienna, Muriel's comrade in her anti-Hitler activities was the socialist Joseph Buttinger, who began life as a shepherd in a Tyrolean village; later on, she married him. After World War II the Buttingers became great friends and protectors of Hannah, and she visited them in America a couple of times; when they came to Paris they would invite a large number of people from Hannah's entourage, including Janka and me, to dinners in Left Bank restaurants. The Buttingers' circle, to which Stephen Spender also belonged, should be supplemented with another of Hannah's circles, which was loosely connected with the first; Dwight Macdonald and his wife, Nancy Macdonald (who was deeply involved in helping Spanish refugees), would have appeared there.

One measure of the high regard that the Buttingers had for Hannah, which was manifested by their fulfilling her every wish, was their purchase of the house in Montgeron. We had been renting, for very little money, an old house in Brie that belonged to a Monsieur Benier, but our lease had expired and M. Benier needed the house for his family. In 1956 we were searching for a new place, in the country (because Paris was expensive, and also because Janka felt that the city was not a good place for children). But everything that we looked at cost more than we could afford. Then Hannah had an inspiration. With an interest-free loan from the Buttingers, we bought the house in Montgeron, with its large garden, near the La Pelouse green belt and right next door to the *lycée* that Tony would be attending. That amount, which today would be ridiculously small, meant a great deal then. When we moved to California, the house was sold and the loan repaid.

I mowed the grass there so diligently and Janka gradually made so many improvements that our neighbors considered us wealthy Americans, even though, despite my backbreaking efforts, we could barely make ends meet. It's interesting that our children, as we learned later, never figured out that Janka often was afraid to go to the store in Brie because of our unpaid debts and that our Montgeron prosperity was entirely a façade.

And now Hannah is here. Certainly, killing people, as has been done with such enthusiasm in this century, is bad. A sudden and unexpected death, however, is merciful in comparison with slow and—even worse— fully conscious, dying. This eternal, unchanging sediment of horror, with that festive noisy spectacle on the surface, provides, for me at least, an argument against the goodness of the Creator. This really eats at me and I return to the point I started from, to my metaphysical despondency as a fifteen-year-old. Because, in the final analysis, the construct no longer holds according to which true life begins after death, and the body as the temporary dwelling place of the soul has been replaced by a body which is identical with the individual, cared for, adored, tested, weighed. The only I, corporeal, inescapably traversing the way of all flesh. I do not know if those Christians whose faith is very strong are capable of stepping beyond the body, toward Heaven or Hell, since the pounding of our blood, our greed, our sensual appetites grip us here and carry us along, make us participate in the festival on the surface. As a fifteen-year-old I felt alienated, *not yet* summoned to the festivities, envious of those who strove, ran, yearned, sated themselves, and did not see an illusion. Vincenz has a story about Dobosz the bandit, who was invited to a ball in a castle in the Carpathians. It was a magnificent ball; there were a large number of richly dressed beautiful women, color, pomp, dances to the music of a small orchestra. But one of Dobosz's comrades noticed that from time to time the musicians dipped their fingers in a bowl of some kind of fluid and daubed it on their eyelids. He crept over and did the same thing. Then, instead of seeing a splendid ball, he saw skeletons dancing to the music of devils. He grabbed Dobosz by the arm and they ran from the castle, which was a ruin atop a dark mountain. It seems that now, in old age, I am once again falling into a state of alienation and the ball does not make me happy. Or it does, but less and less often.

Hannah says she wants only one thing—to die—and that she cannot kill herself, how could she, because "I never even killed a fly in my entire life." She tells me her dream: she was in the Opera and was walking up the stairs, but when she reached the doors, they were locked. And then more stairs and locked doors. "How can one exit from life?" she asks. "What can I do to fall asleep and not wake up?" Who could succeed in convincing this helpless being, whose one desire is not to be, that she should feel the hope inherent in being alive? Let us note that in calling this arrangement of the world monstrous, we enter into a purely human solidarity, we underline our, our species', uniqueness in the universe, and our consciousness and our moral protest are backed by a bright and weak God against the dark and powerful God of Nature.

Lev Shestov could not stand stoicism: Why should we bow before the inevitable only because it is inevitable, instead of crying out "No"?

But what does it mean to cry "No"? I was here in this hospital with all my knowledge of our so-called goodness, from behind which leers the child-ishly simple and obvious play of ambition. Nothing has been spared me, not even the underside of what is considered to be love. I did not fall apart, I did not have a breakdown, and I somehow have to bear that. This is a kind of experiential addendum to that fifteen-year-old's *Weltschmerz*.

"Lord, to whom shall we go? Thou hast the words of eternal life" (John 6:69). And with this, rebellion ends.

ℳ AY 25, 1988

Brie-Comte-Robert is a small town on the Ile-de-France plain, thirty kilometers from Paris. The pointed spire of its ugly cathedral, built over several centuries in various mixed styles, is visible from a great distance. It also contains the ruins of a castle. It is surrounded by fields of wheat and sugar beets. When Janka and the children arrived from America in the summer of 1953 and we moved to Brie after a few months in the village of Bon on the French side of Lake Leman, the center still contained a town pond in which horses were watered, and the women often washed their linen at the *lavoir.* You didn't see any foreigners there, because there was no good transportation other than the bus to the Place de la Bastille, which took an hour.

ℳ AY 29, 1988, ℒ AUSANNE

A couple of days ago I visited Józef Czapski in Maisons-Laffitte. He was just about to leave for Switzerland and he invited me to his exhibit in the Aeschliman Gallery in Chexbres, outside Lausanne. I had planned to visit Mrs. Irena Vincenz on Saturday, May 28. But I'd had a poetry reading in Polish the day before at the Pallotini Fathers', in the large hall next to the church. On the way there, I got soaked to the skin, and although the reading was a success (plus an hour's autograph orgy), I felt lousy. Despite this, I took the train to Lausanne, and as soon as I arrived at Mrs. Vincenz's we left by car for Józef's exhibit. With a runny nose, afraid of sneezing in her direction (she is eighty-eight years old and is prone to bronchitis), I had a rather miserable afternoon. Spent the night at Basia Vincenz's with fever and pills.

Mrs. Vincenz and Czapski, even though he is ninety-two, have minds as sharp as Hannah's. I am surprised by his ongoing youth as a painter. I don't understand how he can paint so much and so well, even though he is almost blind, or at least that's what he says. Especially the paintings of the last couple of years; those are what he wanted me to see. In particular, one still life with a rag in shades of gray and white.

To what extent did my conflict with *Kultura* in the fifties spill over onto Czapski? I have to interrogate myself on this point, since my awe and even

veneration might suggest that there was no friction. He became a legend
during his lifetime and will become even more of a legend—as a painter, a
witness, a writer, the author of a monumental work (his diaries, both the
text and the drawings). He is still writing his diary, but he can no longer
decipher his own handwriting (no one can), and it will be a long time before
they are read.

It was Czapski who introduced me to Simone Weil's *La Pesanteur et la
Grâce*. Her first published book. It was also he who showed me Gobineau's
pages about Ketman. I could have a real conversation with him. And yet
there was a barrier. My hypothesis: he was right in everything he said, while
I resisted because my mind was polluted. My second hypothesis: due to
defects in my own character and mind, I maintained a (dialectical!) distrust
of "yes-yes," "no-no," and I managed to put my finger on a number of
Czapski's characteristic features. The ones that linked him with a certain
Polish milieu—aristocratic, chivalrous, idealistic, romantic, *vieux Polonais*
—while his other traits opened him up to art, philosophy, religion. I accused
the first Czapski of a somewhat exalted moralistic fervor—in other words,
the feature that spoiled the books his sister Maria Czapski wrote.

I cannot decide which of these hypotheses is correct. It reminds me somewhat of my special, lofty, but at the same time not exactly innocent place
in my class at school. I—an internal hunchback; they, my classmates—just
like boys ought to be. But a hunchback, with his fine-honed consciousness,
knows what they do not know, about themselves, about himself. At a price:
in place of that "yes-yes," "no-no," he harbors a hodgepodge of uncertainty.
Czapski was an exceptionally positive variant, then, of my high-school class,
and I was a suspect mutation.

MAY 30, 1988, RUE DE RENNES

A couple of days ago I phoned Stephen Spender in London about a certain
practical matter. Here in Paris I had read his book on T. S. Eliot, at night,
when I do all my reading. The book is good up to the chapter in which he
discusses Eliot's "contemporary" theater pieces on "upper-middle-class" life.
Perhaps tact prevents him from uttering further criticism other than the
assertion that the characters are hardly realistic. But it cannot be ruled out
that as an Englishman he doesn't see the comedy of this social stratum and

its rituals. For me, a foreigner, it was incomprehensible that Eliot, a great poet, could dream up something like this: plays which are set in the highest social sphere and in which the characters speak in verse. The grotesqueness of this combination, the unwitting parody, probably derive from the fact that while psychological and religious problems are being debated with great dignity in the living room, the customs of these sahibs (let us imagine a Hindu as servant and witness) cause us to double over with laughter. The specific features of this society make it impossible to treat seriously a character like Celia Copplestone, for example, who craves martyrdom, becomes a missionary, and is crucified in Africa by savages. At best, she might be a representative figure in some two-bit farce. I think that every society has similar comic aspects in its customs that it is unaware of. In France, for example, André Gide traveling through Africa. While black men were carrying him in a sedan chair, he was reading Racine (*Voyage au Congo*).

In a certain sense, the poet's dependence on his class and nation reveals his weak side; it unmasks him, as it were. To a certain extent, Eliot's "drawing-room" poetry spoiled his more elevated texts for me, because they were, after all, spoken by the same voice.

Czapski's paintings bring us back to the secret of human individuality. They are so easily identifiable from a distance; one knows instantly that they're Czapski's. Works of art as essence.

> And Kasia burned up in a flash.
> What was left was a handful of ash.

And over this ash rises the essence, the ethereal vapor, unequaled since the beginning of the world, inimitable.

MAY 31, 1988, RUE DE RENNES

The desire *to be somewhere else*. One could write a thick tome about the shape this desire has assumed in the modern era, especially in the nineteenth and twentieth centuries. One variant of *somewhere else*, obviously, is the future; the entire Russian intelligentsia was afflicted with that ailment. Later, after the Russian Revolution, the French and the English tried to locate in the East the solution to the excessively quotidian, exasperating reality that surrounded them. Sartre even relocated his ideal country from Russia to Cuba, and then to China.

I write this in connection with my reading of the new edition of Malcolm Cowley's *Exile's Return*. The migration of voluntary exiles from America to Europe after World War I gives some indication of the changes that have occurred. America as a provincial backwater, a country of materialistic obtuseness, in which one could not create or write. And now, some sixty years after that exodus of artists, novelists, poets—America as a magnet, the center relocated there from Paris and London, those culturally frozen capitals.

The *somewhere else* of the American expatriates was geographical: Europe. Cowley provides quite a good look at the role played by the colleges and universities, for they instilled "culture" understood exclusively on the model of the European indoctrination of the young: Latin and Greek were studied, the classics were read, history was understood to be the history of the Mediterranean lands and of Western Europe. One should not be surprised, then, that the most impressionable people fled to their true fatherland of the spirit. The more so since life in Paris, for instance, was sweet and cheap. Weren't the yearning eyes of artists and writers from our "worse" Europe turned toward Rome, Munich, Paris, for decades? Styles and fashions were imported; the people who traveled there on fellowships, which were often privately financed, were introduced to Naturalism, Symbolism, Impressionism, Cubism.

Somewhere else belongs to the chimeras of the mind that respond to certain of its needs. I myself received more than enough of an introduction to the power of those chimeras, chasing after them like a dog after a mechanical rabbit. In the dual meaning of the future and of the great capitals of culture. And I was just as snobbish—if not more so—about my Parisian tastes and my French as were the American expatriates.

$\mathcal{J}$UNE 1, 1988, RUE DE $\mathcal{R}$ENNES

America and Europe. The Americans asked: "Who are we?" Russia and Europe. The Russians asked: "Who are we?" Two virtual contemporaries—Walt Whitman (*b.* 1819) and Dostoevsky (*b.* 1821). Nineteenth-century American literature as a whole, however, does not bear comparison with the already strong and already autonomous Russian literature, which arose in both friendly and unfriendly rivalry with Europe.

$\mathcal{J}$UNE 2, 1988, RUE DE $\mathcal{R}$ENNES

I walk by the cafés on Boulevard Montparnasse—La Rotonde, Dôme. Seen for the first time in the summer of 1931, they were a miracle, a revelation, that crowd of seemingly celestial human beings sprawling in wicker armchairs, lazily watching the people walking by. This resident of Wilno had never seen anything like it. Nor did he understand how marginally celestial these individuals were. That was the end of Montparnasse, of course. The voluntary exiles were returning to America, forced to leave by the stockmarket crash, disconnected from their "financial breast." The cafés of Montparnasse would once again approach their 1920s apogee, but more poignantly this time, when the German emigration settled there in flight from Hitler.

Ought I to write a book, as Ola Wat insists I should, about independent Poland during the two decades from 1918 to 1939? No one else will do it, because it would have to be written by an eyewitness. *La Pologne est un pays marécageux où habitent les Juifs*—Poland is a marshy country where Jews live. That is one image in the consciousness of Western Europe. Another image—the opposite—has been created and will continue to be created as a result of the idealizing vision of those who do not know and cannot know what it was really like.

I disqualified myself a long time ago, because I grew up not in Poland, after all, but in Polish enclaves, isolated, alienated. Although it may well be that I have an acute consciousness of the absurd, owing to that experience. I am incapable of re-creating my thoughts and it is possible that the word "consciousness" is inappropriate, because it suggests a sphere of clearly defined concepts. Perhaps I am doing myself an injustice by not fully valuing my clairvoyance and agony, which were deeply rooted in me. In the final analysis, *Three Winters* does testify to something; those poems could have been written only by a poet who had already composed a dirge.

One would have to begin with how the people in the east were accustomed to tsarist Russia; in the south, to the Habsburg monarchy; in the west, to Germany. For many people, perhaps for the majority, the Polish state seemed to be an anomaly or, perhaps, a bitter surprise. After all, virtually all of Congress Poland was antagonistic toward Piłsudski's Legions. And what was the purpose of that state in the minds of the millions of Jews and even more millions of Ukrainians, or the Germans from Bielsko, Bydgoszcz, Sopot? Or all those "locals" who answered "Orthodox" or "Catholic" to questions about their nationality? From a more distant perspective, only the religious divisions were still meaningful; a Pole was equivalent to a Roman Catholic, but he also had all the members of other faiths against him. Besides which, in Wilno, Grodno, Białystok, one could appreciate the durability and powerful influence of Russian culture. I can't say very much about Galicia and Vienna's influence there, but our Jews and those in Congress Poland responded to Poland either with indifference or with reluctance, as to an obviously temporary creation. Which is not very surprising. After all, only Polish ethnocentricity could succeed in obscuring the facts of the international situation. In the twenties, perhaps, immediately after the 1920 victory, those facts may still have been favorable to Poland, but the radicalization of the intelligentsia begins with the economic crisis everywhere, including America; the experiences of our group in Wilno, then, correspond perfectly to the experiences of the New York intellectuals. The Jews simply did not view the world through Polish ethnocentric lenses; in other words, they saw the situation somewhat more objectively. Our group's roots in the ethnically mixed territories may have had a similar impact.

Artur told me about a trip he took from Bielsko to Warsaw in the thirties. The Jewish street was talking about politics; politics meant assorted shades of red. The evolution of our group seems to me now to have been inevitable, as can be seen most clearly in Henryk Dembiński—from his right-wing Catholicism in school to Communism. In my opinion, only two positions, two rationales, made sense in Poland. Either the "national" rationale (meaning the primacy of Church and Nation), or the leftist, or "Masonic," rationale. Either to denationalize and/or expel the "minorities," or to love each other, to choose multi-ethnicity and internationalism, which in turn inclined many people to take the internationalism of the Communists seriously.

In Paris I have been trying, unsuccessfully, to track down Jean Le Louet. Yesterday, at dinner at Pierre and Betty Leyris' in Meudon, I read the poem "Attitudes" from my just-published book, L'Immoralité de l'art. They all agreed it is a lovely poem. But it is a translation into French of my translation into Polish; the French original was lost. Its author, Jean Le Louet, a French poet of the second wave of Surrealism, was in Warsaw in August 1939, possibly for romantic reasons (he was gay). I have a vague recollection that he knew Iwaszkiewicz and was even at Stawisko. The outbreak of war caught him in Warsaw; the Germans sent him to Lake Constance as a French citizen, and he was interned along with another French citizen, Stanisław Dygat. That is where he wrote that poem, immediately after the fall of France in 1940, I believe. Dygat brought it to Warsaw and gave it to me; I translated it and put it in my anthology The Invincible Song (1942).

Attitudes

At that time I saw three men. The first was covered with blood, and because they had beaten him, the blood kept pouring out of him. The second was kneeling, and because they had tied his arms, he remained on his knees. The third was sitting at his enemy's table, and because the enemy treated him with respect, he remained at that table.

Then I called the first by name and cried out to him, "Don't die." But the blood continued to flow and through the blood he replied, "I'll make it, because I love."

Then I named the second man and cried out to him, "Cast off your bonds." He replied, "I am weak, and the man who tied me up is very strong."

And I named the third man and said to him, "Stand up, won't you!" And he replied, "I shall remain here, because my enemy is cunning and I wish to outwit him."

Then I summoned the angel of unity and said to him, "Unite these people or destroy them." At that the angel of unity took the first man's blood and smeared it on the other two.

And he who had been kneeling and he who was sitting were strengthened.

The bleeding man leaned on them for support. And the blood flowed less freely from his wounds. And the blood removed the veil from their eyes.

Leyris, who is very old and knows all of literary Paris, said that he re-members Le Louet, but only vaguely: thin, delicate, almost feminine, with a sickly throat, speaking in a whisper. From someone else (Pierre Boutang, Jr.?), I heard that after the war he led the life of a *clochard*. No one knows when he died. And that is all. Completely forgotten as a poet, with that one title to his fame—a poem in Polish translation. An unusual poem, having nothing in common with Surrealism, as Leyris points out, but referring to biblical tradition (as if it were written by a Polish romantic poet); a prophetic poem, because how in 1940 could he have foreseen collaboration? If one were to compile an anthology of the best texts of the Second World War in various languages, it would have to be included. I think it is better than the poems of the young underground poets of Warsaw—tighter, denser, like a parable from the Gospels.

"Now that I have observed you in the company of American poets and with your Polish friends here," says Carol, "I can see that the Americans appreciate you more as a poet, because for the Poles you are, more than anything, a famous personality." And that is undoubtedly true. Today, an-other letter: "I congratulate you on the well-deserved laurels with which you have adorned our unfortunate fatherland."

JUNE 4, 1988

I was in Broca again visiting Hannah in the hospital. We talked about Janka.

No matter how often my pen tempts me, I hesitate to describe our life in Brie and Montgeron. Because if I were to do it absolutely honestly and openly, I would reveal virtually everything that I know, or at least think, about myself. I am restrained by my concern for the other people who are involved in this. Janka above all, who can no longer correct anything, so that only my version would be preserved. And what kind of a court hears only one of the parties? I have no doubt that our versions would be very different.

JUNE 6, 1988, RUE DE RENNES

Yesterday, Sunday, just as I did one year ago, I went to Fontainebleau, this time by car with André Silvaire and his son. The ceremony of placing flowers on Oscar Milosz's grave, and as always the long ritual breakfast in the Hôtel l'Aigle Noir.

A sequel to my search for Jean Le Louet; Silvaire, it turns out, knew him. The last couple of years before the war, Le Louet published a journal, *Les Lettres Nouvelles*. His volumes of poetry had strange titles. Gallimard wouldn't publish them because *Les Lettres Nouvelles* was somewhat competitive with *La Nouvelle Revue Française*. Some individuals—Jean Cassou, for instance—hailed him as a young genius, almost as a new Rimbaud incarnate. He was given a fellowship to travel to Poland. Silvaire met him in Toulouse, after the *débacle*. Le Louet told him that he was trying to get out of France. And he spent the rest of the war in Spain. I ask myself: When was he released from the camp at Lake Constance and when did he write that poem? I don't remember when Dygat returned from the camp, and in any case Le Louet might have been released earlier. He might have written the poem immediately after the fall of France and given it to Dygat or, if he was no longer in the camp, sent it to him in a letter. If, however, the poem was written before the fall of France, as is beginning to seem likely, then it relates not to the French situation but to the Polish one as the author imagined it, and in that case it is in essence a Polish poem from a French pen.

After the war, Le Louet did not return to literature. People speak of his decline with pity and horror. He was a *clochard* in the literal sense and lived that way for a long time, because he died no more than a couple of years ago; in other words, I could have found him. Silvaire insists that he published nothing after the war.

I return to Brie.

This is very difficult. Whenever I speak about Brie, I resort to self-pity. It really was a harsh existence, in the wilderness. Brie was close to Paris, but whenever I went there I had only enough money in my pocket for one glass of wine and a return ticket. The Goodmans and Hannah used to visit us; Poles showed up, too, but only occasionally—more frequently after the Thaw, when we were already living in Montgeron, and then there was a lot of wine and the raucous conversations of compatriots. We hardly ever went into the city together, so our social life was very limited. We thought it very funny when an elegant woman from Poland was appalled by our life in Brie. You call this France, Paris? Ugh. It's the most out-of-the-way provincial backwater. And such poverty.

JUNE 12, 1988

Back in Berkeley; what a relief. Piles of mail; just sorting through it will take many hours, and how and when will I answer all these letters and proposals? I spent the day before yesterday preparing for a seminar on Polish and American poetry which I taught yesterday at University Extension in San Francisco—more than four hours, from 10 a.m. into the afternoon, with a break for lunch. A good, receptive class of adults, real poetry lovers, probably poetry writers, too. The seminar was a success and I told myself that once again I managed to pull a rabbit out of a hat. The bliss of sunshine after a cloudy, rainy May in Europe.

JUNE 13, 1988

Last night, when we were having supper with Tony and Joanna, the house swayed, and then it swayed once more. We waited, but nothing else happened. It was a moderate earthquake, probably about a 5.0 on the Richter scale.

I devoted the seminar to objective poetry. Not attempting to define what I mean by that, but rather using examples from various poets: Cendrars, Cavafy, Jeffers, Whitman; also a poem written by a Chinese woman poet in, approximately, the year 1200. Then Polish poets: Herbert, Swir, Zagajewski.

I spoke a lot about reality purified by the passage of time. Thus, the past of a particular individual, the melancholy of ephemerality (the most poetic tone, according to Edgar Allan Poe), and alongside it, the historical past. My reconstructions of the Belle Epoque with their clear aspiration to an (objective?) synthesis of the personal and the historical. But, I say to my students, let us not forget the contradictions that are concealed in this. After all, by focusing entirely on tangible objects, which were independent of my existence or nonexistence, I have a sense of my power that derives from my choice: I cut out some images and not others, and piece them together. As in Cendrars, what appear to be snapshots ("Kodak") are often a collage of sentences taken from Gaston Le Rouge's novel *Dr. Cornelius*, so that despite my anxiety about being faithful to detail, my Belle Epoque is quite subjective. In someone else's reconstruction, it might have been entirely different.

In self-defense, I might cite Schopenhauer or Simone Weil: in relation to the past my contemplation is *truthful*, that is to say, *disinterested*; in that sense I approach objectivity, although I will never achieve it.

Was Mickiewicz disinterested when he wrote *Pan Tadeusz*? "There is but one land remaining / in which there is a bit of joy for Poles: / The land of our childhood . . ." Perhaps, in all fairness, one should say that Mickiewicz was not disinterested when he allowed himself that leap into the past, into reminiscence (his goal: to fortify the heart), and that afterward he disinterestedly followed his most profound need? It's just that *Pan Tadeusz* is a fairy tale, an idyll, an embellishment. The real Lithuania, the one from Salomon Maimon's memoirs, for example, or from Johnston's description of his journey from Moscow to Warsaw in 1813, had little Jewish towns swarming with the poor; it had cruel estate stewards, a benighted peasantry, the machinations of village poachers over beaver pelts and elk meat, innumerable twisted, crippled lives; in other words, it was, like this Earth, a most ordinary vale of tears.

When I think about the typhus epidemic in our district and the funerals throughout that winter of 1919 (if I remember correctly), *The Issa Valley*— even though it is a novel and not a documentary—acquires the coloration of a fairy tale. And I am ready to put all literature on trial for inaccuracy.

It's all very well for those who insist that there is no objective truth about reality, that the kaleidoscopic variability of reality under our pens matches the only aspect of reality that is accessible to us. They are on fairly solid philosophical ground, but unfortunately in practice they are putting a weapon in the hands of those who engage in *l'écriture*, who let reality run loose, transforming it into a dream and a mere pretext for words. There is a difference, after all, between the man who focuses on his inner life and the hunter who grieves because the "wild swan of the world" (as Jeffers's poem puts it) cannot be captured.

JUNE 15, 1988

Yesterday I gave a poetry reading in Black Oak Bookstore to mark the publication of *Collected Poems*. It's difficult to comprehend how four hundred people could have crowded into the bookstore's two rooms; that's the delighted owner's count. I had total control over my audience; I could have read for another half hour. A successful evening, in other words. Then a lot of book signing, not just this new one. Even a couple of my Polish books. I was introduced by Leonard Nathan.

The horror of this world. I once read something about Cézanne's youth. Now, *he* was sensitive to horror, but you wouldn't guess it from his later canvases. His early painting is violent, obsessive, sarcastic, grotesque, hostile to sexuality. One should remember that sex, like death, introduces a true, pitiless, measure into a sphere where the deceptive colors of mellowness somehow manage to hang on. I am thinking of the Marquise Brie-Serrant and her daughter from my poem about the little town of Pornic. "Drunken men punished them for their pride." To have their thighs forced apart and a revoltingly alien organ stuffed into their virginal vagina has been the fate, after all, of innumerable women from time immemorial. But the reverse is true, too—the terror experienced by innumerable young lads when confronted by the rapacious, perhaps toothed, maw of the female genitalia.

Whenever I see a daddy longlegs moving across a smooth floor on its long legs, or recall the dreamy but ominous movement of a snake as it coils, I think about my own death. To abandon this earth, sever my ties with it? How should I do this? How many more illnesses, or the slow ebbing of my strength, still await me? It's better not to write about horror and to be satisfied that somehow or other I have isolated myself from it by praising tangible forms in spite of it, just like the mature Cézanne.

$\mathcal{J}$UNE 26, 1988

After a trip to a music festival in Bend, Oregon, in which poets participated, too: Ursula Le Guin, Leonard Nathan, Gerald Ramsey, Czeslaw Milosz. After France, the relief of open spaces, sunshine, the ease of traveling by car down the right lanes of empty freeways. Snowy peaks above pine forests. My American side is growing stronger and stronger, after all, and I am reluctant to contemplate a lengthier stay in Europe. One month in Paris was already too long. Anyway, since Western Europe is barely acquainted with the public reading of poetry, I value the festival in Bend. Instead of a hall, a large tent has been erected in the park, on the riverbank. The audience is a bit too eager to laugh, anticipating the wisecracks that my colleagues supply with alacrity. Years ago I would have found this irritating, but now, no longer so quick to take offense, I am more mellow and therefore more fair. Since it is a good audience, I don't make any concessions, I read what I want to, eliminating only poems that are too long, and I elicit a good response.

The difference between the fates of poetry in Western Europe and in America. The myth of European culture commands American poets to envy their European colleagues, whereas it ought to be the other way around.

This brief trip was chiefly a treat for the eyes. Nonstop from Berkeley to Bend, with snow-covered Mt. Shasta and the expanses of meadows below the mountain range on the California–Oregon border. On the way back, a day spent driving along mountain roads: Mt. Bachelor, Crater Lake with its snow just melting and the early spring flowers, then Klamath Lake, abounding in fish and aquatic birds, a night at Klamath Falls, then on to Berkeley, over three hundred miles without growing tired, relying on cruise control most of the time.

July 1, 1988

So, yesterday was my seventy-seventh birthday. Carol made a barbecue and we ate in the garden; Rose was the only non-family guest. The pure azure of the sky. The weather just as it was seventy years ago in Szetejnie, when my little chair was decked with peonies. Of all my birthdays (or name days) I remember that one best, that June of 1918 after our, the repatriates', return from Russia, or, to be precise, from Dorpat, but crossing Soviet territory.

Reading *Al-Kemi*, a book about René Schwaller de Lubicz published by Lindisfarne Press, I learn the reasons why O. Milosz broke with the man he had considered his closest friend, almost a brother, so close that he gave him half his name: he had allowed Schwaller, an Alsatian, to add Lubicz (the name on the Milosz coat-of-arms) to his name. In 1919 they both belonged to the Veilleurs organization, which Schwaller founded; Oscar's close friend, Carlos Larronde, whom I knew, was also a member. It was an occult organization, but with political inclinations that we would call fascistic today, even with uniforms that were similar to the uniforms the SA would later adopt. The occultist connections of Hitlerism in its early phase are well known, after all. Afterward, Oscar never allowed anyone to speak about Les Veilleurs or about Schwaller. He lost one friend because of right-wing politics, and later he lost Carlos Larronde because Larronde, who was a theater director in a working-class community, showed Communist leanings. The chosen, those who *know* how to make society happy, the right or the left. Oscar's powerful yearnings in that direction after the First World War came to an end when he realized that, by organizing, one falls into a trap. There was yet another serious reason for the break with Schwaller. According to

this book, *Al-Kemi* by André Vanderbroeck, very little of which I understand,
it seems that Schwaller was not a Christian; he was concerned exclusively
with elite, secret knowledge, while Oscar was a religious writer and, after
1927 or thereabouts, a practicing Catholic.

July 4, 1988

I learned in Bend that half of all birds of prey (hawks, falcons, owls) die
during their first year because they do not develop the agility required for
hunting. These birds become skilled hunters, possessing the know-how
needed for survival, only after they are a year old. To think that natural
selection has been taking place in a given species for millennia, and *despite
that*, half the young are doomed to extinction!

July 9, 1988

"When you lived with Janka's parents." Nothing of the sort ever happened.
We were very poor then, during the war years, but her parents were even
poorer and we invited them to live with us.

First, Dynasy Street. Memorable because it was there that the three of
us—Janka, Andrzejewski, and I—prepared my first book of poems, probably
the first mimeographed volume in occupied Warsaw. Also memorable for
the great roundup throughout the center of town; we didn't know then that
it was for Auschwitz. Carefree, returning home from Stawisko with Andrzejewski, I had walked from the commuter railway station to our house.
A couple of minutes after I entered, I could hear shouting in front of the
building: they were rounding up all the men. Urbański, the building janitor,
was standing in front of the house and he was taken away. A couple of
months later, Mrs. Urbański (they had two children) received word of his
death. Those were the men who built Auschwitz. I don't think I would have
survived if I had landed there. Both Urbańskis remain in my memory with
their proletarian sullenness and class hatred of the privileged. And our empathy with them on that score.

Then Dynasy Street became part of the German quarter and we had to move. To Mazowiecka Street, at the corner of Kredytowa, or to Kredytowa at the corner of Mazowiecka—to the home of Antoni Bohdziewicz, a Wilno Parisian, formerly chief announcer for the newly established Polish Radio in Wilno, later a filmmaker from the Start group and a radio broadcaster— in other words, Janka's and my colleague. It was an ultramodern building; the finishing touches had just been completed when the war broke out. We rented a room from Antoni, next to a large photography studio, etc. All sorts of things went on there, including work for the underground. Next door was the Arria Café, which people referred to as "At the Actresses," where Antoni worked as a bartender; this explains our privileged access to alcohol. Witold Lutosławski and Andrzej Panufnik played the two pianos there. Antoni was a stickler; if we were a couple of days late with our room rent, he'd slip a reminder under the door.

In June 1941, when Hitler attacked Russia, there were many empty apartments in Warsaw that had been vacated by the army. Through connections with the municipal authorities—that is, on the basis of an appropriate recommendation from the underground hierarchy—I was given an apartment on Independence Avenue. Three rooms and a kitchen, with a view of the fields. The Mokotów Fortifications beyond the fields. And, from 1941 to 1944, some sort of communion with nature, walks. During the last year, Janka nursed a flycatcher that had fallen out of its nest, feeding it flies (Janka was able to catch them in flight, something I couldn't do). But flycatchers and swallows, which we also had, are unable to hunt if they don't learn how from their parents. Finally, we released the flycatcher in the gardens of the Polytechnic. Big and fat, it behaved like a nestling, flapping its wings, and the other flycatchers actually started feeding it. This happened a day or two before the Uprising began, in an area where violent battles would be fought. As for Independence Avenue, it wasn't idyllic all the time. Roundups and executions took place in the immediate vicinity, and later, during the Uprising, our building, which was closest to the fields, was destroyed by artillery fire.

*J*uly 10, 1988

I swear I have no idea which of my poems and prose works will be valued. I receive letters from readers who tell me what an important role I have played in their lives. The letters come from Poland and from America, from people who read me in English. (Letters from Germany are a special case: 99 percent of them are requests for autographs.) It is a pleasure to learn that you have helped someone and that someone else feels that you are close and important to them. I shall never figure out, however, what my reception is in reality, and I always suspect such a radical transformation of the text according to the reader's own needs that I would not recognize my intentions in it.

Thinking about one's own death always involves speculation about salvation or damnation; I, at least, cannot do otherwise. This takes the form of concrete individuals who in my opinion are models of virtue and therefore ought to be saved. We have a tendency to cite our artistic merits, but after a moment's reflection we have to admit they are not worth very much. What they mean, if we agree, is that a bad man is incapable of creating a truly outstanding work, and that therefore the perfection of the artistic product provides indirect testimony to the ordinary, hidden human virtues of its creator.

*J*uly 11, 1988

A letter about a trip to Lithuania:

"The wooden church in the Sventybrastis settlement is still standing. It was recently listed as an architectural landmark. Mass is celebrated in it every Sunday at 2 p.m. The church is painted yellow and the cemetery is immaculate, although a few old Polish crosses are leaning precariously. The rectory houses a school. There are no beginning classes, however, because the entire village is fated to die out. The last child was born in Sventybrastis in 1978. All the young people find ways to move to the city. But Kiejdany (which now numbers fifty thousand inhabitants) is also no paradise. They built enormous chemical plants there, which poison the entire region. You can't drink the raw milk and the vegetables aren't fit for consumption. There is a high concentration of sulphur dioxide and nitrous oxide which cause acid rain. The Niewiaża River is no longer a river in which biological life is renewed. It is simply a channel for flowing mud . . . Szetejnie has also been developed; one can only say that from an ecological point of view it is not very different from Kiejdany."

July 16, 1988

One should give thanks for the gift of being mentally active. Even if the poems I wrote this year are dark in tone, too dark for me to have a clear conscience about wanting to print them. Nevertheless, they exist, and that in itself is something, considering that poetry is in the habit of visiting twenty-year-olds, thirty-year-olds; it is not associated with maturity, to say nothing of old age. Poems or prose, in the morning the thought that I will be able to sit at my desk arouses the same excitement in me that I used to feel in my childhood at the thought that I would soon run out into the garden for a whole day of frolicking.

July 21, 1988

In Henryków, at the Priory.

The greatest loss that I have had to bear while living abroad for decades was the absence of theater. In America, the theater does not exist. It does not exist for me; whether it exists for others, and to what degree, is not for me to say. I have seen various productions which left me indifferent, as if I hadn't seen them at all. But I could say almost the same thing about the theater in Paris, from which I harvested only three evenings: before the war, a Pirandello play with Ludmiła Pitoëff, in which the heroine's makeup is changed so that she is transformed within a few minutes from a young girl into an old woman; after the war, *Waiting for Godot*—but that, I think, was largely because of my irritation at the audience, who only laughed at it; and, finally, Brecht's *Caucasian Chalk Circle*, because of its rhythmic simulation of a long journey on foot. I might add to this a performance by the Beijing

Chinese opera company. For me, the theater is primarily language, or, to be more precise, what constitutes the play's background, the associations that accompany it. When the language is foreign, not my own, I prefer action on stage, but that is insufficient. So, life deprived of theater, with the cinema as a substitute.

I am a contemporary of the cinema. From the flickering images with German subtitles in Dorpat in 1918, from the silent films in Wilno with the stormy accompaniment of a piano and violins at moments of high drama ("Baldie, play!" from the gallery), to the refined-nihilistic products of the seventies and eighties. I was moved by the misfortunes of Mary Pickford, Lillian Gish, Silvia Sidney; I was in love with Greta Garbo; I performed extraordinary feats with Douglas Fairbanks (*The Thief of Bagdad*); I laughed at Buster Keaton and Chaplin. I imbibed potent draughts of melodrama and kitsch. Yes, film was melodrama and kitsch above all. It came to us uninvited, unheralded by any theory, a plebeian entertainment to which well-educated people were also addicted, although secretly, and somewhat embarrassed by it. Analogies with the origins of the novel are obvious and unavoidable. The novel made its appearance in just the same way, as "true adventures," as sentimental romance, as a variant of common fairy tales about knights and dragons. In fact, one of the fathers of the novel, Cervantes, wrote *Don Quixote* as a parody of the chivalric romance.

$\mathcal{J}$ULY 22, 1988

Despite its modest beginnings (the novel around 1800 was still not considered a respectable genre like lyric poetry, the epic, and tragedy), the novel matured rapidly and became a "mirror" of customs, of human psychology, of ideas that were in circulation in society, and it even participated in philosophical and theological disputes. The question arises: Is film developing in the same way, from frivolousness to high seriousness, not only competing with the novel, but even trespassing on its terrain, exploring every problem that my contemporaries are preoccupied with?

Nicola Chiaromonte insisted that this analogy is misleading. I am trying to reconstruct those conversations around a table in the village of Bocca di Magra near Carrara in the summer of 1963. Lots of red wine. All of us motorboating over to the bay with its marble cliffs, where the swimming was magnificent. And those discussions—Nicola, his wife Miriam, Mary McCarthy, Janka, and I. Chiaromonte is one of those heroic figures of the twentieth century who have to be forgotten so that someday, when just deserts are fairly distributed, their fame will be even greater. He was an intellectual with an honest, independent mind; he understood the totalitarian systems he fought against. He had fought against Fascism in Italy, his fatherland; against Franco in Spain as a pilot in Malraux's division (reading Plato); after the war, against Soviet Communism, as co-editor (with Ignazio Silone) of the journal *Tempo Presente*. I had come across his name during my first stay in America when I read, with appreciation, his essays in *Partisan Review* and *Politics*. Well, Nicola, who at that time was a respected theater critic in Rome, argued over wine that the ambitions of film directors—Fellini, Antonioni, for instance—don't match their intellectual preparation, that in their effort to equal the great writers of the nineteenth century they reveal their intellectual poverty and their susceptibility to social clichés. I remember his harsh pronouncements whenever I go to the movies in the hope of nourishing both my eyes and my mind, only to walk out into the street afterward with a bad taste in my mouth, a feeling of shame, or simple rage. Such superb technique, such expertise at taking beautiful photographs, and such trash? One might even think that the medium itself, due to the necessity of introducing action to keep the viewer from falling asleep, contains within itself the unmasking of the novel's devices, which are unpleasantly revealed in it, while the writer, working with verbal material, has many other ways of grabbing his readers' attention. One way or another, the characters and their mutual relations lose their multidimensionality. Words, should a director attempt to rely on them, vanish with the passing moment once they are uttered; they do not remain before our eyes as in a book. Perhaps responsibility for these meager results should be placed on financial and social pressures, on the character of a given civilization, or on the selection (artistically *in minus*) of the type of person who is suited to be a director, who has to be too much a man of action, a politician, a financier, for the Muses to love him.

July 23, 1988

"But," someone will object, "film has produced masterpieces."

True enough. But it may well be that these are solely film masterpieces, limited to that medium, and untranslatable into the thoughts and sensibilities that were the strength of the novel in its prime. There have been exceptions, but, nonetheless, a viewer such as I has the constant feeling of the almost limitless possibilities of film that have not as yet been realized. Perhaps the chief contribution of cinema in this century is that its formulations and devices have fertilized literature—both poetry and prose—quite wondrously, and painting, too.

I have constructed my own imaginary films without being at all eager to write screenplays. There is one film in particular that I watch on my private screen. I am not the only one who knows the first and last names of the people who appear in it.

Leon Schiller. At that time when I used to get together with him, along with Stefan Jaracz, Edmund Wierciński, and Bohdan Korzeniewski, Schiller lived on one of the top floors of the Prudential building in Warsaw and was famous for his wide-ranging reading, which was exceptional even among the well-read people of occupied Warsaw. It was simple: he needed no more than four hours' sleep and could devote the rest of the night to reading. For us who were so much younger than him, he was a looming presence, replete with his whole past as a director—and as a singer. He would sit at the piano and sing the cabaret songs of Young Poland, which I would never have heard were it not for those evening gatherings. Try as I might, I cannot recall where this took place. But I hear distinctly:

> The wind is laughing outside the windowpanes.
> Damn it, this life is so bad.
> No, I won't drink anymore,
> Tomorrow I'll start living differently.

Or from another song, warmer and more heartfelt, though only the beginning:

> My beloved is so ugly,
> Her little teeth are rotten . . .

I owe my near certainty that Young Poland's popular songs derived chiefly from Paris to my participation in those sessions with Schiller, and often with Teofil Trzciński. Schiller, after all, had lived in Paris from 1907 to 1909, then again from 1910 to 1911, when he belonged to the Society of Polish Artists on rue Denfert-Rochereau (just like Oscar Milosz).

I can't picture Schiller, a legendary figure in the history of the Polish theater, as a director and a theater critic; but I can see him taking his seat at the piano and singing. The texts and notes could probably be found, even though his collections burned up along with his apartment in Warsaw. He was a short man, with a large head, a heavy, somewhat athletic build; dark-complexioned, blue-eyed, dark-haired. He struck me as very advanced in years; he wasn't sixty yet, but he was one of those people who look older than their years.

Schiller took his secrets to the grave; I don't think they were preserved anywhere. He was so multidimensional that any attempt to tailor him to a cinematic model would inevitably trivialize him.

Henryków. Warsaw's underground theatrical life can be divided into two periods: before the shooting of Igo Sym, and after that event, when Schiller and Jaracz were arrested (1941) and sent to Auschwitz. They were gotten out with great difficulty several months later. Not long ago, at Charles de Gaulle Airport in Paris, I purchased a book called *Des Écrivains et des artistes sous l'occupation (1940–1944)* by Gilles Ragache and Jean-Robert Ragache; reading it, I came to the conclusion once again that the German occupation of France was fundamentally different from the occupation of Poland. It is possible that this can be explained by the German inferiority complex with regard to French culture and their utter contempt for the "subhumans" to the east of Germany. But the behavior of Poles and Frenchmen was also different. Had Igo Sym gotten a license to operate theaters in France, it would have been seen as nothing special; and yet in Poland he was executed as a traitor (because he had declared himself a Reichsdeutsch, since he was born in Austria) and as a demoralizer of actors (by inciting them to collaboration; i.e., to playing in a theater licensed by the occupying powers). Who shot him is still unknown; the Germans suspected Dobiesław Damięcki, who had to change his name and flee Warsaw with his wife, Irena Górska-

Damięcka. After the attack on Sym, attempts at founding an official theater virtually ended; there were a few departures from this principle later on, at the very end of the occupation. Most actors worked as waiters and waitresses (for example, in the elegant Arria Café on Mazowiecka Street, "At the Actresses"). Readings of new plays, in Polish and in translation, took place in private apartments, where numerous theater productions were also mounted. The underground Theatrical Council monitored all this, issued pronouncements on what was permitted, prepared a repertoire for after the war, commissioned translations of plays, and devised plans for the organization of theaters. Leon Schiller had the deciding voice in the Council, although Edmund Wierciński and Bohdan Korzeniewski were the most active members.

People in Poland didn't immediately understand the Germans' intentions of carrying out their policy of extermination, and many people believed at first that it was an ordinary occupation by victorious forces in wartime. That explains, for instance, why people registered in the appropriate German office for permission to practice various professions, including the profession of man of letters. In our circle, Ferdynand Goetel advised people to register, and several were persuaded by him, including Jerzy Zagórski, for instance. Jerzy Andrzejewski and I were opposed, but I have loyally to declare that at that time, in 1940, it was still possible to be deceived.

It was Jerzy Andrzejewski, I believe (I saw him very often), who told me one wintry day before Christmas 1942 that we were invited to visit the nuns in Henryków for a performance of Schiller's *Pastorałka* [Christmas Play], which he himself had edited. I had never heard of Henryków. It turned out it was somewhere on the other side of the Vistula, to the northeast; I had never been in that area. The Benedictine Sisters had a nunnery there and also an institution for female juvenile offenders, mainly prostitutes who had been rounded up on the streets of Warsaw by the blue (Polish) police.

July 25, 1988

So, the trip to Henryków. First, Janka and I went by tram from our stop on the corner of Independence Avenue and Rakowiecka Street to the city center; there we met Jerzy and took the tram to Praga across the Kierbedź Bridge. The grayness of the city under the occupation, the grayness of a wet winter;

being crammed into the jam-packed tram, the first car of which was reserved for Germans. From Praga, a suburban rail line. I don't remember it at all, other than that we had already met people we knew who were traveling with the same goal in mind. I also remember nothing about Henryków, up to the moment when we were led into what I think was the chapel, with rows of low benches; the audience, about a hundred people, were seated on these benches; mainly well-known faces, actors, writers, painters, people from the university.

Stanisława Umińska. Let us go back in time. The city of Warsaw in the early twenties does not fit easily into the imagination, chiefly because the era that began before World War I developed slowly and over a long time and was still alive in the twenties, although it was already making way for the fashions and customs of the new era. Caps, lots of visored caps—the insignia of the lower classes; soft-brimmed hats—the indispensable accessory of the upper classes (no one would dare go outside with a bare head); the flat-crowned black hats of pious Jews in their long overcoats; women liberated from their corsets but still in nineteenth-century attire; on the streets, wagons pulled by horses, horse-drawn cabs, automobiles. And definitely in the air the triumph of independence regained against all odds, self-assurance stemming from the victory in the 1920 war with Russia (how many Poles had ever experienced a victorious war?), along with the poverty of the working-class districts and the unemployed, the shouts of newsboys crying out the sensational headlines, with the mutual accusations of the parties in the Sejm, the frequent dissolutions of the government. Photos of London or New York at that time may be of help, because in every decade large cities share the common spirit of the time. Warsaw's specific feature, most likely, was its transformation from a "western Russian" city with strong provincial residues into the nation's capital. Cafés, newspaper offices, theaters, many theaters, poets reciting on stage, already famous even though so young, barely past twenty, like a sign that everything was just beginning, but all those things —literature, art, fashion—are separated from today by the hiatus of war, just old stuff packed off to a museum forever.

JULY 26, 1988

What did it mean then to be young and a talented actress? Stanisława Umińska quickly made a name for herself. She was famous for playing Puck in Shakespeare's *Midsummer Night's Dream*. It was said to be an exceptionally well-acted Puck. For that, one needs charm, boyish beauty, a light step. *The Literary News* of June 15, 1924, features a large photograph of her with the caption: "One of the most marvelous and interesting actresses of the young generation, the splendid creator of Consuelo (*He Who Gets Slapped*), Lidia (*What Is Most Important*), has achieved a new success with her intelligent, focused realization of the role of Berta (*A Cricket in the Hearth*)."

One might conclude that the editor printed this praise because he was aware of Umińska's liaison with his collaborator on *The Literary News*, Jan Żyznowski, and knew of the couple's journey to Paris to seek medical treatment for him. I read about Żyznowski in *The Dictior¬ry of Contemporary Polish Writers*:

> b. June 15, 1889, in Warsaw, to a family of landed gentry. The son of Antoni and Michalina (*née* Jamiołowska) Żyznowski. He went to Paris a couple of years before the First World War to continue his literary and artistic studies. He was in Paris when the war broke out and was one of the first in the Polish community to join the Polish Legion of Bayonne. After his discharge in 1915 he went to Russia and worked on the Petersburg daily *The Voice of Poland*. After his return to Poland, he took part in the 1920 war. After demobilization, he became the director of the art-criticism department in the journals *Res Publica, The Illustrated Weekly*, and *Miss*. For a few months in 1924 he was in charge of the department of art-exhibition reviews at *The Literary News*. Terminally ill with cancer, he traveled to Paris for radiation therapy. Shot at his own request by his fiancée, the stage actress Stanisława Umińska, he died July 15, 1924, in Paris.

JULY 28, 1988

Paris in the year 1924 will always be a mystery for me because of the artistic explosion there. After all, only a few years had passed since the great slaughter, and people were walking along those streets who not so long before had been in the hells of Verdun or the battles on the Somme. It would seem that after such a descent into the abyss the general tone of thought, of art, of literature ought to have been gloomy. And in neighboring Germany it was, and also in England, which had lost a significant percentage of its young elite. T. S. Eliot's *Waste Land*—a satiric and catastrophic poem—was well suited to the mood over there. But France, where every little town erected a monument with the names of the fallen, in some places amounting to two-thirds of the male population, acted as a conductor for the current of euphoria that was encircling the planet and once again attracted all the enthusiasts of a revolution in art and literature. It was the time of the "expatriation" of numerous American writers and artists, too; Hemingway and Gertrude Stein were the most famous among them. The peak years of Montparnasse and its cafés—not so much the Closerie des Lilas (it peaked before 1914), as La Rotonde and La Coupole with their chairs occupying the entire width of the sidewalk, and their cosmopolitan crowds that did not, however, include tourists as they would in a later Paris (which creates a fundamental difference in atmosphere).

The two of them in that euphoric Paris: Żyznowski and Umińska. On the terrace of La Coupole, sipping Dubonnet and looking at the parade of pedestrians. Just to think that never, not for all eternity, will anyone know what they talked about and how they reached their decision. They had come to seek hope from the doctors. When there was none, what remained was the faithful love of a woman who did not recoil from a helping act, from a remedy that must have horrified her. And immediately afterward, the Paris newspapers filled with a sensational story that exactly matched the expectations of this city of modernist bohemia's daily scandals: an actress had shot her lover.

JULY 29, 1988

The trial, too, was sensational. The faces of the French jury, the rituals—
is it possible to penetrate closed doors? The story was a moving one and must
have struck people right in the heart, especially women, even though the
accused was the wrong nationality. At that time, the little towns of northern
France were swarming with Poles who had come to work in the mines and
factories, often straight from the countryside, who were not necessarily considered members of the white race, but rather were perceived as the sort of
foreigners whom people frighten children with, like Algerians later on. In
the police blotters the Poles were the chief perpetrators of theft and murder,
which is where the expression *les bandits polonais* comes from.

The verdict was an even greater sensation: Not guilty. This meant not
only that murder is sometimes not an offense but also, perhaps, that murder
to shorten (or, in this case, to avert) someone's suffering should not be
punishable.

Perhaps Umińska, seeking anonymity above all, fleeing human eyes and
tongues, found a haven somewhere in France; perhaps she returned immediately to Poland. But not to the theater, in any event. She considered
that chapter in her life to be over. She entered a nunnery. One can explain
this decision in various ways, and all explanations are based on conjecture.
In a Catholic country, a nunnery was, traditionally, a shelter for unmarried
women who belonged to that category for a number of reasons: familial,
financial, personal, not necessarily because of vocation. "Entering a nunnery" was also a synonym for escape from the world after some personal
drama. Umińska could fall back on a certain tradition, and the nunnery
gave her the anonymity of an assumed name, which was important to her.
It is also possible to conjecture that, in choosing the discipline of the cloister,
she was meting out punishment for her deed, which she could not forgive
herself, or for forsaking Żyznowski by not having accompanied him in death.
The most difficult thing, obviously, is to come up with hypotheses about
the nature of her religious faith and her gift of prayer. One ought not to
forget that our inner life is never static, that every month and every year
introduces changes, that therefore some of our features atrophy while others
develop.

In the course of many years spent in the cloister, Umińska, as happens
to all nuns, must have been moving simultaneously in both a vertical and
a horizontal direction. The former describes the history of the human soul

in lonely contemplation, striving toward God; the latter refers to the daily affairs of a closed community of nuns, the numerous and multifaceted relationships among the sisters. Individuality is forged then in the inescapable collision of characters. It could not have been easy for Umińska, because she was very different from her new environment; she was above it on the intellectual level, perhaps, but most of all, despite her youth, by virtue of the experience that the theater, love, and her personal tragedy had given her. Adaptation was first of all a matter of humility, or of working at humbling her separateness. She may have been helped in this also by her ability to feel her way into various roles. One way or another, she became a model nun, valued by her order for her piety, tact, and kindness toward others. In 1942 she was the prioress of the cloister in Henryków.

We do not know if she had completely broken with the theatrical community during her years as a nun, or if, on the contrary, she had maintained certain friendships or at least had followed what was happening in the theater. When, however, Schiller was invited by her to Henryków after he was ransomed out of Auschwitz, her conversations with him were certainly an extraordinary moment for her. One would have to explain how it came about, at whose initiative—his, hers, or perhaps friends who sought a safe place for him, especially after several months of imprisonment in Auschwitz.

Schiller and a cloister—the two didn't fit. Although at that time in occupied Warsaw the old divisions were less clear and Schiller's past was less important than his status as the most prominent figure in Polish theater. Before the war he was known as a leftist, but I, for one, found out just how engaged Schiller had been only when I was recording my interviews with Aleksander Wat. Schiller supported the Communist *Literary Monthly* financially and it was only out of tactical considerations that he didn't join its editorial board. Many meetings of Communist sympathizers took place in his (exquisite) apartment. That Schiller was a confirmed Communist cannot be questioned, a "salon Communist," as it were; after all, his value for the Party consisted exclusively in the politicization of the theater—that was his language, he spoke his mind in it. He was the object of attacks in the right-wing press and from time to time he would lose his theaters. After the war, when he joined the Polish Workers' Party and wrote his autobiography in 1946 as a candidate for the Sejm, he spoke a great deal about those persecutions, but he did not mention the typical Polish arrangements—that is, his friendships with government dignitaries who somehow managed to protect him. There is also, of course, no mention of his attitude toward religion, even though a theoretician and practitioner of "grand theater," a director of Mickiewicz's *Forefathers' Eve*, Krasiński's *The Undivine Comedy*, and Słowacki's *Silver Dream of Salomea* could not possibly *not* have thought about such matters.

In Henryków, Umińska put at his disposal her young prostitutes as raw acting material, and in this way Schiller was able to keep his director's hand in practice. His stays in the nunnery, however (he moved there permanently in 1943), were not limited to that. "At that time he became a Benedictine oblate and took the monastic name 'Ardalion,' " according to the *Biographical Dictionary of the Polish Theater* (1972). An oblate is a lay person who adheres to the rules of monastic life but does not take vows. The monastic rules included partaking regularly of the Eucharist, which means that Schiller became a practicing Catholic. Various hypotheses are possible. A revolutionary change had taken place in him in an extreme situation; that is, in Auschwitz. Stanisława Umińska converted him. Or else, despite the anticlericalism he had developed in his youth in clerical Cracow, this man of luminous erudition and intelligence was sufficiently endowed that he could exist on several levels simultaneously, reconciling his revolutionary beliefs with his secret religious experience. Perhaps my intuition misled me, but I sensed a great inner concentration in Schiller, a core that was not revealed to anyone, as happens with people who have mystical inclinations. As far as I know, Schiller never attempted to write anything about that. Shortly before the Uprising, he returned to Warsaw from Henryków; he was deported to Germany after the Uprising. Immediately after the war ended, he organized a theater there for Poles under the aegis of the YMCA. Afterward, in People's Poland, he acted effectively and in every way as a committed revolutionary and Party member, a delegate to the Sejm, so there could be no cause to speak of any private deviation. In general, during the Stalin years, people believed that he was zealous out of a deep conviction and was becoming more fanatic than was appropriate, than even the Party wanted him to be. Nonetheless, I wasn't at all surprised when I learned from Wat that this dogmatic Communist by day prostrated himself before the crucifix at night.

July 30, 1988

Pastorałka. "She makes the entrance of a great actress," said Jerzy when the prioress entered the hall with her nuns to occupy the first rows of benches.

He was expressing what we all felt: respect for her beauty (still present) and her dignity.

I did not know *Pastorałka*. In 1919, Schiller had arranged folk carols and folk songs as *An Old Polish Manger Scene*; later, in 1922, he presented it as *Pastorałka* in the Reduta Theater. I pass on this information now; I don't think that I was aware of it at the time; at most, I'd heard something or other about it. Lo and behold, it was not a Greek tragedy, not a work by Shakespeare, not a romantic drama that afforded me the most powerful theatrical experience of my life, but a folk spectacle, a Manger scene, a Nativity play, performed by poor girls from the Warsaw streets who had never been in a theater. Without a doubt, Polish carols possess a particular charm, freshness, sincerity, good humor, that simply cannot be found in such proportions in any other Christmas songs, and perhaps one ought to look at them for the essence of Polish poetry. My susceptibility to that performance can be explained by my having listened to carols from childhood, but also because only the theater has such an impact, appealing to what is most our own, most deeply rooted in the rhythms of our language. One might say, then, that the cause of my later bad relations with the theater abroad was its foreign intonations.

In a Nativity play, just as in Greece once upon a time, the plot is not at all surprising, because it is already decided, known by heart. Also, the characters are already formed and everything takes place in between: between the character and its incarnation by the actor, between the text and its enactment, in speech, in song, in dance.

The Mother of God was dressed in blue, of course; small, almost childlike, thin, blond. She appeared against a background of many centuries of tradition in which she had been depicted just that way in painting and in polychrome sculpture, although another tradition also exists of a Madonna with olive skin, black-eyed and black-haired. The director had chosen her unerringly, perhaps because of her voice. It was a tiny, mouse-like voice which, when she sang, made my throat constrict with emotion. I was partaking of a mystery which, simultaneously, revealed the essence of theater. That essence is, most likely, the human possibility of *being someone else*, which, if you think about it, means that every man is the home of many personalities that dwell within him potentially, that are never realized, because only one of them appears on the outside and proffers the mask that is accepted by others. A change in a configuration through a change of participants brings forth other hidden and heretofore suppressed personalities. The purity and holiness of the Mother of God were undoubtedly her own, this girl actress's, although at the same time she was someone else and that someone else had recently sold herself to German soldiers for a couple of zlotys. Thus, the theater is, or ought to be, a celebration of human multifacetedness and plasticity which make it possible for every man and every woman to bear within himself or herself an entire range of experiences and aptitudes, from the highest virtue to common evil, while being vaguely aware of this and therefore capable of resonating with the actors on the stage. The question arises: To what degree is it necessary for us to be aware that we are watching dual beings on the stage, that that girl, for example, is "playing" the Mother of God while being both "herself" and her? In the "lifelike" theater, we are told to forget about that duality, and probably that is why it is a low genre of theater. But here, in Henryków, an amateur spectacle was transformed into a professional act by an excellent director, so I insist that the trenchancy of that theatrical performance can also be explained by our knowledge of who those children were who had been so clearly transformed into a theater company. And, perhaps, more than one of us was thinking that, in order to play the Mother of God like that, it would be difficult not to undergo an inner transformation, so that she, the performer, was also present, along with her unimaginable future life story.

St. Joseph was dressed in a sort of brown burnoose, with the staff of a wanderer; he gently escorted Mary in their flight across Egypt. I can see that scene and hear Mary singing in her thin little voice; although I am not absolutely certain of the words, I shall write them down from memory:

> *Just a few steps, Joseph*
> *Just a few steps, Joseph*
> *After all I cannot*
> *Run so far away.*

In *Pastorałka*, tender, quiet melodies are interwoven with bursts of joyous carols and triumphal dances. At the very beginning, the arrival of the shepherds in the manger and their presentation of their gifts offers an occasion for this *vivace*. In Poland, it isn't easy to separate "folk" elements from the contributions of Church writers and musicians, not to mention seminarists and minstrels who worked for the parish. The most intense activity occurred in the seventeenth century; thus, old Polish "folklore" and, most of all, the carols bear a strong imprint of the Baroque. The shepherds bring with them the earthy humor of the countryside, their games and buffoonery, but the seminarist who is in charge of keeping order also joins them:

> Contrabasses and tenors
> We split up into two choirs
> Hey, hey, hey!

I remember the melodies of those merry carols and the joy of the performers, who seized the opportunity to discharge their energy in a permissible fashion—a discharge of energy that was doubtless very necessary in that severe institution. The dramatic part escapes me entirely, the dreadful adventures of Herod and Death, but to this day I am united in enthusiasm with Janka and Jerzy, who are sitting beside me, and with the entire audience, when *Pastorałka* concludes with a Dionysian dance. This is total madness, an unbridled frenzy on stage, a letting-go beyond all bounds, although the words are as plain as can be.

The rapture of the dancers, their crazy leaps and turns were like elemental movement.

Since I saw that *Pastorałka*, I have held on to the conviction that I know what true theater is, and I have applied that measure to my later evenings at the theater, usually with negative results. Obviously, one could say that specific conditions coalesced into that fervid reception (not only mine) of Schiller's spectacle: visual starvation in the drab colorlessness of the occupied city, and the absence of theatrical or cinematic entertainment; the exceptional nature of the production as a reward for the lengthy jostling on the tram and suburban rail line; and even the surprise discovery of so much acting talent among that accidental collection of girls. Perhaps an audience's receptivity is always helped by somewhat similar conditions, for, after all, the creation of a magic space, of a colorful spectacle unfolding despite the surrounding insufficiency of color, belongs to the very essence of theater. A sudden change in inner rhythm, due to the leap from one reality to another, is also necessary. *Pastorałka* in Henryków belongs to a series of somehow therapeutic performances in a Europe contaminated by the totalitarian plague; these performances took place in the occupied cities, the ghettos, the prisoner-of-war camps. I do not want to believe, however, that a true theatrical experience is possible only in times of great upheavals.

No, I would not want to transfer to the screen the film I have fashioned in my imagination. The more intensely Schiller is present, the more Umińska is a tangible presence, and even Żyznowski, of unknown appearance, the more clearly I see the girls from *Pastorałka*, who today, if they are still alive, are old women—the more powerfully can I sense the poverty of cinematic devices compared with the richness of human characters and fates. All these individuals exist simultaneously in their various phases, but it is impossible to capture that temporal dimension in linear fashion, in an unfolding plot, despite the ever more frequent use of the flashback technique. Nicola Chiaromonte was probably correct when he denied the possibility of film ever rivaling literature. Fine. But then where are those exceptional virtues of literature? No doubt they, too, are modest. But the impotence of literature when it attempts to capture and preserve reality in words is a separate topic entirely.

JULY 31, 1988

Leafing through the *Anchor Book of French Quotations*, I found a passage which is a proper closing for this year of my notes:

Lord, I did what I could. Is it my fault Thou didst not speak more clearly? I tried my best to understand. —Maeterlinck

BIOGRAPHICAL GLOSSARY

Andrzejewski, Jerzy. Novelist, friend of Milosz's from their time in Nazi-occupied Warsaw, engaged in underground activities.

Bem, Józef (1794–1859). Polish artillery officer, hero of the Hungarian revolutionary war, called affectionately by the Hungarians "Daddy Bem"; the uprising of 1956 against Soviet rule began at the monument to him in Budapest. A poem in hexameters by Cyprian Norwid on the funeral of Bem elevates the dead hero to a mythical dimension.

Białoszewski, Miron (1922–83). Poet who made use of Warsaw street slang; author of *Memoir of the Warsaw Uprising* (Northwestern University Press, 1991).

Bierut, Bolesław (1892–1953). Communist activist, president of Communist Poland.

Borowski, Tadeusz (1922–51). Poet, prisoner at Auschwitz; some of his stories were published in English under the title *This Way for the Gas, Ladies and Gentlemen*; committed suicide.

Broniewski, Władysław (1897–1962). Revolutionary poet in the romantic-socialist tradition.

Bujnicki, Teodor (1907–44). Poet of the Żagary group in Wilno; killed by the Polish underground for his collaboration with a Soviet-sponsored newspaper.

Byrski, Tadeusz, and his wife, Irena Byrski. Actors, members of the theater group *Reduta* in the 1920s; after World War II, theater directors in Poland.

Chwistek, Leon (1884–1944). Painter, creator of "formism"; mathematician.

Curzon line. Lord Curzon, Britain's Minister for Foreign Affairs, made a proposal in 1920 for a peace treaty between Poland and the Soviet Union, intentionally drawing the border close to the line between ethnically Polish and non-Polish areas.

Czapski, Józef (1896–1992). Painter and writer, connected with the émigré monthly *Kultura* in Paris. During World War II, interned together with other Polish officers in the Soviet Union. One of the few who were not executed at Katyń.

Czechowicz, Józef (1903–39). Poet, killed in a bombardment during the German invasion of Poland.

Dembiński, Henryk. With Stefan Jędrychowski, leader of a political leftist (in fact, Communist) group in Wilno that emerged from the literary group Żagary.

Dmowski, Roman (1864–1939). Politician, theoretician of nationalism as a doctrine that assigns to the state the role of instrument wielded by one dominant nationality. His political party, National Democracy, was called ND or *endecja.*

Dziewicka, Muta. A colleague of Milosz's from Wilno; a Communist militant.

Elzenberg, Henryk (1887–1967). Philosopher.

Fini, Leonor. Painter, Jeleński's life companion.

Gałczyński, Konstanty Ildefons (1905–53). Poet; highly popular because of his greatly inventive humorous poems and his "Green Goose, the Smallest Theater in the World."

Goetel, Ferdynand (1890–1960). Novelist; before World War II, an admirer of the Fascist Italian system.

Gombrowicz, Witold (1905–69). Novelist and playwright; exerts great influence on Polish letters with his irreverent philosophy directed against the traditional system of values.

Głowacki, Janusz. Playwright.

Herbert, Zbigniew (b. 1924). Poet.

Hersch, Jeanne (b. 1910). Philosopher, professor at the University of Geneva.

Hertz, Zygmunt. Member of the team of the monthly *Kultura,* founded in 1947 and still published today; he died in the summer of 1980. A huge volume of Hertz's letters to Milosz, 1952–79, was published in 1992.

Ivask, Astrid. Latvian poet; wife of Ivar.

Ivask, Ivar. Estonian poet.

Iwaszkiewicz, Jarosław (1894–1980). Poet and novelist of Skamander literary group.

Jastrun, Mieczysław (1903–83). Poet.

Jędrychowski, Stefan, called "Robespierre." With Henryk Dembiński, a leader of the Communist group in Wilno that emerged from Żagary; after World War II, a member of the Politburo in Warsaw.

Jeleński, Konstanty (Kot). A brilliant essayist and translator of Polish poetry into French.

Kisielewski, Stefan, also known as Kisiel (1911–91). A brilliant journalist, novelist, and composer, he was very popular because of his unrelenting satirical campaigns against the Communist authorities.

Kochanowski, Jan (1530–84). Renaissance poet; considered the most important Polish poet before Adam Mickiewicz.

Kolbe, Father Maksymilian. Before World War II, created a powerful Catholic press center in Poland with a rightist orientation. Imprisoned by the Nazis and deported to Auschwitz, he offered his life in exchange for that of another prisoner who was to be executed; canonized as a martyr by the Vatican.

Krasiński, Zygmunt (1812–59). Poet, considered one of three "bards," together with

Mickiewicz and Słowacki; author of the prophetic play on social revolution in Europe, *The Undivine Comedy* (1833).

Lebenstein, Jan. Polish painter living in Paris.

Malewska, Hanna. Catholic novelist.

Maritain, Jacques (1882–1973). French Catholic philosopher; came to America after the defeat of France in 1940. His book against collaboration with the Germans, *A travers le désastre*, was translated by Milosz and was published by the Polish underground, earlier, incidentally, than the clandestine edition in France.

Micińska, Nela. Sister of philosopher Bolesław Miciński, a friend of Milosz's from Warsaw. She and her husband, Jan Ulatowski, lived in the South of France, in Menton.

Mickiewicz, Adam (1798–1855). Major Polish poet combining in his oeuvre elements of classicism and romanticism, the ideas of the Enlightenment, and visionary beliefs of the first half of the nineteenth century in a new age of humanity; his language, simple and vigorous, is a model for Polish poets to this day. Among his works are *Grażyna* and *Konrad Wallenrod*, tales in verse about medieval Lithuania. *Pan Tadeusz*, his epic poem written in couplets, is considered the highest achievement of Polish poetry; it described the everyday life of the Lithuanian–Polish gentry in 1811–12. *Forefathers' Eve*, a drama in verse, is considered a sacred Polish play, a mainstay of the "monumental" theater.

Milosz, Oscar V. de L. (1877–1939). Milosz's cousin, he was a French poet, though he stressed his Lithuanian origins and was, after 1918, the first representative of independent Lithuania in Paris.

Mycielski, Zygmunt (1907–87). Composer; of aristocratic origins, from the south of Poland, the site of a bloody peasant rebellion in 1846 led by Jakub Szela.

Napierski, Stefan (Marek Eiger). Poet, translator, and literary critic; executed by the Nazis in 1939.

Norwid, Cyprian (1821–83). An important Polish poet preoccupied with the history of Poland and of Europe, he spent most of his life abroad as a political émigré, mainly in Paris, in utter misery; highly valued as a precursor of modern poetry and as a thinker.

Orzeszkowa, Eliza (1841–1912). Novelist; widely translated in her time because of her liberal views (the emancipation of the Jews and of women); wrote about the life of ordinary people in her native province in Lithuania.

Pankiewicz, Józef (1867–1940). Important Post-Impressionist painter; lived mostly in France, and died there.

Piasecki, Bolesław. Leader of the extreme right Falanga before World War II; then, in People's Poland, collaborated with the Communist authorities and founded Pax, an organization that combined Catholic rightist and Communist programs.

Piast. A half-legendary first King of Poland in the tenth century A.D., who rose to that position from peasant origins and started the Piast dynasty, which ruled the country for a couple of centuries.

Prus, Bolesław (1847–1912). An important Polish novelist of the nineteenth century, author of *The Doll*, a novel of life in Warsaw in the 1870s, and of *Pharaoh*, a novel-parable about ancient Egypt.

Pruszyński, Ksawery (1907–50). Journalist, soldier, diplomat.

Putrament, Jerzy. Colleague of Milosz's from Wilno, a writer turned Communist politician; after World War II, ambassador of People's Poland in Paris, then supervisor of writers; i.e., secretary of the Writers' Union.

Rodziewiczówna, Maria (1862–1944). Novelist who wrote about provincial life; very popular among less sophisticated readers.

Ryńca, Władysław. Colleague of Milosz's at the university in Wilno; a socialist. In addition to his multifaceted activities in the country under the German occupation, he volunteered, though he was not Jewish, to serve as a courier between the Jewish Bund in the Wilno ghetto and the Bund in the Warsaw ghetto.

Sadzik, Father Józef. Author of a book on Heidegger and director of a Catholic publishing house, Les Editions du Dialogue, Sadzik was a priest, a member of the Pallotini religious order; he died a year after his friend Zygmunt Hertz.

Scherer, Olga. Professor of literature and novelist.

Shestov, Lev (1866–1938). Russian philosopher.

Skiwski, Emil. A gifted literary critic; the only instance among the Polish writers of open collaboration with the German occupying forces—curiously enough, for ideological reasons.

Słonimski, Antoni (1895–1976). Poet of the Skamander literary group.

Słowacki, Juliusz (1809–49). Important poet of romanticism, a visionary; developed his own philosophy of history in his poems.

Stempowski, Jerzy (1894–1969). A brilliant essayist and memorialist, whose knowledge of Greek and Latin is evident from his writings; often wrote under the pen name Paweł Hostowiec.

Stolypin, Piotr. Prime Minister of Russia, assassinated in 1911. He used to vacation on his estate in Lithuania, neighboring on the estate of Milosz's grandfather, Kunat. Milosz mentions Stolypin's visits in one of his poems.

Stoss or Stwosz, Wit (*ca.* 1447–1533). Sculptor from southern Germany who worked and lived in Cracow; his masterpiece is the altar of polychromed wood in the Church of St. Mary.

Szczepański, Jan. Novelist.

Szumska, Danuta. Literary director of Editions du Dialogue.

Szymanowski, Karol (1882–1937). Composer.

Tarski, Alfred (1902–83). Professor at the University of California, a great name in mathematical logic.

Turowicz, Jerzy (b. 1912). Editor of the Catholic weekly, *Tygodnik Powszechny*, in Cracow, Poland. Respected by the entire spectrum of political opinion for his integrity, he is a personal friend of Pope John Paul II.

Tuwim, Julian (1884–1953). Poet from Skamander literary group.

Uniłowski, Zbigniew (1909–37). Fiction writer of great promise, unfulfilled because of his premature death.

Venclova, Tomas. Lithuanian poet, professor at Yale.

Vincenz, Irena. Widow of a Polish writer, Stanisław Vincenz, who for many years lived in Switzerland and died there.

Wat, Ola. Widow of the poet Aleksander Wat, whose *My Century: An Odyssey of a Polish Intellectual,* based on his conversations with Milosz, was published in English by the University of California Press, 1988.

Weyssenhoff, Josef (1860–1932). Novelist of a conservative orientation; depicted life in the gentry manors of Lithuania.

Wielopolski, Margrave Aleksander (1803–77). Chief of the civil government in the Russian-dominated Kingdom of Poland. A sincere believer in loyal collaboration with the Russians as the only means of improving economic conditions in the country. The 1863 uprising against Russia made his program moot.

Wierzyński, Kazimierz (1894–1969). Poet of the Skamander literary group; political émigré after 1939.

Winnicka, Wiktoria. Physician, half sister of Józef Wittlin.

Witkiewicz, Stanisław Ignacy (1885–1937), called Witkacy. Painter, playwright, novelist.

Wittlin, Józef (1896–1976). Author of *Salt of the Earth: A Tale of a Patient Infantryman* (1936), a novel about World War I.

Zagajewski, Adam (b. 1945). Poet and essayist.

Zagórski, Stefan, called "Elephant." Arrested by the Gestapo as an activist in the Resistance, he committed suicide by jumping out of a window of a high-rise while being tortured.

NOTES

PAGE

7 Isaac Bashevis Singer, *Shosha* (New York: Farrar, Straus and Giroux, 1978), pp. 234, 237.

14 Leopold Staff, "The Bridge," trans. Czeslaw Milosz. In *Postwar Polish Poetry*, ed. Czeslaw Milosz. 3rd ed. (Berkeley: University of California Press, 1983), p. 2.

26 Leszek Kołakowski, *Religion* (New York: Oxford University Press, 1982), p. 157.

45 *Congregation: Contemporary Writers Read the Jewish Bible*, ed. David Rosenberg (San Diego: Harcourt Brace Jovanovich, 1987).

56 *The Complete Works of Montaigne*, trans. Donald M. Frame (Stanford: Stanford University Press, 1958), pp. 668–69.

62 Czeslaw Milosz, "Slow River," trans. Renata Gorczynski, *The Collected Poems 1931–1987* (New York: Ecco Press, 1988), pp. 18–20.

69 Stanisław Ignacy Witkiewicz, *Insatiability: A Novel in Two Parts*, trans. Louis Iribarne (Urbana: University of Illinois Press, 1977).

72 Keiji Nishitani, *Religion and Nothingness* (Berkeley: University of California Press, 1982).

93 Lev Shestov, *Penultimate Words and Other Essays* (New York, 1916).

132 "Of Vanity," *The Complete Works of Montaigne*, trans. Donald M. Frame (Stanford: Stanford University Press, 1959), pp. 732–33.

140 Teresa Torańska, *"Them": Stalin's Puppets* (New York: Harper & Row, 1987).

143 Gustaw Herling-Grudziński, *A World Apart*, trans. Joseph Marek (London: William Heinemann, 1954).

170 Chaim Grade, *My Mother's Sabbath Days: A Memoir*, trans. Channa Kleinermann Goldstein and Inna Hecker Grade (New York: Alfred A. Knopf, 1986).

178 Harrison Salisbury, *Journey for Our Times: A Memoir* (New York: Harper & Row, 1983), pp. 212–13.

199 From "Dreams from the Shore of the Mediterranean," in Aleksander Wat, *With*

the Skin, trans. and ed. Czeslaw Milosz and Leonard Nathan (New York: Ecco Press, 1989), p. 70.

203 Number 5 from the cycle "Throughout Our Lands," in Czeslaw Milosz, The Collected Poems 1931–1987 (New York: Ecco Press, 1988), p. 149.

227 Donald Davie, Czeslaw Milosz and the Insufficiency of Lyric (Knoxville: University of Tennessee, 1986).

235 A transcript of this encounter can be found in Cross Currents: A Yearbook of Central European Culture 9 (1990), pp. 75–124.

257 L'Immoralité de l'art is the French translation of Ogród nauk [The Garden of Knowledge], which has not been translated into English in its entirety. Essays from that miscellany are included in Czeslaw Milosz, Beginning with My Streets: Essays and Recollections, trans. Madeline G. Levine (New York: Farrar, Straus and Giroux, 1992).